Undocumented Latino Youth

LATINOS:
EXPLORING DIVERSITY AND CHANGE

Undocumented LATINO YOUTH

Navigating Their Worlds

Marisol Clark-Ibáñez

BOULDER
LONDON

Paperback edition published in the United States of America in 2018 by
Lynne Rienner Publishers, Inc.
1800 30th Street, Boulder, Colorado 80301
www.rienner.com

and in the United Kingdom by
Lynne Rienner Publishers, Inc.
3 Henrietta Street, Covent Garden, London WC2E 8LU

Hardcover edition published in 2015 by Lynne Rienner Publishers, Inc.

ISBN 978-1-62637-595-6 (pb)

Printed and bound in the United States of America

The paper used in this publication meets the requirements of the American National Standard for Permanence of Paper for Printed Library Materials Z39.48-1992.

10 9 8 7 6

There are no borders from what I can see up here.
—José M. Hernández, author of *Reaching for the Stars: The Inspiring Story of a Migrant Farmworker Turned Astronaut,* speaking to a reporter from space

Being undocumented for thirteen years made me feel dehumanized. When I was a child I really believed I was an alien from another planet because I internalized my invisibility and my oppression. I write to affirm my humanity and to remind myself that I am human.
—Josefina Lopez, Chicana novelist and playwright of award-winning projects such as *Real Women Have Curves*

Contents

List of Tables ix
Acknowledgments xi

1 Undocumented Immigration: Dreams of Education and Beyond 1

2 Immigration Policy: Living with the Law 15

3 Elementary School: The Beginning and the Promise 43

4 Middle School: Creating New Paths 63

5 High School: Aspirations with Uncertainty 83

6 Community College: A Gateway 107

7 The University: A (Mostly) Safe Haven 127

8 After College Graduation: Bittersweet 143

9 DREAMer Activism: Challenges and Opportunities 163

10 Being a "DREAM Keeper": Lessons Learned 179

11 Rethinking the American Dream 193

Appendix A: Sociology *con y en la Comunidad* 209
Appendix B: Brief Overview of the Field 227
Appendix C: Summary Tables of the Participants 235

References 239
Index 263
About the Book 273

Tables

1.1 High School Graduation Rates in North County School Districts, 2009–2010 8

1.2 High School Graduates with UC/CSU Required Courses in North County School Districts, 2009–2010 9

2.1 Restrictive US Immigration Laws 18

2.2 Immigration and Nationality Act of 1965: Preferential Ranking System 20

2.3 Supreme Court Cases Related to Latino Children 24

2.4 DREAM Act and Similar Legislation Proposed in US Congress 27

2.5 States Granting In-State Tuition for Undocumented Students 28

2.6 Anti-Immigrant State Policies 31

2.7 Local Anti-Immigrant Ordinances 33

2.8 Approaches to Immigration Reform Bills 36

Acknowledgments

This book could not have been written without the trust and generosity of our participants in the greater North County of San Diego, South West Riverside, and Palm Springs Desert regions of California. We promised to take care of your stories, and I hope we delivered.

The book could not have been completed without the integrity and dedication of the student researchers and educator-community collaborators. Since 2008, we have been colluding, resisting, organizing, and aiming to conduct meaningful research that would tell not only our participants' stories but ours as well.

I wish to thank the three anonymous peer reviewers who offered valuable insights. For two reviewers in particular, I truly am thankful for the chapter-by-chapter feedback that took seriously this collective endeavor with the goal of making each chapter "sing" clearer notes.

Andrew Berzanskis, editor/magician, plucked my colleagues and me from a conference presentation, guided me through the book proposal process, and offered his keen insights, patience, and humor through the revision stages of the book. Valerie Mendoza, personal editor and friend, helped polish our many voices to create a choir. Melanie Stafford, copyeditor, provided clear and thoughtful improvement to the prose.

Ricardo Levins Morales, whose art graces the cover of this book, is an internationally known and extraordinary social justice artist. Since college, I have collected his posters on women's rights, indigenous sovereignty, incarceration, human rights, and environmentalism. What luck to have married into a family who considers him a close friend. I am deeply grateful for being able to collaborate with him on creating the image for the book cover.

Participants at scholarly conferences, ally workshops for undocumented students, and immigration-justice community events shared their experiences and comments related to this project and book. They also offered enthusiastic support of its publication. You know who you are. It's finally here!

My colleagues in the Department of Sociology at California State University, San Marcos (CSUSM)—along with committees awarding internal university grants and a sabbatical leave—have offered incredible support for this endeavor. Sharon Elise and Kristin Bates are senior colleagues who were steady cheerleaders. Xuan Santos has enriched CSUSM students' lives through his activism and mentoring. Richelle Swan, best friend and colleague, offered insights, analysis, expertise, and lots of wonderful food with wine.

Graduate students helped with important details. Matthew Chase tracked down citations. Joe Briceño assisted with data analysis of quantitative middle school data. Diana Garcia helped me think through issues of mixed-status families.

Many CSUSM colleagues work tirelessly on behalf of undocumented students—both current and future college students—in the North County San Diego region. I am particularly grateful for the friendship and support of Lisa Bandong, Arcela Nuñez-Alvárez, Ana Ardón, Sandra Carrillo, Minerva Gonzalez, Marivel Rojas, Arlene Toya, Norma Larios, Patricia Diaz, Silverio Haro, Gerardo Gonzalez, and Arturo Ocampo.

Outside of my immediate locale but deep in my heart are Ursula Castellano, Susan Miller, and Jennifer Myhre, sociology sisters since our doctoral study at the University of California, Davis. They are resolute champions of social justice. My actual sister, Giselle Clark-Ibáñez, is my life coach. Whether advising on how to write about homelessness or choosing our children's birthday party decorations, she combines a critical perspective with pragmatic sensibility.

My coproducer in life, love, and social justice is Luke Lara. He stayed up late with me as I finished chapters or worked on analysis of data while he played charango, composed songs on the piano, or worked on his own duties as counselor, department chair, and student advocate. Because of Luke, working at 1 a.m. never seemed like a lonely time but one full of loopy laughter and deep conversations—often both! I am so lucky to have his parents, Kathy and Leo Lara, educators and performers, supporting our journey.

My children were born during various stages of this project. Pablo Vicente (now six years old) and Cecilia Catalina (now four years old) attended numerous research meetings, community events, and presentations related to immigration and educational access. Their love and vivid imaginations energize me. Their insistence to "stop working" and play keeps me sane.

I thank my parents—Mercedes Ibáñez and Bill Clark—who raised me with progressive values, deep respect for others, and an appreciation for our Peruvian-Irish-American heritage. My parents are smart, fun, creative, and caring people. I hope my own kids will be able to say that about me!

Finally, I am grateful to the many *familias,* adults, and youth who continue to fight for humane immigration reform.

1

Undocumented Immigration: Dreams of Education and Beyond

Bodies running fast in all directions. Gravel spraying behind feet sprinting away.

¡Corran! ¡Corran! ¡La migra! (Run! Run! The border patrol!)

¡Por aquí! ¡Por aquí! ¡Corran! ¡Escóndanse! (This way! This way! Run! Hide!)

Brown faces straining. Sweat running down foreheads and behind ears.

Omar and the other children take cover in bushes, up trees, and behind rocks. They climb over fences.

Wham! A front door slams. Inside is the last place you should hide.

Grown-ups holler, "*¡Vayan a jugar allá fuera y no azoten la puerta!*" (Go play outside and don't slam the door!)

Wham! Running. Looking. The sun is setting, and shadows help with hiding. Where is the best place to sneak past *la migra?*

Heavy breathing you could hear in the darkness.

Shhh, ay' viene. (Shhh, he is coming.)

Deep-voiced, gringo Spanish, "*¡Halto Uh-hee! Halto Uh-hee!*"

Screams erupt and then transform to laughter.

Streaming bodies once again run around like chickens trying not to get caught.

Shirts yanked from behind, just enough to slow you down.

Got you! Your arm grabbed behind your waist.

¿A dónde crees que vas? ¡Vaz pa' tras! (Where do you think you are going? You are going back!)

¿A dónde? Where?

Back to where you came from!

This group of cousins and neighborhood children in Encinitas, a Southern California coastal town, creates scenarios based on conversations they overhear among the adults. "*¿Escuchaste que a Mario lo agarraron en el Depot?*" (Did you hear that Mario got picked up at the Home Depot?) Seven-year-old Omar and the rest of the children who had previously crossed the border were *los pollos* (the chickens, slang for migrants). The migrant smuggler was *el coyote,* the kid with the most experience with *el cruce* (border crossings). The kids born in the United States were *la migra* (Immigration and Customs Enforcement [ICE], also known as border patrol).

Sometimes the games reenacted crossing the border, or *el cerro* (the hill), which took a physical form, such as a line of trees, a set of cars, or the street. Other scenarios reflected current activity in the community: going to the swap meet, park, or store. It always ended with getting chased by *la migra*, which meant being sent back across the border to Tijuana or kept out of the game by going to jail.

Through these exhilarating games, the children reenacted a journey many of them or their parents experienced. Omar's childhood was *peppered* with deportation fears and realities. His brother had been taken by border patrol on multiple occasions. Once, it took place in front of their driveway. Omar recalled the many times his mother urgently told him and his sisters to hide in their bedroom because *la migra* was outside. His sister was detained for more than a year and eventually deported. She returned to the United States, but she has suffered anxiety and depression.

During the school year, Omar and his undocumented peers attend public elementary schools. The 1982 Supreme Court decision *Plyler v. Doe* granted all undocumented youth the right to attend public schools, from kindergarten through high school. Yet, the context and conditions in which undocumented students learn are often stressful.

We intentionally use the term *undocumented.* The terms *illegal immigrant* and *illegal alien* are inaccurate because it is not possible for a person to be "illegal."[1] They strip people of dignity and are therefore considered derogatory.

Alfredo, a participant in this study, attended school every day. He was a seventeen-year-old, undocumented high school student who crossed the border by himself several years ago. Similar to other unaccompanied migrants, he left a violent family situation in Mexico (UN High Commissioner for Refugees 2014). Alfredo was good at math and wanted to go to college to become a lawyer. Yet, sometimes concentrating in class was hard. He began to sweat and panic, seemingly out of the blue. His mind started racing, and he wondered if today was his last day in the United States. Alfredo's everyday existence—going to work and walking to school—required that he negotiate border patrol encounters in and out of the Escondido city limits. He lived in town but worked in the avocado and citrus groves on the weekends. He had been chased three times (but not caught yet) by the border patrol—twice near his work and once during a routine traffic stop.

My coauthors and I describe the experiences of undocumented children, youth, and young adults. Because of the scope of the community projects, most of the participants were Latino/as in the San Diego, Riverside, and Palm Desert regions. Many of the participants voiced concerns about the dilemmas of walking to school or work, driving, trying to get by, and working hard to succeed in the face of intense stress about their immigrant status. Life for these students involves risk and faith. Immigration for them means coping with daily life-altering decisions, the sense of being from neither here nor there, and the enduring quest for a better life. Deysi, one of our undocumented community college participants, explained what sometimes feels like the impossibility of her situation:

> I think that nothing is impossible; it's just that if you believe it. But, no, since I don't believe that . . . no. Nothing is impossible for me. I feel like I am a bee. Because bees are impossible . . . because the scientist say[s] they . . . because their bodies are so big and their wings are so small that they are not supposed to fly. But they fly anyways. Because they don't listen to humans! So they do whatever they wanna do; because they have wings they fly! And that's how I feel. Even though someone is telling me, "Oh, you cannot do that!" I know I am able to do that. I have two hands, two arms, two legs. I have everything I need. So, I just do it!

We began this study to understand the experiences of young migrants at each stage of the educational pipeline: elementary school, middle school, high school, community college, four-year university, and beyond. Through the research experience—interviews, photos, and qualitative online surveys—the participants in this project invited us into other social worlds: peer, family, community, work, and legal worlds.

Education was a fundamental goal for the undocumented young people we interviewed. It is why their parents risked everything to bring their children to the United States. The hope for a better future is the time-honored goal of all immigrants to the United States and the basis for many proposed legislative paths to citizenship. However, what goes on in school is only a portion of the story they wanted to reveal. So, as the chapters focus on groups of students at different points of their educational journey, we also share their fears of deportation, desire to work, terrible workplace conditions, and mixed-status family dynamics, in which some are "legal" and some aren't. We tell the stories of career and educational aspirations, of depression, of hope and hopelessness, and ultimately of struggle. *Ganas*, determination.

The United States has more than 11 million undocumented immigrants and about 1.8 million of these are undocumented youth under eighteen years old. The College Board (n.d.) estimates 65,000 undocumented students graduate from high school each year. Latino/as represent the largest group of undocumented immigrants in the United States. Although they are legally allowed to attend public K–12 schools, the Supreme Court in *Plyler v. Doe* left decisions about higher education access to individual states.

As is often the case, however, law and lived reality can be quite different. The law does not assure undocumented Latino/a students that they are safe to attend school. States are enacting laws to undermine the spirit of *Plyler v. Doe*. After Alabama passed a law requiring school officials to check birth certificates, 2,300 of the 36,000 Latino/a public school children vanished from classrooms (Dias, Gray, and Scherrer 2011:14). Responding to outrage in the Latino/a community, state officials created ads on Spanish-speaking radio to explain that schools would not check existing students' citizenship if they came back to class.

As we worked in our communities, we discovered local practices of law and immigration enforcement also negatively affect the ability of families to send their children to school. Colleagues in Riverside County (southeast of Los Angeles) who work for migrant education programs have been dismayed to see ICE trucks trolling local elementary, middle, and high schools during drop-off and pickup of students. A school psychologist in a local San Marcos elementary school commented with dismay that deportation of students or their parents is no longer treated as a crisis but is, in fact, such a regular occurrence that school officials have developed protocols and interventions for students. The students featured in our study (some of whom are authors) have described the horror of immigration raids taking place in family friendly settings, such as the local swap meet on a Saturday morning. This constant law-enforcement surveillance in our region has a chilling effect on the undocumented Latino/a community and families.

Although my name is on the spine of the book, I consider the project a collaborative monograph. My collaborators include student researchers (some undocumented), educators, and community members. Throughout the book their individual voices and contributions are highlighted and credited. For a full discussion of the methodology and team behind the book, see Appendix A. Since 2009, my collaborators and I have been involved in an ongoing public sociology project that includes education, activism, outreach, and data collection. We strive to embody Michael Burawoy's (2005) notion of organic public sociology by working closely with the "visible, thick, active, local" members of the undocumented Latino/a communities in our region (7). This book honors community-based knowledge and elevates the voices of undocumented students along with the educators who support them. This collaboratively written monograph also bears witness to their stories, the firsthand accounts and experiences of living undocumented in the twenty-first century.

As a sociology professor tenured at a teaching-oriented state university, I trained my collaborators in rigorous research methods, facilitated meetings, kept track of data, and cowrote most of the chapters in this book. During the analysis and writing stage of this project, I worked side by side with them to discuss data and write up the results. We met at taco shops, Panera, Noodles and Company, Starbucks, or at my house. In the case of one student collaborator, Fredi, I Skyped with him in Tijuana. We shared, deliberated, analyzed, and revised this work repeatedly. As an illustration of one of my roles in this project, I recall when Omar and I worked back and forth on this introduction to the book. When I sent him the last draft of our collaboration, he responded on e-mail, "Lots of work. End result will be a great book. Piece by Piece. *Tejiendo Palabras* [weaving words]. That is your art."

We, the authors, believe this book exemplifies one of the most important tasks of public sociology: to "make visible the invisible" (Burawoy 2005:8) by including the lived experience of the authors. We intentionally highlight their agency or navigation along with what Negrón-Gonzales (2013) described as "the numerous daily practices undertaken by undocumented young people which require them to bridge the schism between belonging in a place they do not have a legal right to" (1286). This book is firmly entrenched as a social justice project that connects with the community by drawing on personal narratives—both visual and oral. Drawing upon diverse forms of data collection, we offer compelling snapshots of undocumented students, educators, activists, and authors themselves who actively experience the undocumented context. I hope this book paints rich, complex, and diverse portraits of undocumented Latino/a immigrant experiences.

The (Leaking) Educational Pipeline for Undocumented Students

Education represents the roots and wings of the undocumented young people featured in this book. Understanding that their parents have sacrificed to provide them better opportunities leads to immigrant students' increased engagement in school. This awareness becomes a source of resiliency for young migrants. Many of the immigration reform policies—both federal and state—rely on educational attainment to determine future educational opportunities for young migrants.

The metaphor of the "pipeline" represents the pathways taken by students through the educational system (Solórzano, Villalpando, and Oseguera 2005). The normative trajectory through this public school pipeline entails a student progressing through each grade level beginning with kindergarten, arriving at her or his high school graduation, and possibly going beyond to college. The educational pipeline has significant "leaks"—that is, low-income students and/or students of color who are pushed out. These leaks result in "push-out" rates[2] and/or create phenomena such as the "school to prison" pipeline.[3] (Please see Appendix B for a brief overview of research that describes various explanations for undocumented Latino/a student attainment or lack thereof.)

Covarrubias and Lara (2013) offer powerful evidence of the "leaking" educational pipeline for undocumented students, especially when compared with documented (naturalized) and US-born students of Mexican heritage. They use data from the US Census Current Population Survey of 2010 to explore ways in which citizenship and gender shape educational outcomes. The pipeline begins with 100 students in elementary school. We clearly see the loss of students as they move through the educational pipeline. Covarrubias and Lara find that only about 50 of 100 young men and 40 of 100 young women who are undocumented graduate high school; they graduate at lower rates than naturalized or US-born Mexicans. The undocumented students also enroll in college less frequently than their naturalized Mexican peers, and about half of the undocumented students are pushed out of college before completing a degree. Fewer undocumented immigrants earn associate's, bachelor's, or graduate degrees than naturalized students. This is not surprising given the additional stress and insecurity undocumented students face in their educational journeys.

Those who do not make it through the educational pipeline experience potentially serious and long-term consequences for future earnings. According to the US Bureau of Labor Statistics (2013), education levels make a substantial difference in salaries. In 2012, the average worker in the United States made $816 per week. Those with less than a high school degree earned a weekly average of $471, high school diploma $652, some college $727, associate's degree (community college) $785, college degree $1,066, master's degree $1,300, professional degree (e.g., law) $1,735, and doctorate $1,624. Of course, these averages vary in real earnings by race and gender.

The pipeline research approach, although a powerful descriptor of inequality, typically does not acknowledge that we begin to lose students during elementary school and middle school. Some parents of undocumented elementary school children choose to keep their children out of school when there is a strong or sustained presence of border patrol around the neighborhood. As a result, absences from school may accumulate and thus predict student push-out rates. Robert Balfanz (2011), a Johns Hopkins professor and director of the Everyone Graduates Center, found that if a sixth grader in a high-poverty school attends school less than 80 percent of the time, fails math or English, or receives an unsatisfactory behavior grade in a core course, there is a 75 percent chance that without effective intervention, he or she will be pushed out of high school. California has a 3.5 percent push-out rate for middle school children. Trends in longitudinal studies of children from kindergarten or preschool through high school show predictors for educational outcomes begin as early as preschool (Heckman et al. 2009). Some argue the best predictor of educational outcome occurs before a child is even born because it is based on a mother's educational level (Gándara 2010).

Also, as useful as the educational pipeline metaphor is in describing the push-out rates, it leaves out some of the causes and the nuances of what happens in the pipeline, stage by stage. We hope the rich nature of our stories—across grade levels and beyond—yields a compelling narrative and social snapshot of current education and immigration policies in practice.

A Regional Context for Education

This project is mostly situated in a San Diego region called North County. The resource-rich cities of Encinitas, Carlsbad, and (to a lesser extent) Oceanside serve as the West Coast boundary of the region. Vista and San Marcos are in the middle. Escondido and Ramona make up the eastern side. Some might know of the region because of LegoLand (Carlsbad) and the San Diego Zoo Safari Park (Escondido). Others might be familiar with California State University, San Marcos (about 12,000 students) and two community colleges, Palomar College (about 30,000 students) and MiraCosta College (about 15,000 students). In Oceanside, Camp Pendleton is the largest West Coast marine training facility; it is also the largest employer in North County, and 36,000 families are housed on base.

Given this economically diverse region, Arcela Nuñez-Alvárez and Ana Ardón (2012) of the National Latino Research Center analyzed educational trends with a focus on Latino/as. US Census data from 2010 show Latino/as have reached close to 50 percent of the total population in the cities of Escondido (49 percent) and Vista (48 percent). The number of Latino/a children in the North County region is 43.6 percent compared with about 23 percent in the United States. Latino/a student enrollment surpasses any other group, reaching more than 50 percent in Escondido, Fallbrook, Oceanside, and Vista. (Note: In contrast, Latino/as are poorly represented among the teaching faculty in these districts, constituting only 16.4 percent of all teachers in the county.)

Focusing on North County San Diego school districts, Nuñez-Alvárez and Ardón (2012) drew upon data from the California Department of Education. Latino/a students represent 76.9 percent of economically disadvantaged students compared with 50.2 percent in the United States. Latino/a students have the lowest graduation rate in North County; more than one in four Latino/a twelfth graders did not graduate. In the San Marcos Unified School District, the general graduation rate is 92 percent, but the graduation rate for Latino/as is 47.8 percent. It is difficult to know how many *undocumented* Latino/a students are represented in these numbers. Most of the participants in this study lived and went to school in North County. Table 1.1 presents the overall findings across school districts in the region for the general population and for Latino/as.

Most of the school districts in this region are graduating students at fairly high rates except those in Vista. However, when we separate out and examine rates for Latino/a graduation, we can see some profound differences. The lowest graduation rate is 25 percent, for Latino/as in Carlsbad, and the highest is 60 percent, in Escondido. The percentage point differences in rates range from a gap of 72 (Carlsbad) or 67 (Ramona) to a smaller gap of 21 (Vista) or 32 (Escondido).

The San Diego North County region is failing Latino/as in regard to college preparation. As seen in Table 1.2, Latino/as also lag behind students who graduate high school having completed the courses required by the state public four-year colleges, the University of California (UC) and California State University (CSU) systems. Students who do not complete these required courses are not eligible to enter directly a four-year university (but could enroll in community college).

Some school districts, such as those in Oceanside and Vista, are struggling to prepare *all* of their students for university. In Vista, only 20 percent of the students have taken the courses required for enrolling in a four-year

Table 1.1 High School Graduation Rates in North County School Districts, 2009–2010 (percentages)

School District	Overall Average	Latino/as	Percentage Point Difference
Carlsbad	97	25	72
Escondido	92	60	32
Fallbrook	90	48	42
Oceanside	86	53	33
Ramona	94	27	67
San Marcos	92	48	44
Valley Center–Pauma	94	30	64
Vista	68	47	21
Total averages	89.13	42.25	

Source: Nuñez-Alvárez and Ardón 2012.

Table 1.2 High School Graduates with UC/CSU Required Courses in North County School Districts, 2009–2010 (percentages)

School District	UC/CSU Ready, Overall Average	UC/CSU Ready, Latino/as	Percentage Point Difference
Carlsbad	50	37	13
Escondido	33	23	10
Fallbrook	30	18	12
Oceanside	27	21	6
Ramona	53	38	15
San Marcos	69	58	11
Valley Center–Pauma	42	28	14
Vista	20	13	7
Total averages	40.5	29.5	

Source: Nuñez-Alvárez and Ardón 2012.

university. San Marcos and Carlsbad are preparing their students much more rigorously. Yet, there are still gaps in the course completion by Latino/as. Ramona suffers the worst gap at 15 percentage points, whereas the other districts have gaps less than that.

Regardless of comparisons with non-Latino/as, the percentages for Latino/as alone are concerning. For example, only 13 percent of Latino/as in Vista have taken college preparation courses. Taking college prep courses makes a difference. Oseguera (2012) reports that, of the youth in poverty who completed their college preparatory work, about 75 percent went on to attend a four-year college. Giving students a chance—a pathway—to take college requirements results in strong college attainment rates. It is clear most of the school districts are not adequately serving Latino/a students. The regional data here offer a glimpse into the community context in which Latino/a students are embedded.

The Undocumented Sociological Imagination

As sociologists, we have a particular lens through which to view and understand the educational pipeline. Through a social lens focused on disparities and educational inequality we can clearly examine the leaks in the pipeline and the critical points at which Latino/a students leave the educational system. We give primacy to institutional and structural explanations for students' successes and failures. We examine the personal "troubles" of those in the educational pipeline through the "sociological imagination" (Mills

1959). Individual people tell the joy of graduation or the pain of dropping out of high school early. The sociological imagination allows us to focus a broader lens on students' journeys, to step back and consider broader social forces, and to examine the impact of history and current events on this issue.

To understand immigration and undocumented students from a sociological perspective, we also draw upon the concept of *social location*. We are all "socially located" within specific social systems, and our social location has a profound influence on our identity. Social location affects how we think, feel, and behave and, as such, shapes the range of possibilities we envision (Johnson 2008).

Undocumented students are structurally located within overlapping social systems of inequality. Race, class, gender, sexual orientation, ability, and immigration status all play a role in the undocumented student's educational journey. Undocumented families live and work within various community and regional contexts that affect their access to resources, their employment opportunities, and their contact with border patrol. Undocumented immigrants currently exist in an era that differs from those past in terms of the laws and policies affecting their lives. The specter of future comprehensive immigration reform as well as current federal, state, and local laws shape their everyday lives. Legal and financial circumstances often curtail educational opportunities for undocumented immigrants. The undocumented immigrant is embedded in a legal framework that currently denies rights and opportunities by law.

Undocumented immigrants' social locations are intrinsically linked to their aspirations, living conditions, opportunities, and futures. They face numerous hardships and challenges related to having low income as recent immigrants. They also cope with being denied many social services available to low-income children who are citizens. Undocumented youth and their educational journeys are negatively affected by frequent changes in residence and by living in crowded housing environments (Seif 2004). Lack of health-care access, future substance abuse, and mental health challenges are all cited as potential risks for undocumented immigrants (Abrego 2008; Perez et al. 2009). These challenges affect school experiences and work against aspirations and educational advancement (Suárez-Orozco et al. 2011). A sociological lens is a powerful tool for understanding the diversity of lived experiences of undocumented Latino/a students.

Multiple Methodologies

Our data collection spanned three years, from 2010 to 2013. As we describe in the following chapter, during this time period state legislators passed significant laws that supported undocumented students, and President Obama took executive action offering temporary resources to undocumented students. (In each chapter, we indicate which specific legislation was on the horizon or at play for our participants.)

We drew upon Latino/a critical race theory, which encompasses the following principles: the notion that race is socially constructed; the centrality of race in the analysis; the primacy of immigration and language in daily life; the importance of challenging dominant ideology; the explicit linkage of theory, practice, and community; the presentation of a structural perspective and use of personal voice and experiences; and a commitment to social justice (Delgado Bernal 2002).

Thus we developed diverse approaches for capturing the students' experiences. Additionally, we strive with this project to reflect what Paris and Winn (2014) describe as a "humanizing research" approach, which aims to bring a meaningful and explicit social justice agenda into the research. For elementary school students, we used photo-elicitation interviews in which the undocumented child took photos of his or her everyday life, and the researcher used those photos as a basis of the interview (Clark-Ibáñez 2004, 2007, 2008).

For high school, community college, and university students we conducted in-depth, qualitative interviews. For postgraduates, we developed an anonymous open-ended online survey that would reach more participants.

Two community members engaged in professional autoethnography. A teacher reflected on teaching practices based on more than twenty years of teaching undocumented students. A director of a middle school program for more than ten years presented the struggles facing undocumented students.

Appendix A details more of the collectivist ideals that shaped our methodology and author collaborations.

Chapter Guide

In Chapter 2, Fredi García-Alverdín expertly guides us through the complexity of immigration policy and how these laws shaped educational opportunity (praxis). We argue policy is the basis of the "undocumented" experience because the very category is created through law. García-Alverdín provides historical background, shows federal attempts at immigration reform, explains the state legislative arena, and concludes by analyzing the anti-immigration forces at the local, state, and federal levels.

In Chapters 3 to 8, we focus on undocumented immigrants in the educational system: elementary (Rhonda Avery-Merker), middle school (Cecilia Rocha), high school (Yeraldín Montiel), community college (Bettina Serna), four-year university (Griselda Alva-Brito and Fredi García-

Alverdín), and postgraduate (Omar Canseco). In all but the middle school chapter, the authors were student researchers. I cowrote and collaboratively analyzed data for each chapter. For the middle school chapter, Cecilia Rocha and I collaborated to discuss the many undocumented middle school students with whom she has worked since 2005. She describes her successful program for positive interventions to help youth through the pipeline. She is also my community partner for many of the events and outreach efforts that emerged from our Pipeline Research Collective.

We conclude with chapters that feature ways to change the educational and legal systems. In Chapter 9, Carolina Valdivia Ordorica provides an overview on the activism that has emerged since the creation of the Development, Relief, and Education for Alien Minors (DREAM) Act in 2001. She situates herself as an activist-scholar-DREAMer and paints a rich landscape of the youth-led *online* social movement. Her expert "insider" view counters the arguments that the Internet is leading to a decline in meaningful social change (e.g., "clicktivism" and "slacktivism").[4] This chapter highlights the agency among vulnerable members of society. We want to inspire the reader to join us in the struggle for educational opportunity and a humane approach to immigration policy and praxis.

Chapter 10 focuses on a teacher who successfully educates undocumented students. Alma Ruiz-Pohlert is a "DREAM keeper." She has been my collaborator on many academic and mentoring projects related to undocumented students. She has been generous with her insights and passionate about helping immigrant families in the region. Through our friendship and collaborations over more than ten years, I have come to ask myself, "What would Alma do?" In this chapter, she shares her experiences, advice in terms of what she has observed, and what she believes should be done. She has been a bilingual teacher for more than twenty years, and she herself came to the United States from Tijuana as a young girl. We integrated academic analysis to give a broader perspective on pedagogical and institutional best practices.

In Chapter 11, I reflect on the lessons learned and future directions in research and policy based on what we have discovered about the educational pipeline for the undocumented Latino/a students interviewed for this book. I focus on social, human, and cultural capital and highlight the cultural wealth upon which the students draw to survive and thrive in the United States. Ultimately, I believe the participants in this study offer a variety of ways to reconsider the "American dream" and how we contextualize undocumented immigrants.

Appendix A is a methodological discussion of the varied data sources, processes, and approaches we undertook. I also outline the various community efforts that emerged from the project. I invite those interested to reach out to me directly so that I can share the English and Spanish informed consent forms and IRB applications created for this study. Appendix B is a short essay giving an overview on research about undocumented immigration and education. Appendix C lists the research participants' demographic details not provided in their corresponding chapters.

Notes

1. In 2013 the Associated Press decided not to use the term *illegal* to describe undocumented immigrants, and other news outlets and publishers have changed the way they describe them as well. See Colorlines.com for its campaign to "Drop the 'I' Word."

2. "Push-out" rates is a concept that replaces "dropout rates" because it more accurately describes the dynamics of school (the institution) that undermined the success of the student; "dropout" overly emphasizes the individual without considering the microinteractional, institutional, or structural factors for a student leaving school (Doll, Eslami, and Walters 2013).

3. The "school to prison pipeline" refers to disciplinary rules (e.g., zero tolerance) disproportionately applied to low-income students of color. Schools rely too heavily on school police and the juvenile justice system to administer discipline. As a result, students experience extreme consequences, such as suspensions and misdemeanors, that place them at risk for leaving school or for further exposure to the criminal justice system.

4. There is concern that the prevalence of online options, such as clicking on a website to donate funds to a particular social cause or signing an online petition, could negatively impact the occurrence and possibility of "real" social change. See Roberston (2014) for an example of this argument.

2

Immigration Policy: Living with the Law

I am writing this chapter as a DREAMer in political exile and a scholar living and working in Tijuana, Mexico. I lived in the United States for two decades, from August 1990 to May 2011. During that time, I obtained my bachelor of arts degree in sociology and political science as well as a master of arts degree in sociological practice at a California public university. During my last semester of graduate school, I was detained by the police and then turned over to US Immigration and Customs Enforcement (ICE). This was a result of the Secure Communities Program, a partnership between local and state police agencies and the Department of Homeland Security (DHS) to enforce immigration laws. I completed my master's thesis while in removal proceedings. I did not have the resources to fight deportation, so I talked to my family about my decision of seeking *voluntary departure*,[1] which was granted by an immigration judge on January 4, 2011. ICE gave me four months to leave the United States or the department would have an order of deportation reinstated. Finally the date arrived, and on May 2, 2011 (my sister's birthday), I left the United States and registered with the US Consulate in Tijuana two days later. I did not walk across the graduation stage for my master's degree hooding nor did I have the chance to participate in other graduation celebrations.

The intersection of immigration policies, law, and education has shaped my life. It began in my junior year of high school, when I sat down with my counselor from the Migrant Education Program to discuss the low odds of

---

Fredi García-Alverdín wrote this chapter.

acceptance to a four-year university because of my undocumented status. I still remember her words, "*¿No perdemos nada con intentar, verdad?*" ("We don't lose anything by trying, right?") In the spring of my senior year (1994), I received a letter from San Diego State University granting me "provisional admission." This meant I could register but would have to pay additional nonresident fees. This was impossible because my parents barely made enough to make ends meet, and, as an undocumented youth, I did not have a job. The letter stated I also needed to provide a Social Security number and proof of my legal residency in the United States. Again, it was impossible for me because I was undocumented. This was my first experience, of many to come, in which immigration law deferred my educational goals and opportunities.

As I walked my high school hallways and sat in my senior classes, many students talked about college: where they were accepted and where they would choose to go. It was emotional for me to hear such conversations because I knew I had been accepted to a four-year institution, but because of my immigration status, I would have to give up my dream of pursuing higher education. When students asked me about future plans or whether I was accepted to any colleges, my response was always, "I'm going to take a break, maybe one or two years, because I want to work and save money." In reality, I was undocumented, and I knew pursuing a higher education was out of the question. I realize now many students like me were in the same situation.

The purpose of this chapter is to highlight the effects of key immigration policies that have shaped immigration today, the impact of immigration law on undocumented students' education, and current discussion on immigration.

Immigration Law Overview

Prior to discussing immigration and educational policies and their effects on undocumented students, I will look back at historical events that led to an increase in the undocumented population in the United States.

The United States was founded on the premise of immigration. This has shaped US society culturally, socially, and politically (see Alba and Nee 2005; Martin and Midgley 2003; Portes and Rumbaut 2001, 2006). It has also served as a key factor for economic development because many industries have relied on immigration in different periods of US history for growth. During times of economic expansion and hope for prosperity for industry owners and developers, there was an open immigration policy. In fact, labor recruiters traveled to certain parts of the world to entice and even pay for immigrant passage to the United States.

During times of economic uncertainty immigrants have been used as scapegoats and blamed for such troubles (Flow of History 2013; Starkweather 2007; Stawski 2008). As a consequence, throughout US history restrictive policies were set for immigrants from specific countries, such as quotas, preferential systems, and deportation statutes. (See Table 2.1 for restrictive US immigration laws.)

Initially, restrictive immigration laws did not directly affect Mexican and Latin American immigrants as much as they did immigrant groups from Asia and Europe. It was not until the Immigration and Nationality Act of 1965 that Mexican immigrants began to see the effects of restrictions imposed upon them through the use of caps. Focusing on the effects of US policy on rates of Mexican/Central American immigration, Rosenblum and Brick (2011) identified three main historical phases: "limited flows before World War II, primarily Mexican government-sponsored guest worker flows during and after the war, and mainly illegal flows beginning in 1965 and accelerating over the next four decades" (3).

The Bracero (Farmworker) Program and the Immigration and Nationality Act of 1965

After leaving the United States, I had the ability to travel freely in Mexico. In the summer of 2013, I journeyed to the towns of El Huamuchil and San Sebastian El Progreso in the state of Oaxaca. My goal was to visit my grandparents, whom I had not seen for twenty years. Growing up, I heard that both my grandfathers had traveled to the United States to work as braceros. During my visit, my eighty-seven-year-old maternal grandfather shared some of his experiences while in the United States, including the times he crossed the border through Calexico, California. While my grandfather was telling me his stories, he reached into his shirt pocket and pulled out his "Alien Laborer's Identification Card." For me it was a magical moment. Here was a part of my family's history new to me; I had in my hands a document that confirmed the history of immigration within my own family.

My paternal grandmother shared stories of my grandfather, who had passed away a few years back, working as a bracero. Some former braceros or their families, including some of my relatives, had received a small compensation from the Mexican government as part of a settlement for which they had fought for decades. During the Bracero Program, "about 10 percent of the wages earned by Braceros between 1942 and 1949 were withheld by U.S. farmers and sent by U.S. banks to Mexican Banks" (*Rural Migration News* 2006). The Mexican government has claimed it misplaced such records and funds. However, many bracero families are still seeking payment from the Mexican government (León 2014; Macias 2014).

Table 2.1 Restrictive US Immigration Laws

Immigration Act and Year	Description
Page Act of 1875	Restricted immigration for individuals classified as "undesirable"; under this category numbers of Chinese, Japanese, and immigrants from other Asian countries were restricted
Chinese Exclusion Act of 1882	Suspended Chinese immigration to the United States; a ban intended to last ten years
Geary Act of 1892	Extended and strengthened the Chinese Exclusion Act of 1882
Immigration Act of 1903	Also known as the Anarchist Exclusion Act. Codified previous immigration laws and included the following classes as inadmissible: anarchists, beggars, people with epilepsy, and importers of prostitutes
Immigration Act of 1917	Also known as the Asiatic Barred Zone Act. Banned immigration based on the following terminology: "homosexuality," "idiots," "feeble-minded persons," "criminals," "epileptics," "insane persons," "professional beggars," "mentally or physically defective" individuals, polygamists, and anarchists; also banned persons from most of Asia and the Pacific Islands
Immigration Act of 1918	Expanded the Anarchist Exclusion Act of 1903
Emergency Quota Act of 1921	Also known as the Emergency Immigration Act of 1921, the Immigration Restriction Act of 1921, the Per Centum Law, and the Johnson Quota Act. Originally a temporary measure, in the long run set numerical limits on European immigrants and implemented a quota system
Immigration Act of 1924	Limited the number of immigrants admitted by imposing a 2 percent cap per country; further restricted southern and eastern European immigration
Immigration and Nationality Act of 1952	Retained quota system for some nationalities and regions; established a preferential system for desirable immigrants; labeled and defined three types of immigrants: those with special skills or relatives of US citizens, average immigrants, and refugees; allowed deportation of immigrants and naturalized citizens considered subversive
Immigration and Nationality Act of 1965	Replaced the national origins quota system with a preference system based on labor skills and family relationship with US citizens and Legal Permanent Residents; restricted number of visas allowed to 170,000 per year to the Eastern Hemisphere and 120,000 per year to the Western Hemisphere
Illegal Immigration Reform and Immigrant Responsibility Act of 1996	Stipulated the punishment for immigrants unlawfully present in the United States as well as deportable offenses, including minor misdemeanor violations

It was not until World War II that an official guest worker program was created between the United States and Mexico to deal with labor shortages caused by US workers going to war. This was named the Bracero Program and lasted from 1942 to 1964.[2] Although initially the Bracero Program was implemented out of wartime necessity, it was extended as demand increased from produce growers and other industries (Akers-Chacón and Davis 2006). Nearly 5 million Mexicans participated in the program (Ortiz Uribe 2013). Braceros experienced poor working conditions and exploitation.[3] Mize (2006) cites Mexican American scholar and activist Ernesto Galarza, who conducted interviews with braceros during the 1950s: "For instance, Galarza collected hundreds of pay stubs that detailed shifting pay rates, illegal deductions for blankets and carrot ties, exorbitant deductions for insurance and food, and a substantial number of instances where workers did not receive their guaranteed wage" (86).

Many laborers, after their contracts ended, started to come into the United States without immigration documents. This meant they were not protected by the meager guarantees of the Bracero Program (Akers-Chacón and Davis 2006). The legacy of these policies shaped people's lives today.

Eventually, those who participated in the Bracero Program formed enclaves and served as contacts in towns across the Southwest for future migrants. I jokingly told my grandfather, "*Si se hubiera quedado en los Estados Unidos todos fueramos Americanos*" ("If you had remained in the United States, we would all be American"). He laughed but told me it was very hard labor and such extreme exploitation that he stopped going back and decided to stay in Oaxaca. (For more history on the Bracero Program, see Craig 1971; Galarza 1964; Gamboa 1990.)

After the Bracero Program, a major immigration policy was enacted in 1965. The Immigration and Nationality Act of 1965 made it difficult for immigrants to seek citizenship. It eliminated national origin quotas but implemented caps for the Eastern and Western Hemispheres (170,000 and 120,000 respectively). It also limited the number of immigrants who could emigrate from a specific country to 20,000 (Institute of Portland Metropolitan Studies 2011). Furthermore, it established a preferential system that benefited low-skilled workers and family members of US citizens and permanent legal residents (see Table 2.2 for the preferential ranking system).

Because the 1965 law restricted immigration and required an arduous application process that often resulted in being rejected for admittance repeatedly, those workers looking for seasonal work found it easier to enter the United States as undocumented immigrants. It became more convenient to cross the border outside the legal system. After the implementation of the 1965 immigration law, undocumented apprehensions rose drastically at the border: from 1966–1975, 500,000 on average were apprehended each year (Institute of Portland Metropolitan Studies 2011).

Table 2.2 Immigration and Nationality Act of 1965: Preferential Ranking System

1. Unmarried adult children of US citizens
2. Spouses and unmarried adult children of permanent residents
3. Members of the professions and scientists and artists of exceptional ability
4. Married children of US citizens
5. Brothers and sisters of US citizens over age twenty-one
6. Workers in occupations for which there is insufficient labor supply
7. Refugees given conditional entry or adjustment
8. Applicants not entitled to preceding preferences

Source: Teaching American History Project, Institute of Portland Metropolitan Studies, Portland State University, 2011.

The framers of the Immigration and Nationality Act of 1965 did not anticipate an influx of undocumented immigrants. As mentioned previously, the combination of immigration caps, a time-consuming visa approval process, emphasis on family reunification, and lack of an adequate system for employers to have access to low-skilled workers contributed to such an influx (Massey, Durand, and Malone 2002). Rosenblum and Brick (2011) mention that, in addition, the Immigration and Nationality Act of 1952 "made it illegal to aid or harbor unauthorized immigrants, but explicitly exempted businesses from being liable under the law" (5). Employers therefore continued to hire undocumented immigrants because of the demand for low-skilled employees and lack of enforcement of that law by the US government. This arrangement continued during the 1970s and early 1980s (LeMay 2007). It is important to note that during the 1970s and early 1980s economic troubles and civil wars in Latin America also led to an increase in undocumented immigration.

The Immigration Reform and Control Act (IRCA) of 1986

During the early 1980s, my family and I lived in Mexico City. I have memories of my uncle coming to stay with us; he lived and worked in the United States, so he hardly visited. I would hear my parents and uncle talk about his experiences in the central valleys of California, Oregon, and Washington State. One aspect of those conversations was always his experiences with *la migra* (border patrol). This changed with the passage of IRCA in 1986; my uncle was able to change his status to temporary permanent resident, and eventually he achieved legal permanent resident status. This law also benefited other relatives who helped my father to migrate and then the rest of my family to cross the border into the United States.

The US Congress passed IRCA as a way to deal with undocumented immigration into the United States. Its main provisions included legalization of undocumented immigrants present since 1982, legalization of agricultural workers, employer sanctions for hiring undocumented workers, and greater border enforcement (US Citizenship and Immigration Services n.d.a).

According to Kerwin (2010), IRCA benefited about 1,596,913 immigrants via its general legalization program, 1,093,065 under its special agricultural worker program, and 14,907 by late amnesty. Many critics of this legislation suggest that instead of deterring undocumented immigration, it created more social enclaves that further encouraged migration and made it possible for future settlement of immigrants. IRCA had flaws, certainly. Kerwin (2010) attributes the rise of undocumented immigration to the lack of an accurate employment verification system and to backlogs of petitions from legal permanent residents attempting to bring their families to the United States via the opportunity created by IRCA (8).

IRCA allowed the legalization of many undocumented immigrants, but at the same time it affected the structure of immigrant families. Because the cut off date was 1982 and implementation of the act started in 1987, those with unauthorized entry during this five-year gap were not able to benefit from IRCA. Thus, close relatives, spouses, and children of IRCA immigrants remained undocumented immigrants. This increased the occurrence of mixed-status families with both authorized and unauthorized members (Cooper and O'Neil 2005).

IRCA served as the conduit for many of the estimated 11.7 million undocumented immigrants to enter the United States just as it did my family (see Passel, Cohn, and Gonzalez-Barrera 2013 for this estimate as well as estimates of the undocumented populations in California, Florida, Illinois, New Jersey, New York, and Texas). I explored the impact of IRCA for my master's thesis by interviewing immigrants who had benefited under this law (García-Alverdín 2010). Their lives changed drastically. Former undocumented immigrants began to have better job opportunities, access to government programs, and greater protection under the rule of law. Most important, immigrants began to petition for the legal status of their families (Paral, Wijewardena, and Ewing 2009). Economically, the United States benefited from this influx. The Immigration Policy Center (2013) reports that previously undocumented immigrants who benefited from legal status earned higher wages, increasingly became homeowners, and contributed more to local and state taxes.

The Immigration Act of 1990 and the Illegal Immigration Reform and Immigrant Responsibility Act of 1996

I was a teenager in the United States when I witnessed the effects of two major immigration laws. First, it was the Immigration Act of 1990, a family-based policy. In my community and school, many students had crossed as undocumented immigrants, others had individual and family petitions to the former Immigration and Naturalization Service (INS; now US Citizenship and Immigration Services), and still others were receiving their "green cards" because family members were becoming US citizens. This scenario reflected the complexities of immigration itself and mixed-status families across immigrant communities (for more studies on mixed-status families, see Capps, Kenney, and Fix 2003; Fix and Zimmermann 1999; Passel and Cohn 2011; Passel and Taylor 2010; Sutter 2005).

The Immigration Act of 1990 *increased legal immigration* to the United States. It was a relatively flexible law that benefited immigrants by granting family-based, employment-based, and diversity-based immigrant visas (Greenwood and Ziel 1997). As stated on the US Citizenship and Immigration Services website: "It increased the limits on legal immigration to the United States, revised all grounds for exclusion and deportation, *authorized temporary protected status* to aliens of designated countries, revised and established new nonimmigrant admission categories, revised and extended the Visa Waiver Pilot Program, and revised naturalization authority and requirements" (US Citizenship and Immigration Services n.d.b). However, this increase in immigration into the United States created a public outcry.

States were already passing anti-immigrant legislation. Immigrants were blamed for overly using social services and public assistance. For example, in November 1994 California voters passed Proposition 187, the purpose of which was to screen individuals for citizenship and to prohibit undocumented immigrants from accessing health care, education, and other social services. Eventually, Proposition 187 was rendered unconstitutional in federal court, but it created a hostile environment for immigrants, including incresed stereotyping and harassment.

I constantly watched the news and read different newspapers, hoping for the government to pass some type of relief for undocumented immigrants. Life was becoming difficult because states were requiring a Social Security number and legal presence documents for simple chores such as going to the bank, obtaining a driver's license, and even going to the emergency room. Then it happened. The Illegal Immigration Reform and Immigrant Responsibility Act of 1996 (IIRIRA) and the Personal Responsibility and Work Opportunity Act of 1996 (PRWORA) were passed and signed into law by President Bill Clinton.

The IIRIRA was a *restrictive immigration policy* of which the main purpose was to deter undocumented immigration into the United States by increasing interior and border enforcement, instituting employer sanctions, and strengthening deportation statutes. Furthermore, it restricted permanent resident immigrants' access to various social services, such as public benefits, driver's licenses, Social Security benefits, and federal student financial aid.

Immigration Reform and Education

The IIRIRA negatively affected immigrant communities by imposing many restrictions, including access to higher learning institutions. Interestingly, the law did not deter unauthorized immigration; as the economy worsened in Mexico because of the North American Free Trade Agreement (NAFTA), migration to the United States actually increased. Since the federal decision *Plyler v. Doe* in 1982, undocumented immigrant children and youth were able to attend public schools, kindergarten through high school. However, the court left the decision about higher education eligibility and admission to the states. As the young undocumented children journeyed through the educational pipeline, they were graduating and not finding college accessible.

By 2000, significant numbers of undocumented youth were graduating from high school and joining the formal or informal economy. Many had a dream to pursue higher education but were limited by accessibility and funding, which resulted in politicians starting to address the issue by introducing the first bipartisan legislation to help undocumented students find a pathway to citizenship, among other benefits.

Setting Precedent: Latino/as and Educational Equity

The struggle for equality and fair treatment for Latino/a children is not new. In particular, two Supreme Court cases set the precedent for undocumented youth, many of whom were Latino/as (of Mexican origin) in the United States. *Lemon Grove* (1931) and *Mendez* (1947) were cases based in Southern California, a region with large Latino/a and Mexican immigrant populations (see Table 2.3 for a summary of the court cases shaping educational access for Latino/a children).

Several state court cases also determined opportunities for undocumented students in the United States. First, *Leticia A. v. the University of California Board of Regents and California State University Board of Trustees* (1985) allowed undocumented students to qualify for in-state

Table 2.3 Supreme Court Cases Related to Latino Children

Court Case by Year	Description
Roberto Alvarez v. Board of Trustees of the Lemon Grove School District, 1931	First desegregation court decision in the United States; established right to equal education for students of Mexican descent
Lopez v. Seccombe, 1944	Southern California court ruled that San Bernardino violated the Fourteenth Amendment of the US Constitution by banning citizens of Mexican and Latino/a descent from public schools and park facilities
Mendez v. Westminster, 1947	Ninth Circuit Court ruled segregation of Mexicans in California's public schools was a violation of the Fourteenth Amendment of the US Constitution
Brown v. Board of Education, 1954	The US Supreme Court ruled "separate-but-equal" segregation of public schools a violation of the Fourteenth Amendment of the US Constitution
Romero v. Weakley, 1955	Two lawsuits charged two Imperial County public schools with segregation of African American and Mexican American children
Regents of the University of California v. Bakke, 1978	US Supreme Court ruled that a university could not use race or quotas in admissions decisions
Crawford v. Los Angeles, 1963 (settled in 1982)	Challenged school segregation in Los Angeles

Source: University of California, San Diego, Social Science and Humanities Library, 2010, "Timeline: *Brown v. Board of Education:* The Southern California Perspective," retrieved March 25, 2013 (http://sshl.ucsd.edu/brown/timeline.html).

tuition within the UC and CSU systems. They also could qualify for financial aid and the Cal Grant Program. However, *Bradford v. the University of California Regents* (1991) overturned this decision and instituted nonresident tuition for undocumented students (Olivas 1995, 2004). I graduated high school in 1994 and therefore could not afford to attend college because of the *Bradford* ruling.

In other parts of the country there was also a growing immigrant population. As noted earlier, states had the right to restrict their laws regarding access to education for undocumented immigrants. For example, in 1975, Texas enacted a law allowing school districts to charge tuition to the parents of undocumented students. The superintendent of the City of Tyler began charging an annual tuition fee. A US district court and the Fifth Circuit Court of Appeals ruled the Texas law unconstitutional. Ultimately, it made its way to the US Supreme Court, where it was declared a violation of the Fourteenth Amendment equal protection clause. This court ruling, known as *Plyler vs. Doe* (1982), stated that all students, including undocumented students, have the right to a K–12 public education (Olivas 2010).

Plyler v. Doe was pivotal for future generations of undocumented children arriving in the United States. They were guaranteed access to primary and secondary schooling, but their access to higher education was restricted or forbidden. In rare cases, access was granted: during the 1980s, the City University of New York (CUNY) and the State University of New York (SUNY) granted in-state tuition to undocumented students (Flores 2010: 240; Rincón 2008).

Development, Relief, and Education for Alien Minors (DREAM) Act

As undocumented students were graduating from US high schools, they were not able to attend a community college or a public university as a result of the restrictions imposed by Section 505 of IIRIRA. Yet, there were loopholes in the law. I, for example, was able to attend community college. In 1998 institutions of higher education lacked support systems for undocumented students. Those of us who found a way to attend college created a support system among ourselves to help us navigate the system. Even though we had created this sense of community, I never disclosed my status to anyone except a couple of good friends because of the stigma attached to being undocumented and resulting intergroup discrimination. Also, I wanted to protect my family from being detected.

Then, on August 1, 2001, the Development, Relief, and Education for Alien Minors (DREAM) Act was introduced in the US Senate by Richard Durbin (D-IL) and Orrin Hatch (R-UT). This bill would have granted conditional permanent residency to those immigrants with good moral character who arrived as minors, had continuously lived in the United States for five years, and graduated from US high schools. At first they would obtain temporary permanent residency for six years. During this period of time, beneficiaries would have been required to complete two years of community college or a bachelor's degree or military service (Immigration Policy Center 2011).

I greeted the introduction of the DREAM Act with great enthusiasm. I was joyful and very optimistic about it. It was a light at the end of the tunnel. I said to myself, "Keep working on your education, and soon it will pay off." The day after the introduction of the bill, we talked about it at school, and everyone within our close circle was excited. Unfortunately, it was just an illusion—a dream (ironically). The bill has yet to be enacted, and it has been changed as it has been reintroduced over the years. The DREAM Act has come before Congress many times (see Table 2.4), and it also has been included as part of other legislation such as the Comprehensive Immigration Reform Act (2006 and 2007), the Defense Authorization Bill (2008), and the National Defense Authorization Act (2011).

State Laws and Access to Higher Education

Since its introduction, the DREAM Act has been the hope of many undocumented immigrants in order to become eligible for financial assistance and achieve higher education. At the national level, politicians have failed repeatedly to pass the DREAM Act. However, various legislators have proposed state-level DREAM Acts with some success. State legislatures cannot propose a path to citizenship. They typically focus on access to higher education and funding opportunities. Undocumented students achieved their first such victory when some states granted them the ability to pay in-state tuition rather than out-of-state fees, which can be more than three times the amount. In addition, select states have passed laws that allow undocumented students tuition assistance in the form of eligibility for scholarships and even state financial aid.

In-State Tuition Eligibility

Several states provide in-state tuition or some kind of relief for undocumented students at either community college or university levels (see Table 2.5). In 2001, Texas set the precedent as the first state to pass a significant law benefiting undocumented immigrants. Texas House Bill 1403 granted nonimmigrant students access to in-state tuition for higher education institutions that included state financial aid. The bill required residing with a parent or guardian in Texas, graduating from high school or having received a general education development (GED) diploma, having resided in Texas for three years, and signing an affidavit stating intent to adjust to documented status if the opportunity presents itself (Texas Higher Education Coordinating Board 2008).

Similarly, California Assembly Bill 540 (AB 540) was signed into law on October 12, 2001, by then governor Joseph Graham "Gray" Davis Jr. It allows undocumented students to qualify for in-state tuition at institutions of higher education such as the CSU system, the UC system, and the community college system. In order for undocumented students to benefit from this law, students need to meet certain criteria that include having attended a California high school for three years or more, having graduated from a

Table 2.4 DREAM Act and Similar Legislation Proposed in US Congress

Senate Bill	House of Representatives Bill
S 1291 Development, Relief, and Education for Alien Minors Act of 2001 (8/01/2001)	HR 1582 Immigrant Children's Educational Advancement and Dropout Preservation Act of 2001 (4/25/2001)
S 1545 Development, Relief, and Education for Alien Minors Act of 2003 (7/31/2003)	HR 1918 Student Adjustment Act of 2001 (5/21/2001)
S 2075 Development, Relief, and Education for Alien Minors Act of 2005 (11/18/2005)	HR 1684 Student Adjustment Act of 2003 (4/09/2003)
S 774 Development, Relief, and Education for Alien Minors Act of 2007 (3/06/2007)	HR 5131 American Dream Act (4/06/2006)
S 2205 Development, Relief, and Education for Alien Minors Act of 2007 (10/18/2007)	HR 1275 American Dream Act (3/01/2007)
S 729 Development, Relief, and Education for Alien Minors Act of 2009 (3/26/2009)	HR 1751 American Dream Act (5/14/2009)
S 3827, S 3962, S 3963, and S 3992 Development, Relief, and Education for Alien Minors Act of 2010 (various dates)	HR 6497 Development, Relief, and Education for Alien Minors Act of 2010 (12/07/2010)
S 952 Development, Relief, and Education for Alien Minors Act of 2011 (5/11/2011)	HR 1842 Development, Relief, and Education for Alien Minors Act of 2011 (5/11/2011)

California high school or obtained a GED, and submitting an affidavit stating he or she meets the AB 540 requirements and is in the process of adjusting his or her immigration status or will do so as soon as he or she qualifies (Mexican American Legal Defense and Educational Fund 2009). These requirements have been used with similar legislation across the United States.

Table 2.5 States Granting In-State Tuition for Undocumented Students

State	Year of Passage and Law Number	State Financial Aid[a]
Texas	2001, HB1403	Yes
California	2001, AB 540	Yes
Utah	2002, HB 144	No
New York	2002, SB 7784	No
Washington	2003, HB 1079	Yes
Illinois	2003, HB 60	No
Oklahoma	2003, SB 596 (revoked in 2008)	No
Kansas	2004, HB 2145	No
New Mexico	2005, SB 582	Yes
Nebraska	2006, LB 239	No
Wisconsin	2009, A 75 (revoked in 2011)	No
Maryland[b]	2011, SB 167/H 470	No
Connecticut	2011, HB 6390	No
Colorado	2013, SB 33	No
Minnesota	2013, S 1236/HF 1692	Yes
New Jersey	2013, S 2479	No
Oregon	2013, H 2787	No
Florida	2014, HB 851	No
Virginia	2014, via DACA	No

State University Systems Granting In-State Tuition
2011, Rhode Island Board of Governors
2013, Hawaii Board of Regents
2013, Michigan Board of Regents

Notes: a. States granting financial aid to undocumented students might have passed additional bills separate from an in-state tuition bill to grant financial assistance to undocumented students.
b. Community colleges.

Analysis demonstrates, however, that in-state tuition is not enough to ensure students' success. Conger and Chellman (2013) analyzed the academic performance of New York State college students, where undocumented students have access to in-state tuition. They found that although "undocumented students perform well in the short term, earning higher grades," for example, they were less likely to earn their bachelor's degree in four years compared with their US citizen counterparts (364). Thus, undocumented students experienced higher costs than anticipated for completing their four-year college degree.

Many undocumented students take semesters off because their financial situation is dire. Throughout my educational career I had to work to pay tuition fees and buy books; I borrowed money from my parents and friends so that I could pay tuition fees and enroll in my classes.

State Tuition Assistance

Some immigrant advocacy groups have successfully pressured politicians to grant in-state tuition, but it is a struggle that continues in many states with a high percentage of undocumented immigrants. Because there was no action on the DREAM Act at the federal level, advocacy groups and pro-immigrant politicians have begun to pressure the US Congress by drafting and pushing for state-level DREAM Acts. See Table 2.5 for states that have granted in-state tuition in the United States.

The California DREAM Act, championed by Gilbert Cedillo, was passed in 2011 (California DREAM Act 2011a, 2011b). The act was divided into two pieces: AB 130 and AB 131. AB 130 allows those students who qualify as AB 540 students to receive only privately funded scholarships in the CSU system, the UC system, and California community colleges. AB 131 allows AB 540 students to receive state-funded financial aid, which includes institutional grants, fee waivers, Cal Grants, and Chafee Grants (California Student Aid Commission 2011a, 2011b). These bills were initially estimated to benefit about 2,500 students, with a state cost of $14.5 million, just *1 percent* of the annual budget for Cal Grants (Wilkey 2011). According to the California Student Aid Commission, the highest number of applications came from Los Angeles, San Jose, Santa Ana, and San Diego. In San Diego County alone, undocumented immigrants submitted approximately 920 applications (Aguilera 2013).

In March 2011, the Maryland legislature passed its DREAM Act. Opponents to the bill were able to get enough signatures to pose it as a referendum in the November elections of 2012. Voters ratified it with 58 percent in favor. In comparison to other state DREAM Acts, the Maryland version requires the beneficiaries to have attended high school for at least three years and for their parents to have filed income taxes for at least the past three years. Furthermore, if undocumented students attend a community college in their county, they are eligible for in-county tuition. Then, after having obtained or earned sixty units, they can qualify for in-state tuition at four-year universities (Tilsley 2012).

Whereas the laws described above enhance access to higher education, several states passed laws severely restricting it. Arizona, Indiana, and Georgia deny in-state tuition to undocumented immigrants, and Alabama and South Carolina prohibit enrollment in higher education. As discussed in the next section, the United States is experiencing a flurry of anti-immigration policies aimed beyond educational outcomes.

Anti-Immigrant Legislation

During harsh economic times, immigration policies reflect the attitudes of a given historical period (King, Massoglia, and Uggen 2012). The Great

Recession (2008–2010) is a case study in anti-immigration backlash, despite Latino/a immigrant workers losing more union jobs than native-born white workers (Catron 2013). These laws directly and negatively affected immigrants and their communities and cast a chilling effect on the aspirations of and opportunities for undocumented families and their children. Table 2.6 provides a clear picture of recent anti-immigrant sentiment in the United States. It is important to note states that have not traditionally received undocumented immigration flows, such as midwestern, rural, and southern states, have been some of the most active in proposing and passing anti-immigrant legislation.

South Carolina initially passed some of the most restrictive legislation in recent history (2008), and Arizona legislation in 2010 paved the way for copycat laws in other states. Arizona passed the Support Our Law Enforcement and Safe Neighborhoods Act, also known as Arizona SB 1070. This law criminalized undocumented immigrants and granted police agencies the power to detain individuals on the basis of being undocumented. Although this legislation in Arizona garnered the most national attention, it is important to note similar legislation was being considered throughout the United States. The different state bills had key factors in common: status verification for employment purposes and the criminalization of immigrants. As a consequence, cities have tried to follow in the same footsteps by passing anti-immigrant ordinances.

Anti-Immigrant City and Regional Ordinances

Public outcry about undocumented immigrants has affected local communities that have also passed anti-immigrant ordinances. Traditionally, immigrant integration begins at urban centers as a result of existing social networks that include family, friends, or acquaintances. This contributes to better socioeconomic conditions for these groups as immigrants integrate into US society. Jiménez (2011) states that recent migration waves are more complex and that immigrants are moving into suburbs, skipping urban centers altogether (10). Furthermore, he states that immigrants are much more dispersed, and states in the South and Midwest, places with little or no immigration prior to the 1990s, now have a great number of immigrants (11). Over the years immigrants have moved to new "destination" states, and this has changed population dynamics, leading to anti-immigrant sentiments across the country. Table 2.7 lists some of the laws passed that directly affect undocumented immigrants through local or city ordinances.

Local anti-immigrant movements and ordinances can affect undocumented students' education. During the rise of such movements students can experience a whole range of psychological problems. Clark-Ibáñez, García-Alverdín, and Alva (2011) reported on the strategies of undocu-

Table 2.6 Anti-Immigrant State Policies

State and Year	Name and Brief Description
South Carolina, 2008	HB 4400: South Carolina Illegal Immigration Reform Act (signed by Governor Mark Sanford on June 4, 2008). Mandates the use of E-Verify, denies higher education for immigrants, and restricts access to public benefits
Arizona, 2010	SB 1070: Support Our Law Enforcement and Safe Neighborhoods Act (signed by Governor Jan Brewer on April 23, 2010). Requires local and state law enforcement to enforce federal immigration law, establishes criteria for federal and state benefits, prohibits undocumented immigrants from working or soliciting work, and prohibits the transport or smuggling of undocumented immigrants
Minnesota, 2010	HF 3830: Support Our Law Enforcement and Safe Neighborhoods Act (died in House Public Safety and Oversight Committee). Required local and state law enforcement to enforce federal immigration law, established criteria for federal and state benefits, prohibited undocumented immigrants from working or soliciting work, and prohibited the transport or smuggling of undocumented immigrants
Michigan, 2010	SB 1388 and HB 6256: Immigration Law Enforcement Act (both died in Judiciary Committee). Allowed for enforcement of federal immigration law, allowed for detention of undocumented immigrants, allowed civil actions against undocumented immigrants, and provided civil fines and criminal penalties
Pennsylvania, 2010	HB 2479: Support Our Law Enforcement and Safe Neighborhoods Act (died in House Appropriations Committee). Provided local law enforcement power to apprehend undocumented immigrants for deportation; employer sanctions for those who hired undocumented immigrants; eliminated public benefits, welfare, and education for undocumented immigrants
Missouri, 2010	HB 2449: No exact title (died in International Trade and Immigration Committee). Made it a crime to traffic in, conceal, harbor, shelter, or transport undocumented immigrants
South Carolina, 2010	HB 4919 and SB 1446: No exact titles (both died in Judiciary Committees). Provided for illegal alien enforcement verification of immigration status and arrest of people suspected unlawfully present in the United States
Rhode Island, 2010	H 8142: In Support of Our Law Enforcement and Safe Neighborhoods Act (died in Judiciary Committee). Criminalized the presence of undocumented immigrants and allowed racial profiling
Louisiana, 2010	HB 1205: Louisiana Taxpayer and Citizen Protection Act (died in Judiciary Committee). Increased racial profiling and discrimination based on national origin; made it illegal to harbor, conceal, or shelter undocumented immigrants
South Carolina, 2011	HB 3129: Illegal Aliens Enforcement Act (died in Judiciary Committee). Allowed law enforcement to arrest undocumented

(continues)

Table 2.6 continued

State and Year	Name and Brief Description
	immigrants, made it an offense with penalties not to carry immigration documents, and made it a violation with penalties to hire day laborers
	SB 20: Immigration Status and Enforcement Act (signed by Governor Nikki Haley on June 27, 2011, yet challenged in court and many provisions ruled unconstitutional). Allows law enforcement to detain or arrest a person to check immigration status, makes it unlawful to solicit work, eliminates sanctuary policies, and makes it a crime to use fake IDs for establishing legal presence
Georgia, 2011	HB 87: Illegal Immigration Reform and Enforcement Act of 2011 (signed into law by Governor Nathan Deal on May 13, 2011, but key provisions challenged in court). Authorizes law enforcement to demand "papers" for citizenship or immigration status, criminalizes those who interact with undocumented immigrants, and makes it difficult for immigrants to access state facilities and services without proper identification documents
Alabama, 2011	HB 56: Beason-Hammon Alabama Taxpayer and Citizen Protection Act (signed into law by Governor Robert Bentley on June 9, 2011, but challenged in court, and only two provisions dealing with immigration remain in effect). Requires public schools to check students' immigration status, criminalizes the transportation of undocumented immigrants, requires the use of E-Verify, and allows law enforcement to check for immigration status; provisions remaining in effect: police allowed to check for immigration status during routine and E-Verify required for employers
Wyoming, 2011	HB 0094: Illegal Immigration Act (introduced in the state legislature but failed to gain enough support to pass). Allowed police agencies to arrest without warrant individuals who committed offenses and who would be eligible for deportation
Mississippi, 2011	SB 2179: Support Our Law Enforcement and Safe Neighborhoods Act of 2011 (died in Conference Committee). Allowed police to enforce immigration laws and indemnified the officers for doing so; allowed officers to make unwarranted arrests of individuals to verify their immigration status
Virginia, 2011	HB 2332: Arresting officer to ascertain citizenship of arrestee (amended and conjoined to become HB 1465). Allowed police to act as immigration officers by inquiring as to citizenship or immigration status upon arrest
	HB 1465: Higher educational institutions; policies prohibiting admission of illegal aliens (died in the Committee of Courts of Justices Subcommittee on Immigration). Required Virginia's public colleges and universities to deny admission and enrollment to undocumented immigrants
	Other bills would have required enforcement of federal immigration laws and allowed businesses to use E-Verify; required Social Services to verify legal citizenship of applicants for public assistance and withhold funds if violations existed

Table 2.7 Local Anti-Immigrant Ordinances

City or County	Year	Ordinance
Hazelton, Pennsylvania[a]	2006	Prohibits landlords from renting to and businesses from employing undocumented immigrants
Vista, California	2006	Prohibits businesses from employing undocumented day laborers
Escondido, California[b]	2006	Prohibits landlords from renting to undocumented immigrants
Prince Williams County, Virginia[a]	2007	Requires police to check immigration status
City of Farmers Branch, Dallas County, Texas[a]	2007	Prohibits landlords from renting to undocumented immigrants
Fremont, Nebraska[a]	2010	Prohibits landlords from renting to and businesses from employing undocumented immigrants
Summerville, South Carolina[c]	2010	Prohibits businesses from employing undocumented immigrants

Notes: a. Challenged in court and ruled unconstitutional.
b. The city agreed not to enforce the ordinance.
c. The city eventually tabled the proposal due to political pressures.

mented students to circumnavigate a hostile environment in their communities and to use school spaces as a safehaven when dealing with such an anti-immigrant environment. Similarly, Aranda and Vaquera (2015) found that undocumented young adults in Florida shared the stress of everyday movement in their communities due to the police profiling of immigrants.

Current Political Situation

When it comes to comprehensive immigration reform, a 2012 Politico/George Washington University poll showed the US electorate supports immigration reform by 62 percent. Similar results are shown among those registered as Democrats and independents, whereas only 49 percent of registered Republicans support such a measure (Campanile 2012). In a 2014 poll, Politico asked a simple question: "Do you oppose or support comprehensive immigration reform?" Results show that 71 percent support it (Weigel 2014).

Comprehensive Immigration Reform

Immigration has always been a controversial topic, in particular during elections in which politicians use it to gain constituents' support. Barack Hussein Obama was no exception. He used immigration in his political platform to gain the Latino/a vote by supporting the need for comprehensive immigration reform. He won his first presidential bid in 2008, and he promised an immigration bill during the first year of his presidency, yet he was not able to keep his promise because of a Republican-controlled Congress. In the presidential election of 2012, President Obama won reelection with an even greater percentage of the Latino/a vote. After winning reelection, he reiterated his promise of comprehensive immigration reform. He stated: "Before the election, I had given a couple of interviews where I predicted that the Latino/a vote was going to be strong and that would cause some reflection on the part of Republicans about their position on immigration reform. I think we're starting to see that already. . . . And my expectation is that we get a bill introduced and we begin the process in Congress very soon after my inauguration" (Lambert 2012).

The president saw immigration as a key issue that would benefit the US economy (for economic benefits of comprehensive immigration reform, see Hinojosa-Ojeda 2010, 2012; Immigration Policy Center 2013). During his first term, President Obama had to deal with tough economic problems. He spoke about immigration as part of rebuilding the economy, saying "our ability to thrive depends, in part, on restoring responsibility and accountability to our immigration system" (White House 2011).

Latino/a organizations and immigration rights activists pledged to hold politicians accountable if comprehensive immigration reform was not passed by the end of 2013, and it was not. They planned to use a "report card" of politicians' records to make them accountable for their actions. A key strategy would be a massive campaign to naturalize as many Latino/as as possible so they could become eligible to vote. If politicians do not achieve comprehensive immigration reform, Latino/a voters will send a "report card" to show them who supported comprehensive immigration reform so politicians can suffer the consequences for such actions by not receiving the Latino/a vote (Preston 2012).

As a Latino immigrant, I was very excited when President Obama was elected in 2008. He gave me hope for one day having my immigration status fixed. This has not happened. Instead, he has stirred a lot of criticism from immigration rights activists and organizations because of his stance on immigration enforcement, which has led to a record-breaking number of deportations. In the 2012 fiscal year, the number of deportations was more than 400,000 (Foley 2013a). Deportations have skyrocketed since the implementation of the Secure Communities Program, an ICE enforcement policy. The National Council of La Raza, the largest Latino/a advocacy group in the United States, has called the president the "Deporter-in-Chief" (Epstein 2014).

Some argue the president has been prevented from fulfilling his promises for immigration because of federal legislators. In 2013, passing comprehensive immigration reform seemed promising. On April 17, 2013, a group of eight senators, four Democrats and four Republicans, known as the "Gang of Eight," introduced a comprehensive immigration reform bill in the Senate. The "Border Security, Economic Opportunity, and Immigration Modernization Act of 2013" offered a pathway to citizenship for the estimated 11 million undocumented immigrants in the United States. It provided greater benefits to DREAMers and agricultural workers who could apply for a green card and immediate US citizenship. Those who did not qualify for the DREAM Act benefits, however, would have to wait for greater border security reports before they could get a green card and eventual citizenship (for full text, see US Government Printing Office 2014). Critics of the bill believed it was not fair for all immigrants to wait that long because many have been in the country more than ten years or even twenty years. The bill successfully passed the Senate Judiciary Committee with a thirteen-to-five vote, and it passed the full Senate with a sixty-eight-to-thirty-two vote on June 27, 2013 (GovTrack 2013).

Democrats in the House of Representatives introduced their own version of the Senate bill on October 2, 2013. The House bill was drafted by eight representatives and contains similar statutes to those in the Senate bill. However, House majority leader John Boehner preferred to have several pieces of legislation addressing immigration. Meanwhile, the bill has stalled in the House of Representatives because it has been introduced to different House committees that have taken no action. This led Representative Joe Garcia, a Democrat from Florida, to petition for a Motion to Discharge Committee on March 26, 2014, in order to withdraw any consideration of the bill in all committees (Congress.gov 2014). Immigration reform has been on the table for years without any success (see Table 2.8).

Deferred Action for Childhood Arrivals (DACA)

Since 2011, there have been temporary advances in achieving immigration reform in the United States. On June 15, 2012, President Obama signed an executive order granting deferred action to certain immigrants unlawfully present in the United States at the time of enactment of the law (see further discussion later). This was the result of political pressure after many failed attempts to pass comprehensive immigration reform and the DREAM Act. Also, this political pressure resulted from President Obama's failure to cap-

Table 2.8 Approaches to Immigration Reform Bills

Comprehensive Immigration Reform Bills
Secure America and Orderly Immigration Act of 2005 (S 1033 and HR 2330)
Comprehensive Enforcement and Immigration Reform Act of 2005 (S 1438)
Comprehensive Immigration Reform Act of 2006 (S 2611)
Secure Borders, Economic Opportunity, and Immigration Act of 2007 (S 1348 and S 1639)
Comprehensive Immigration Reform Act of 2010 (S 3932)
Comprehensive Immigration Reform Act of 2011 (S 1258)
Border Security, Economic Opportunity, and Immigration Modernization Act of 2013 (S 744 and HR 15)

Piecemeal Approach: House of Representatives Bill[a]	Vote	Date of Passage
Border Security Results Act (HR 1417)	Unanimous	May 15, 2013
Strengthen and Fortify Enforcement Act (HR 2278)	20–15	June 18, 2013
Agricultural Guest Worker Act (HR 1773)	20–16	June 19, 2013
Legal Workforce Act (HR 1772)	22–09	June 26, 2013
SKILLS Visa Act (HR 2131)	20–14	June 27, 2013

Notes: For more information on other bills containing immigration statutes consult www.govtrack.us (https://www.govtrack.us/congress/bills/subjects/immigration/6206).

a. Bills have passed the House of Representatives Judiciary Committee but have not moved to the House floor for a vote.

italize on his promise to pass comprehensive immigration reform after winning the presidential elections of 2008. After Obama was elected, immigrants were hoping for drastic changes in immigration policy during the first year of his presidency, but instead immigrants continue to be affected by restrictive local, state, and federal laws.

Janet Napolitano, former secretary of DHS, announced the protection of certain individuals who would meet certain criteria, a protective status of two years. This deferred action did not grant lawful status but rather protection from removal from the United States or lawful presence in the United States (US Citizenship and Immigration Services n.d.c). Immigrant advocacy groups critical of DACA have stated that such a policy is not enough when dealing with immigration and that it still leaves beneficiaries of the law unprotected. For example, Castillo (2012) stated that the Department of Health and Human Services made it clear DACA beneficiaries would be excluded from the "lawful presence" category as well as other programs such as Medicaid, the Children's Health Insurance Program (CHIP), or subsidies from the Affordable Care Act (ACA).

The US Citizenship and Immigration Services (2014) has accepted 642,685 applications and rejected 30,732. Applicants of Mexican origin (493,669)[4] top the Latina/o applicants' country of origin with El Salvador (24,199), Guatemala (16,472), and Honduras (16,297) the next most frequent. Other countries include Peru (8,007), South Korea (7,904), Brazil (6,709), Colombia (6,062), Ecuador (5,897), the Philippines (4,041), Argentina (3,848), Jamaica (3,377), India (3,097), and Venezuela (2,782). California (183,497) and Texas (105,262) represent the top states of residence for the applicants.

At the federal level, DACA gave temporary relief to some DREAMers, and there was progress in uniting family members of mixed-immigration status. A few states were able to pass legislation benefiting undocumented immigrants based on DACA. In 2012, Illinois passed SB 957 (the Highway Safety and Mandatory Insurance Act), a law granting "temporary visitor" drivers' licenses to undocumented immigrants or foreign nationals unable to obtain a Social Security number if they have resided in the state for a year and to those unable to provide proper documentation of lawful presence in the United States (see Illinois General Assembly 2011, 2012, 2013).

In 2013, the California Assembly passed AB 60 (the Safe and Responsible Driver Act), which grants undocumented immigrants special drivers' licenses (Drive California n.d.). According to a Pew Research Center study, 2.5 million undocumented immigrants live in California, and the Department of Motor Vehicles estimated that 1.4 million would be eligible to apply for a driver's license (Melendez Salinas 2014). California was the tenth state to allow undocumented immigrants the ability to obtain a driver's license. Similar to DACA, despite offering some relief, the bill has caused a stir in the immigrant community because the licenses for undocumented drivers will effectively alert law enforcement of their immigration status. California governor Jerry Brown touted the bill as a victory for undocumented immigrants and proclaimed, "No longer are undocumented people in the shadows" (Taxin 2013). Yet, the Southern Poverty Law Center (2012) is fighting against cases of law-enforcement abuse, such as when sheriffs' deputies enforce federal immigration law (not their jurisdiction).

Nebraska and Arizona denied drivers' licenses for DACA beneficiaries (National Immigration Law Center 2012). Legal challenges similar to the one filed in Arizona are expected in all states denying DACA beneficiaries drivers' licenses. The Mexican American Legal Defense and Educational Fund (MALDEF), the American Civil Liberties Union (ACLU), and the National Immigration Law Center filed a lawsuit on behalf of DACA recipients (Planas 2012). On December 17, 2014, the US Supreme Court ruled that Arizona cannot deny drivers' licenses to DACA recipients, and the High Court is considering whether to hear an appeal of a Ninth Circuit Court ruling in the case *Arizona Dream Act Coalition et al. v. Brewer* (American Civil Liberties Union 2014).[5] Although it is not a perfect long-term solution, it does prioritize the safety and humanity of undocumented immigrants.

Provisional Unlawful Presence Waiver

On January 2, 2013, the secretary of Homeland Security announced a change in policy regarding waivers of inadmissibility for immediate relatives (spouse, children, or parents) of US citizens. Under a previous policy, those individuals who would benefit from an immediate relative living in the United States had to return to their countries of origin in order to benefit from an inadmissibility waiver. This waiver had to be requested after a US citizen had filed a petition for an immigrant visa. The usual process took from six months to a year to grant admission into the United States, which separated families for long periods. The new provisional unlawful presence waiver would allow individuals to stay in the United States while their case moves toward final action. Individuals would still have to leave the country to appear for an interview and obtain an immigrant visa, but separation from loved ones would be for a shorter period. This recent change in policy has been viewed by many as a move in the right direction, keeping families together (US Citizenship and Immigration Services n.d.d).

One of the reasons the driver's license laws, DACA, and the provisional unlawful presence waiver are so necessary is that the surveillance, apprehension, and deportation levels in the United States are alarmingly high and increasing.

ICE, the Secure Communities Program, and Deportations

As noted, US immigration policy has sometimes been more open toward immigrants and sometimes been restrictive in periods that reflected the socioeconomic and sociopolitical contexts of the times. For example, during the Great Depression many Mexicans were repatriated as a way to alleviate the pressures of immigration on the economy. Furthermore, in 1954, the US government implemented "Operation Wetback" as a way to deal with undocumented immigration. This was a program that continued despite the existence of the Bracero Program. The Bracero Program was not bringing in enough unskilled laborers, yet at the same time the government was deporting them.

The US government has passed and implemented various programs as a way to implement some type of control over immigrants. In 2008, the US government implemented the Secure Communities Program with the purpose of targeting criminal immigrants for deportation. President Obama ended this program with his executive order on immigration announced on

November 20, 2014, but substituted the Priority Enforcement Program (Linthicum 2014).[6]

The Bush administration initiated the Secure Communities Program in 2008 as a pilot program that involved fourteen local police jurisdictions. It was a fingerprint-sharing program that involved local, state, and federal law enforcement agencies to identify deportable criminal immigrants. One of the first participants was the Harris County Sheriff's Office (Texas). By the first months of 2011 the program already had more than 1,000 jurisdictions participating. The original intent was to make it a national program in which all police had to participate (US Immigration and Customs Enforcement 2012). The program was to target only criminal immigrants, but in reality it affected noncriminal immigrants and US citizens alike (Sacchetti 2013). For example, many US citizens, criminal and noncriminal, were wrongfully processed under this program. Also, the parents of many US-born children were deported, sending many of these children into the foster-care system. In addition, the program was criticized for racial profiling: Latino/as were 93 percent of arrestees but make up 77 percent of the undocumented population (Rickerd 2012). Furthermore, Rickerd (2012) stated that "more than 56 percent of Secure Communities deportees had either no convictions (26 percent) or one or two misdemeanor convictions (30 percent)."

This policy shaped my most recent experience with immigration as an undocumented immigrant in the United States. When the police asked me about my parked car, I had a clean record; yet I was turned over to ICE when I could not produce a valid driver's license. I was still a sociologist when I was booked into the detention center in downtown San Diego, and I asked other immigrants why they were detained and deported. Most of them in the holding cell were detained at "sobriety" (i.e., driver's license) checkpoints. These checkpoints have been criticized for targeting undocumented immigrants (Gates 2012). Others shared stories about how they were detained because of simple traffic stops. The *New York Times*, through the Freedom of Information Act, requested data about the origins of police/ICE contact. They found that most of the recent deportations affected men under thirty-five years old of Mexican origin and were based on minor traffic violations (Thomson and Cohen 2014). The story also documents the effects on the community. For a primary wage earner to be deported causes economic and mental health stress on the family, along with negatively affecting children's enrollment in school.

Obama's Executive Order of 2014 on Immigration

After President Obama took office in 2008, he struggled to keep his promise on comprehensive immigration reform. Many have blamed Republican

US representatives' inaction on immigration policy. Different studies concur on the negative effects of not passing comprehensive immigration reform. For example, Ye Hee Lee (2014) cites a study conducted by the Center for American Progress that states the US economy is losing $37 million per day in revenue. Furthermore, passing an immigration bill will decrease the federal deficit by $158 billion in the next ten years.

Congressional Republicans' inaction on immigration reform is also creating a divide within the party. There are Republicans who support comprehensive immigration reform, yet they are frustrated by the attacks against those who support any type of action. For example, Senator Bob Corker (R-TN) stated, "I get really frustrated with people on my side of the aisle who say that anything you do on immigration is amnesty" (Schelzing 2014).

Unfortunately, the US Congress has not introduced a bill that will be widely accepted among Republicans, some Democrats, and conservative groups. Prior to the midterm elections of November 2014, President Obama postponed any administrative relief for undocumented immigrants, citing the surge of undocumented children along the US-Mexico border that created a border crisis. This decision also took into consideration the benefits and consequences of acting prior to the midterm elections because many Democrats' seats in Congress were at stake (Meckler 2014).

The midterm elections of 2014 did not turn out well for Democrats. Republicans regained control of the US Senate, taking full control of both chambers of the US Congress. Before the elections, House Republicans made it practically impossible for President Obama to push through any items of his agenda.

Immigrant rights groups and activists have pushed the idea of an executive action for quite some time. For example, in 2011, President Obama addressed the National Council of La Raza at their annual luncheon. He stated, "Now, I know people want me to bypass Congress and change the laws on my own" (Feldmann 2011). In a June 2011 ImpreMedia–Latino Decisions tracking poll, results showed clear support for executive action, with 74 percent supporting such measures as stopping deportation of undocumented immigrants married to US citizens. Also, 66 percent supported stopping deportation of undocumented immigrants eligible for the DREAM Act (Bolton 2014).

Finally, on November 20, 2014, President Obama announced another executive order on immigration called Deferred Action for Parents of Americans and Lawful Permanent Residents (DAPA).[7] The executive order still has enforcement and border security provisions, but the centerpiece includes protection from deportation for certain undocumented immigrants. This includes the parents of US citizens and legal permanent residents. Also, it enhances DACA by eliminating the age limit, which previously prevented many DREAMers from benefiting from this executive action implemented in 2012 (US Citizenship and Immigration Services 2013). Prior to the announcement by President Obama, the Migration Policy Institute issued a brief report on different executive action scenarios, estimating that between 1.6 million and 4.3 million individuals would benefit (Capps and Rosenblum 2014:8). Immigration rights groups and advocates are still divided in their reactions to this executive order; some praise President Obama's action, and other say it is not enough (Walker 2014).

Obviously, there is much work to be done when it comes to immigration reform. Eventually, this issue will be center stage for the presidential elections of 2016, in which the immigration debate could dictate the winner. Congress has lagged in an adequate response to immigration reform, which still continues to affect many undocumented immigrants.

Conclusion

Writing this chapter made me look back at the decision my father made to migrate to the United States in 1989 and for the rest of my family to follow. Knowing we would face major difficulties because of our undocumented status did not stop my parents from migrating. My parents' sacrifices have always been present throughout my undocumented immigrant experience as a DREAMer. Also, this chapter has allowed me to revisit my own educational struggles as a result of immigration law or lack thereof.

As I look back at the history of immigration law, early policies have had an impact on many immigrant families. Undocumented immigration into the United States has a long history during which the US government has implemented policies to deter it, but such laws have had the opposite effect.

Undocumented students have been affected deeply by immigration policy. Table 2.3 provides key court cases that have dealt with accessibility to education. *Plyler v. Doe* set a precedent when dealing with access to a K–12 education. *Leticia A. v. University of California Board of Regents and California State University Board of Trustees* set a precedent with regard to access to higher-learning institutions but was overturned at the beginning of the 1990s. IIRIRA made it more difficult for undocumented students to access four-year higher-learning institutions and community colleges.

I also addressed anti-immigrant local ordinances and statewide legislation because such policies can affect undocumented students in terms of school performance and ability to pursue higher education. Such laws have emerged even though Congress has discussed immigration reform as shown in Table 2.8. Even though undocumented students experience negative policies, they still persist in seeking higher education and eventually achieving legal presence in the United States.

President Obama's executive order on immigration is clearly a positive step toward a solution to a problem that has dragged for decades. People are still hopeful that someday politicians will provide a clear solution to immigration reform in order for undocumented immigrants to be active participants in US society and for them someday to have a piece of paper stating "permanent resident" or "US citizen."

Notes

1. Voluntary departure means an immigrant departs the United States without a removal order. A voluntary departure allows an immigrant 60 to 120 days to depart the country instead of the 30 days required for those with a removal order. Contradictory information exists about the benefits of seeking a voluntary departure; some sources state that it does not render an immigrant automatically inadmissible for future immigration benefits, and others state that inadmissibility bars can be imposed.

2. General provisions of the Bracero Program included protection for any kind of military service, protection from discriminatory acts, payment of living expenses and transportation from and return to places of origin, proper lodging and medical and sanitary services, payment of agreed salary without any deductions, contracts written in Spanish, wages reflecting those of local farmworkers, exclusive employment as agricultural workers, and the formation of a rural savings fund for each worker of which the Mexican government was in charge. There was also a provision preventing the displacement of US workers (Colorado Oral History and Migratory Labor Project 2008).

3. For critical aspects of the Bracero Program, see Durand (2007) and Mandeel (2014).

4. The following figures reflect applications accepted. Figures on approved applications reflect a slightly lower number. For statistics on DACA from 2012 to 2014, see US Citizenship and Immigration Service (2014).

5. Class-action lawsuit by the American Civil Liberties Union (ACLU) and other civil rights organizations against Arizona governor Jan Brewer's unconstitutional executive order denying driver's licenses to DACA recipients.

6. Under the new program only those convicted of serious crimes or who pose a national security threat will be targeted.

7. As of this printing, DAPA has not gone into effect. On February 16, 2015, Andrew S. Hanen, a US federal district judge from Texas, filed a lawsuit to prevent DAPA from being implemented. In the lawsuit, which was brought forth by the state of Texas (and twenty-five other states), Hanen argues that President Obama's actions were unconstitutional for having bypassed Congress. Moreover, Hanen states that the federal government would put undue costs on states and intrude on state laws about granting driver's licenses. On May 26, 2015, the Fifth Circuit Court of Appeals in New Orleans *denied a request* by the US Department of Justice to lift the hold on DAPA.

3

Elementary School: The Beginning and the Promise

We begin our exploration of the educational pipeline with understanding the experiences of teachers and undocumented students at Hillside Elementary School, situated in a low-income, Latino/a immigrant community. In this chapter, we discuss survey data from the teachers and analyze photo-elicitation interviews with undocumented students. I, Rhonda Avery-Merker, also draw upon my five-year experience as a paraprofessional working one on one with students inside and outside of classrooms, and will speak for both authors throughout this chapter. I witnessed their academic promise, excitement to learn, and hopes for a future. I have also been a sociologist. As a white, first-generation returning college student, I was drawn to participate in this project because of my sense of social justice and observation of the direct and indirect discrimination experienced by young, Latino/a undocumented students.

The good news, based on this case study, is that the beginning of the pipeline is promising. The undocumented students revealed they love school and learning, and most teachers were supportive of undocumented students and their families. This point cannot be overstated: students love school and learning, *and* they have relatively supportive teachers. In contrast, as they move through the educational pipeline, many students do not continue to the next stage of their journey. This is considered serious leaking, at each stage, from the pipeline.

In *Plyler v. Doe* (1982), as explained in the prior chapter, the Supreme Court stated that undocumented children have a constitutional right to

---

Rhonda Avery-Merker and Marisol Clark-Ibáñez wrote this chapter together.

attend public schools. The ruling notes that education is a child's only path to becoming a "self-reliant and self-sufficient participant in society." A public school education, the Court reasoned, "inculcat[es] fundamental values necessary to the maintenance of a democratic political system" and "provides the basic tools by which individuals might lead economically productive lives." According to the Court, denying children access to a public school education could doom them to live within "a permanent caste of undocumented resident aliens" (Borkowski and Soronen 2009:4).

Yet, most of the children at Hillside Elementary School—documented or not—will have a hard road to travel to graduate high school. The Latino/a high school graduation rate for this Southern California town is less than 50 percent; of those graduating, less than 30 percent of Latino/as have completed any college preparation courses (Nuñez-Alvárez and Ardon 2012). The children at Hillside Elementary School come from low-income families, most speak Spanish as their first language, and they live in a community with a high immigrant population. Based on the data collected and discussed for this chapter, Hillside Elementary School has at least four to six undocumented Latino/a students in each classroom.

Hillside Elementary School

Hillside Elementary is situated just off a main road and up a long hill. To the west of the school is a prairie-like vacant lot flanked by apartment buildings, a trailer park, and small commercial malls with businesses such as the Dollar Tree Store. The campus boasts an open building plan with clusters of classrooms near the beach, allowing students to enjoy a regular cool ocean breeze. The bright, whitewashed walls provide a contrast to green grass and the gates that surround the buildings. There are two vegetable gardens and a "butterfly and hummingbird" garden. The principal assigns students from rotating classrooms to weed and tend the gardens.

Of the 660 students at Hillside Elementary School, the majority is Latino/a and low income: 87 percent is Latino/a, 3 percent black, almost 2 percent Pacific Islander, and 6 percent white. The percentage of socioeconomically disadvantaged students is high, at 89 percent. English learners constitute 67 percent. Students with disabilities make up 15 percent. Most students are native Spanish speakers, and all students are integrated in the twenty-six classrooms. Structured English immersion is used for some of the students if they need support in that language. In 2013, 287 English learner students received specialized teaching for forty-five minutes every day, which provided the English learners oral and written

English practice and enabled them to access the English and language arts core curriculum. The teaching staff and administrators are mostly white, non-Latina females.

School administrators are aware of the low-income status of the families. For example, in the summer, the school offers free lunch for all students. Their parents can eat as well for a modest fee of $3. During the year, before and after school, classes in math and English are offered, along with enrichment classes on Early Release Wednesday. Students are chosen by teachers once a year to receive the opportunity to obtain free shoes at a Payless shoe store. Toward the end of each school day, the school secretary cheerfully announces over the loudspeaker, "Backpacks are ready for pickup!" The backpacks are loaded with food for children to take home to their families. Last year, the school gave all parents the opportunity to buy new computers with flat screens for only $65. The librarian and several other staff members entered the school into a contest to win iPads for the classrooms.

Yet, some school practices involving parents were less understanding of families' needs. For example, the principal of Hillside expressed that she did not realize there were undocumented students at the school, and over the years there have been different policies about parents entering the school. For several years, the most family friendly option was allowing the parents to walk their children to their classrooms, which also usually involved greeting the teacher. Sometimes parents would linger and watch their children settle into the school day. The children and their parents appeared very happy with this ritual. A new principal changed this policy. Parents were no longer allowed to enter the school grounds without express permission and checking in at the front office. A guard was posted at the entrance of school. The principal offered little explanation, for example in terms of safety, and so the parents were unsettled and offended. Students were also upset by this change; it was common to see children crying and clinging to parents at the gate. In contrast, many teachers were happy with the change and explained that they did not like the parents coming into their classrooms in the morning. This change had a negative effect on how the parents viewed the school and the leadership.

In 2012, responding to the low college-going rates in the district, all schools were asked to develop programs to encourage higher education. At Hillside Elementary, teachers and the principal regularly invoked college through symbols and song. Each morning, teachers hung their college flags outside of their classrooms. On Wednesdays, teachers wore their college T-shirts and encouraged students to wear school logo shirts as well.

In accordance with *Plyler v. Doe*, the school is sending a message about the *existence* of college. This might be an important first step toward achieving the mandates that "public schools should provide equitable access and ensure that all students have the knowledge and skills to succeed as contributing members of a rapidly changing, global society, regardless of . . . immigration status [and] socioeconomic status" (Borkowski and Soronen 2009:i). Although there was a superficial display or a "spectacle" at Hillside of enthusiasm for college, it did not translate to classroom discussions about why students should go to college. Teachers encouraged students to stay in school so that they could one day obtain a job. Additionally, the school lacked resources: there were not enough textbooks for students and not enough paper to copy sufficient handouts for classroom activities. We find conditions similar to Anyon's (1981) research on class and the hidden curriculum: what and how students learned corresponded to their families' socioeconomic class in terms of their likely future occupations.

Teachers and Undocumented Students

Given this school context, we were curious as to what teachers knew about undocumented students. I created an anonymous, open-ended short questionnaire for teachers at the school. I met with the principal to show her the survey and asked permission to distribute it to all the teachers. It was during this meeting that I learned she was unaware of any undocumented students attending the school, yet she was eager to know more about the research on this population.

Twelve educators—eleven teachers and the school nurse—returned the surveys. I promised anonymity and asked that they leave the questionnaires in my staff mailbox. However, they either gave me their questionnaires directly or wrote their names on them. The surveyed group was small (little more than one-third of the thirty teachers employed), and there was a self-selective bias. Nonetheless, it was heartening to discover that all but two of the educators expressed compassion for their undocumented students.

Awareness. Eight respondents knew of students in their classes who were undocumented. They each knew of at least four to six students in their classes and suggested that there could be more. Four teachers were not aware of the immigration status of their students.

The teachers and nurse became aware of their undocumented students in a variety of ways. Two teachers shared that they knew of the students' status "through classroom discussions and parent disclosure." Another teacher overheard students' worried conversation about potential deportation for themselves and their parents. The nurse wrote, "As a district school nurse, I regularly check the . . . database to see where a child was born. This helps me to know which services I am able to refer them to for assistance. If they were not born in the U.S., resources are limited. I could tell you some sad stories."

The teachers also found out about a student's status when there was a crisis in the family. One of the teachers realized one of her students was undocumented when another parent asked her for "a character recommendation letter for a parent who had been picked up [by the border patrol]." Another time, a student was absent so much that the teacher "went on a home visit where the neighbors reported that the family was picked up by the *Migra*."[1]

One teacher did her own investigating. "Some of them give up the information on their own and some I'm able to get info from our database. Parents also make us aware of it during IEPs." (An IEP is an individual educational plan required for students with disabilities.) Another teacher reported, "For four of my students, the student or the parent told me about their status. In response to this questionnaire, I went through the cum [student] files of all the students and discovered two more of my students were born in Mexico and are undocumented." Schools cannot keep records of the students' immigration status. However, teachers looked up the birthplace of students to assess whether they were documented or not, sometimes following up with parents and other times assuming a particular status given their birthplace and no birth certificate on record. Teachers who knew of undocumented students reported an average of six of twenty-five students (or nearly one-fourth) of the classroom could be undocumented.

Empathy. The teachers in this study were aware of the fear experienced by the undocumented students and their parents. One teacher wrote, "Students worry about wanting to get citizenship or legal papers. Many of our students are more concerned about their parents being sent back to Mexico."

Several of the teachers overtly supported their undocumented students. One teacher wrote that she "personally knows an undocumented family," and she has "watched the effects of being undocumented on the children as they have grown up here." Another teacher expressed compassion for what some students go through:

> We had two brothers in our class whose mother was undocumented. (I'm not sure but I think [the brothers] also were undocumented and their baby sister was born here). The grandfather died in Mexico and the mother went home to his funeral. She passed her baby back to relatives at the border crossing (after the funeral) and then went with a Coyote [migrant smuggler] on a trek through the desert. This was the year of the horrible October fires in San Diego County and their group was overcome by fire. Her husband had to identify her at the UCSD Medical Center by the nail polish on her toes because her face was so badly burned. She died two weeks later, and the school personnel had to go to the house to help the father break the news to the kids. Heartbreaking. . . . Our students shouldn't have to deal with these kinds of issues!

Although sympathetic, sometimes teachers do not have accurate information. For example, a teacher wrote that she wanted her undocumented students to prepare as if they were going to college: "An undocumented student should take advantage of all the education possible, especially in computers, science, and language, so that when the day comes when higher education is open to them, they will be prepared." Another teacher shared, "I personally know of an undocumented student who came to this country at age fourteen. She quickly learned English, studied hard, received good grades—very high marks and, had she been born here, she would have been admitted to UCLA! If the day comes when undocumented students can go on to university, these hard working students will be prepared. I do hope that day will come for them." These two teachers believed there are no current pathways to higher education open to undocumented students, when in fact in California there is open access to community college and four-year universities. In this case, empathy must be complemented with accurate information about opportunities for undocumented students.

Resources. Many of those surveyed noted that Hillside Elementary School had done a great job with bringing resources into the school for all low-income students. A teacher wrote, "We don't treat students differently depending on their immigration status, and our school does everything possible to refer families for outside services, etc." The school nurse shared, "Our undocumented students have great teachers and educational resources for basic ed [*sic*] services." Yet, she added that obtaining medical care, especially dental care, was very hard without a Social Security number. She went on, "However, some schools have foundations or PTA's with funds for extensive supplemental programs."

Another teacher explained how the undocumented benefit from such resources. "Our undocumented students would benefit from exposure to outside cultural activities, local sites to gain general knowledge (e.g., science museums, nature centers, theater, etc.). . . . Positive activities such as sports teams, scouting, dance classes, etc., are out of reach for our undocumented students who often live in poverty." Another teacher described, "Due to being undocumented, these children learn to hurry home and do not attend after school enrichment programs."

Most teachers wrote that they give *all* their students equal attention and help in class; for example, one teacher explained, "I don't know who they are so I can't say they get an unequal education. More importantly, I try to give all my students an equal education." Another teacher wrote, "I teach every child in my classroom to my full capabilities. They are all treated with respect and fairness. I have neither seen nor heard of any teachers giving differential treatment." Teachers who believe all students are the same are ignoring structural inequalities and conditions they could work to ameliorate through classroom dynamics and intervention (Grossman and Charmaraman 2009). This lack of awareness could result in a problematic, "colorblind" approach to teaching, in which racism is not overt but subtle and operates through institutional and cultural practices (Bonilla-Silva 2003). It does not serve the students for teachers to believe "they are all equal" (Boutte, Lopez-Robertson, and Powers-Costello 2011). Black lesbian feminist scholar and poet Audre Lorde argued that we do not need to obliterate difference to end oppression and inequality; instead we need to redefine and address what it means. Simply stated, some students need more help than do others, so the task becomes deploying resources in a better way to improve the learning and lives of students.

Understanding. Some teachers and the nurse at Hillside were clear on how undocumented immigration status affected their students. They believe undocumented students and their families experience life (and school activities) differently than students and families who are documented and/or US citizens. One teacher explained, "Resources are needed for the exposure of other things outside of the ordinary everyday living." Another teacher felt that parents were fearful of presence of Immigration and Customs Enforcement (ICE) and that this stress deterred a more intensive involvement at the school: "Parents are often hesitant to take an additional walk/drive to school to see teachers because they could be picked up by [the] *Migra*."

One teacher encountered this fear directly: "When I make home visits, I'm sometimes told that parents are leery to go out because of previous incidents. In one family, the dad was picked up a few times and is now in detention in North Carolina." Another teacher reflected, "When I worked in [another region of San Diego], I saw children of undocumented workers left with neighbors or extended relatives (cousins, e.g.) when parents were deported. . . . I believe undocumented children are vulnerable."

These fears of family separation were not lost on the teachers. Most noted that family was important to their students. All the teachers who knew of specific undocumented children in their classroom stated that the children were fearful of their parents being deported.

One teacher shared, "Students/children of parents who are undocumented have a bigger fear that they will be deported. Some of these children suffer because they are less likely to get out in the community. They will end up staying indoors where there is no threat of deportation. I think this is a huge problem—isolation—and therefore fewer students understand the world around them. They have less experience in the community and being active." She acknowledged that the children were less involved and that the lack of community involvement affected social and cultural capital and upward mobility.

In addition, some teachers mentioned that some class discussions focused on students missing their grandparents and cousins back in Mexico. One teacher explained, "They also have shared that they're sad that they can't visit their grandparents in Mexico because they don't have papers." It is thought-provoking to note that students willingly brought up the issue of their immigration status when discussing their grandparents.

One teacher believed that students' immigration status might influence them in class. "I think some undocumented students are so intimidated by Anglo students and teachers that they sometimes refuse to answer or participate in a classroom setting or a social gathering. But, [I] also know that the Hispanic [people are so] . . . intimidated by their immigration status that they choose not to be heard or seen." Reflecting on issues of invisibility in the classroom and in the community, another teacher felt that the most important change for undocumented students was the "freedom to be visible."

Another teacher wrote that she thought it was easier for undocumented students to "fall between the cracks" in the educational pipeline because they moved around so often: "These students are sometimes more transient as well, so [they] can fall fast through the cracks before anyone is aware of their special and specific needs."

Overall, ten educators (including the nurse) were well intentioned, and some even had a profound, complex understanding of the undocumented students in their classroom. More professional development (e.g., ally training) and accurate information (e.g., regarding legislation such as AB 540 and the California Development, Relief, and Education for Alien Minors [DREAM] Act) could leverage this positive perspective to improve the experience for all undocumented students and their families. The local colleges and universities have programs to connect with high schools in the feeder communities for recruitment of historically underrepresented groups in the community, which include undocumented students. These outreach efforts should expand to elementary schools.

Anti-"Illegal" Immigration Teachers. There were two teachers (one male and one female, both white) in this sample who expressed explicitly negative views on undocumented immigration. One of the teachers, a female, slightly less critical of undocumented immigration than was the male, was aware of undocumented students in her classroom. She was ambivalent, adding the caveat, "This is a really hard one!" but ultimately she felt that undocumented children had a fundamental right to education. She stated, "Since the children are already here and probably want to stay here, we have the responsibility to educate them the same as every other student in America. By educating them, we are improving their future and the country's future." Then, she revealed her political views: "I do not believe people should come to the United States illegally, since there are so many people that have to wait and come legally. The government needs to do something about this and make it harder for illegal immigrants to stay here and use our resources for free."

The other teacher was male, held very strong views, and was unaware of undocumented students in his class. He wrote, "Undocumented children belong to undocumented parents, all of which burden all systems of government. While sad, all undocumented (illegal) U.S. occupants should be deported." This teacher reiterated his perspective in *each* portion of the questionnaire: "Again sadly, although they were placed in a situation they did not create and while—like all children—they need an education, they must receive this in the country from which their parents illegally emigrated." Interestingly, he made it a point to hand me the survey, despite the opportunity to contribute it anonymously, and said, "I would be happy to talk with you about this more." I believe he directly shared his views with me because I am a white woman, and he (mistakenly) may have thought we held similar views.

The teacher with the strongest views against undocumented immigrants wrote extensively, beyond the questions of the survey, "It is resoundingly clear that our government and all its facilities, programs, and services are extremely overburdened due to non-tax paying undocumented, illegal occupants of our country. Our 'humanitarian' mindset has been taken advantage of, causing numerous cutbacks, closed programs, and discontinued services. These resulting outcomes are seen across the board in many governmental institutions as well as private. Although sad, it's time to tell the world, 'We cannot feed, medically treat, and educate all of you (unless you follow our laws).'" He draws upon legal discourse, the economy, and a focus on individual choices to mask the plain and simple "go back where you came from" perspective. Interestingly, he keeps using "it's sad" or "sadly," which may serve to soften a nativist perspective. Pérez Huber (2010) summarizes a nativist perspective in terms of white supremacy and an intense opposition to the "foreigner." It is alarming that this educator works in a school of predominantly new immigrants with a significant undocumented population.

Summary: Mostly Positive Support by Teachers

At Hillside Elementary, all but two teachers who responded to the questionnaire felt that undocumented students were worthy of support and advancement. One teacher listed the benefits undocumented students should have in a classroom: "acceptance, trust, security, safety, stability, and opportunity." Another teacher expressed that undocumented students deserve "security, nurturing their confidence personally and academically, validating their culture and language, [and] provided opportunities."

The one caveat about the teachers who stated that they treat all their students equally is the notion that "we are all the same." Although a noble idea, it creates consequences that hinder students from achieving success. Yes, we are all humans. However, when we ignore structural forms of inequality and think everyone has the same chance at life (or school), we actually do a disservice to those students structurally at a disadvantage. Sociologists believe that when you overlook issues, you overlook people. Citizenship, socioeconomic status, race, and gender are all issues that must not be overlooked.

Perhaps the opposite of this idea is the notion that we seek to understand and address those differences so as to help those in need. The Internet meme depicting "equality versus equity" comes to mind: it depicts two scenes when children of different heights try to peek over a fence to watch a baseball game.[2] *Equality* is when three children of different heights are standing on the same-sized crates, resulting in differential viewing (best, barely, and no view at all). *Equity* is when the children have different-sized crates so that all three can see over the fence. It is foolish to think every student needs the same thing (same-sized crates) in order to succeed. The comparison below aptly demonstrates that we need different sizes of services for different types of students in order to produce successful outcomes for all.

The Students' Photographs: What Is Important to Them

The photo-elicitation interview project asked that students who participated take photographs of what was important to them. It took about a month for me to explain the project to them individually. I knew that they were undocumented, but I did not frame the project as a study of undocumented children. Although many undocumented Latino/a students expressed interest in the project, in the end seven parents allowed me to do the photo-elicitation project with their children. I understood that even though the topic of the photography project was not about undocumented children per se, the parents were very cautious. There is a looming presence of the border patrol in the neighborhood, even sixty miles from the US-Mexico border. There were several times students came to school crying because one of their parents or relatives had been detained or deported. (Note: Our Pipeline Research Collective decided that we could not sufficiently know the consequences of discussing immigration status with young children. See Appendix A for a more elaborate discussion of this ethical issue.)

When parents and students from a given family agreed to participate in the study, I gave the students each a disposable camera for the project. When the students finished taking their pictures, they returned the camera to me, we set a date for the interview, and then I developed the film. Each student I met with seemed to look forward to the interview. They took it very seriously, and each student came to his or her scheduled interview on time, ready to talk about the pictures they had taken.

Fernanda, Inez, Oscar, Andrea, Esteban, Maria, and Giovana all were given cameras to take photos of what was important to them. They completed this part of the project quickly. I developed the film and then made photo albums with each student's images so that she or he could take them home. We used a second set of copies for the student to shuffle through and put them in certain orders during our one-on-one interviews at school in a quiet room. Each interview lasted about thirty minutes, and the children truly led the discussion, explaining the significance of each picture.

Note, we do not display the children's photographs in this book because we could not be certain of the extent that their identity, location, and the identity of secondary subjects in their photographs could jeopardize their immigration status. The photographs were used as prompts to help them discuss their own lives.

All but Esteban wanted to do the interviews in English, so the quotes are taken verbatim from transcripts and reflect their status as English learners. In general, the students were very energetic and positive. Yet, naturally, they became sad if they talked about someone they missed or how hard their parents worked. Most of the students demonstrated positive attitudes toward their school, teachers, family, and friends.

Immigration Status

Although I took care not to directly bring up the children's undocumented status, I learned that they were aware of their status and experienced fear or worry. Through the course of everyday conversation, some students were comfortable enough to trust me and share their thoughts on their undocumented status. A fourth grader told me her mom told her not to tell anyone that she did not have her papers. I asked her how she felt about that, and she told me that she felt scared. A fifth grader told me she was not able to go on a class field trip because her mom did not want anything to happen to her. Another student told me she was afraid to drive with her dad because the police might stop him, and they could "pick him up." Students who knew they were undocumented understood secrets, limited activities, and fear for themselves and their parents' safety. Yet, by reaching out to me (and other trusted educators) they also seemed to know some adults are worthy of trust (Hernandez et al. 2011).

The students seemed to cope with the stress of understanding (at least partially) the meaning and consequences of being undocumented. The students at Hillside Elementary played just like any other children—monkey bars and four square—but their made-up games revealed much about their daily stress. In particular, many students engaged in a "shooting-chasing" game they called "*La Migra*." This is similar to the game Omar played, described at the beginning of the book. (Note: Omar's reflections were from 2004!) Children are still playing this game today. One day, I asked one of my students, "Who are you chasing?" The little boy said, "The bad guys!" I replied, "Who is bad? What did they do?" The boy responded, "Nothing, they didn't do nothing!" I said, "So why are they bad?" The student shrugged and ran off to continue the chasing. Games like "Cops and Robbers" and "Cowboys and Indians" have traditionally had a racial component, distinguishing one group as good (right) and other as bad (wrong). "*La Migra*," broken down into players, involves one "scary guy" chasing undocumented immigrants ("bad guys"). Yet, the boy's comment was telling: he knows the "bad guys" get chased, yet he does not know what the bad guys did. Similar to how children played in times of slavery and concentration camps, undocumented children are enacting and incorporating the external pressures and messages into their everyday play (Eisen 1990; Frost 2005; Mintz 2014; Monning 2014; Wiggins 1980).

Family

The students' photographs were overwhelmingly images of their families. Very common were responses that simply reflected the love of their parents. Andrea responded to a picture of her dad: "Oh I was taking this picture of my dad because he's nice with me. Um, he takes good care of us. And I like him so much." When she explained the picture of her mother, she elaborated more: "I took a picture of my mom because I like her so much. She buys me almost all the things I want. . . . She [clears throat] and she goes like to all the stores. She buys me Cheetos for me and my sisters. And she takes care of my cousins because she want to 'cause she wants to buy us stuff." At her young age, she has connected her mother's child-care job to what her mother does to provide for them, similar to how she conceptualizes her father as "taking good care of us." Most of the undocumented elementary school students in this study mentioned their parents were working or hardworking and seemed highly aware of their economic condition. Although Andrea was happy her mom bought her almost everything she wanted, it appears as though her wants are minimal (e.g., Cheetos).

Two students took photographs of a family outing to a park. In fact, the longest time that Maria spoke about her photographs was about going to the park with her mom, brother, sister, and dad. This is a small excerpt of her narrative: "Uh, that's the park where we went to the work of my dad because he . . . he started the house, and we were playing water balloons and I took a picture about that because I was all set and then we were playing soccer and a boy came and we were playing." In other images, she explained that her dad was working in construction on a house next to the park. She was very excited to be able to spend the afternoon with her entire *familia*. Maria took several pictures of her dad. In one of the pictures, I noticed a large scar on her dad's arm. I asked her what happened to her dad's arm, and she told me that he fell off of the roof of the house he was working on.

Several students took photographs of family photographs. Andrea, for example, took photographs of framed baby pictures of siblings. Other times, it was a photograph of their parents' wedding portraits. For example, Oscar, who was in fifth grade, explained: "It's when my mom and dad got married. It really important to me because they got married and took a picture about them. That's really important to me." Students were capturing images of past family events or memories, not just living in the present moment, which indicates a complex understanding of family in terms of space and time.

I interviewed Oscar on the day of his fifth-grade graduation. Oscar also shared that he wished he could have taken a photograph of his grandmother, back in Guerrero, Mexico. It was the only time when one of the young interviewees explicitly mentioned that he "didn't have papers" and thus could not go back to see her. Researchers find that the loss of meaningful contact with grandparents can negatively affect a child's mental health and lead to depression in the long term (Doyle, O'Dywer, and Timonen 2010; Moorman and Stokes 2013).

Friends

Second to family members, the most popular topic for the undocumented elementary school students was their friends. Most of the friends photographed were at school. Fernanda was the only student who had a friend other than a relative, a close neighbor with whom she played after school. She explained that they played together because "she lives next to me. And, I go play with her in her house. When I finish my homework, I go to her house." We found that friendships were formed with immediate neighbors or within the living space of each child (e.g., an apartment shared with members of extended family).

After reading their narratives about friends, we realized there was a clear vision emerging of friendship for these young undocumented students. Although there are many popular books on helping children make friends, none are geared to low-income or immigrant children. It was exciting that some clear "friendship rules" emerged from their photographs and subsequent interviews. All the interviewees, except for Oscar, mentioned what they liked in a friend.[3]

1. *Friends help you, and you help them.* Inez, a third grader, described why a particular friend was important to her: "Um because when I didn't haded a partner, she way partner, was my partner, then we made friends." Giovana helped her friend not be as shy: "She's um sometimes shy. When I met her and now when we started um hanging out each other a long time, then, um, she's not shy with me anymore."
2. *Friends play with you.* Fernanda had an image of two girls in front of the school and said, "Me and her we play at recess and lunch recess and Maribel too. I took it because she is my best friend." Inez described a friend's photograph: "That's my friend and we always play together. And we share stuff together." Her other friends were described this way: "Those are my friends and they wanted, I wanted, I taked her, I taked them a picture on the monkey bars." She elaborated that they always played on the monkey bars at lunch recess. Yet another set of friends were explained like this: "Um the tall one and that's my friend Marisol and the other one is Karen. She always plays with me too and I like her. They are playing Chinese Checkers."
3. *Friends are nice to you.* Giovana shared about her friends, "She hangs out to me at recess and lunch recess and we never fight." Of other friends in her photographs, she described as "being so nice to me."
4. *Friends give you things.* Giovana took a photograph of her friend and described her, "She's nice and gives me snacks if she asks me and she's really kind." Another friend's image was captured because "she's, um, shares her food with me or sometimes I share food with her."

These friendship rules echo some of the findings for children in diverse socioeconomic contexts and nations (Corsaro 2003). Yet, the students are similar to low-income African American families in Lareau's (2003) study and confirm her findings: "The commitment among working-class and poor families to provide comfort, food, shelter, and other basic support requires ongoing effort, given economic challenges and the formidable demands of child rearing" (5). However, unlike the African American children in her study, who were allowed to play outside more freely with less adult supervision, the undocumented Latino/a children in this study were more constrained to developing friendships at school or within their immediate living space. The parents of our participants were not invested in "concerted cultivation," as there were no indications of the elaborate "play date" schedules or intensive after-school events found in middle-class families.

Yet, the photographs of their delightful play and friendships serve to counter the stereotype that undocumented students are living in the shadows, fearful to connect with others.

Education, School, and Teachers

The photographs demonstrated that the students loved learning and being in school. On a sunny, spring afternoon, seven-year-old Andrea and I sat in an empty classroom looking at the photographs she took as a participant in our study. She flipped through the stack to an image of her mother sitting at a table. When I asked her what was happening in the photograph, she said, "I am playing with my mom." I replied, "What kind of things do you play with your mom?" She proudly said, "Teachers, 'cause she wants to learn English too." She explained further, "Sometimes [my mom] doesn't have time for us because she needs to cook. So just, um, on Saturdays and Sundays we play with her." Andrea also elaborated on a photograph she took of a little playhouse in her apartment and shared, "We play teacher there. Uh, I teach [my sisters] math and reading and sometimes make multiplications."

Esteban had only been in the United States for about three weeks when I interviewed him. Most of his photographs were of various images of Hillside Elementary School. He was very enthusiastic about being in school and in the United States: "*Esta es la escuela que voy. Esta es mi escuela favorita [por]que a mi me gusta porque aquí puedo jugar [y] puedo aprender cosas. Puedo aprender ingles, matemáticas, todo. Y si no puedo ir al escuela—aburrido! No sabría nada.*" ("This is the school where I go. This is my favorite school, and I like it because I can play and learn things. I can learn English, math, and everything. And if I could not go to school, it would be boring. I would not know anything.") Esteban had already made good friends, and he was an enthusiastic participant in the classroom. Esteban's teacher was not Latina, but she was fluent in Spanish, which seemed to help Esteban participate and feel more comfortable.

Other students focused on specific people related to school. All the students took photographs of their teachers and spoke of them fondly. Andrea captured an image of the speech pathologist and her assistant: "Oh I took this picture from Miss Marshall and Miss Marta because they're my best teachers. Because they, um, they just play games and they are nice." Inez took a photograph of Mr. Lopez, who she described as, "I tooked him a picture because . . . he always, we always do art time at after recess. And then we do our spelling bee every time. Then we do time tables."

Giovana, a fourth grader, took photographs of several previous teachers: "Miss Smith, she's been nice to me [even] when I'm mad. She's been nice to us and done a lot of fun projects." Giovana also said of her fifth-grade intervention teacher (gearing her up for the next level): "She's been really nice. She has [been] teaching me a lot of things I didn't know and now I get them. And she is a good person for me and really nice." Giovana also captured images of her sister's favorite teacher and her best friend's third-grade teacher. Fernanda took a picture of her speech teacher, and when I asked her if she liked speech, she explained, "I like it. I umm learn about pronouns and adjectives." Oscar took a photograph of his best friend and me (a paraprofessional). Inez described a photo saying, "That is Noon Duty. I told her if I could take a picture and she said yes. She lives in my apartments."

Esteban took photos of what he learned in school. For example, he took a photograph of a bottle of water and then explained how he is learning about the environment—not only to save water usage but also to recycle bottles when they are empty. He described how much he loved learning about science.

Yet, the pathway to college is not totally clear for these students. Oscar mentioned that he might not finish high school because he wants to play soccer, explaining: "You have a lot of money and you have fun." I asked Maria if she was going to go to college, and she hesitantly told me yes. I asked her what she would study; she shrugged her shoulders and said, "I don't know." In previous years, a third grader mentioned to me that she was not going to college. When I asked her why not, she said that her dad told her she could not because she did not have papers and would be home working in the kitchen. In this child's case, gender and immigration status seem to play a role in educational decisions by her father.

Material Things

The children took photographs of material things, but these were the fewest in each sample. For example, they documented their computers, dolls, or shoes. For most, it appeared to be an inventory of what their families owned. Maria's mother told her to take a photograph of their computer "to show the computer we have." Esteban took photographs of money, fruit, and his shoes saying that he was glad his family had these things. Fernanda captured images of her toys, dolls, a PlayStation, a shelf of movies, and even "gelatina" (Jell-O). In contrast, Oscar explained why he did not take very many photographs: "I didn't have a lot of stuff. . . . Yeah, like, we threw [a lot] away when we moved . . . two years ago."

More popular were images of meaningful moments or gestures represented by material items. Maria took a photo of flowers her father gave her mother for Mother's Day. Giovana took a photograph of a plant and said: "I took it because my mom, she planted it in my house. So, I like it. And I like it to be there. And, my mom, she works a lot." Andrea explained the photograph of her teddy bear: "I sleep with the teddy bear. I have it, um, I got it for Christmas. My dad bought it for me. Um, I like it so much." She also took a photograph of her brother's drawing of a clock, explaining: "That picture was my little brother's and what he made in kindergarten."

Self-portraits were evident in some students' images. Sometimes a mother or sister would encourage them to take one, and other times the students felt inspired on their own.

Adults and other children were influential in the photographs. This was also found in other photo-elicitation interview projects, such as in Clark-Ibáñez's (2004, 2007) studies of inner-city childhood. Maria told me she took a picture of her mom because her mom wanted one to put in a frame. Andrea revealed the story behind the funny photograph of her brother, "Um that was when my little brother was laughing so much and he made the face. So my mom wanted me, she wanted me to take a photo of him and he made a face." Some yard monitors and peers asked the students to take their photos too.

Summary: Playful and Engaged

The seven undocumented children in this photo-elicitation study were in many ways much like most other elementary school children. They loved recess, their families, and their friends. All but one of the students was engaged with school and had a least one teacher they deemed important enough to include in their collection of images. Suárez-Orozco and colleagues (2011) have discussed the multitude of ways unauthorized children are affected developmentally by their immigration status. They also describe the "conditions of exclusion" that shape their experiences (465). Indeed, our findings support much of their research in terms of the families' hardships and fears. In this study, the photographs and the children's commentaries on them, however, offer an on-the-ground perspective of how children actually experience their daily life at school. At this point in the educational pipeline, they show enormous promise and positive energy as demonstrated through their interviews.

Of particular note is their connection to the family, or *familismo* (rooted in the family), as a factor in Latino/a children's resiliency. Immigration is inherently stressful—the change in culture and homelands, traumas of crossing the border, and disruptions in marital or family routines. Chapman and Perreira (2005) report that a strong family orientation can improve the physical health, emotional health, and educational well-being of youth. Xu and Brabeck (2012), drawing on social-work case studies, found that undocumented children demonstrate impressive resiliency through their work ethic, solid moral compass, positive self-image, and emotional coping skills even though they face challenging barriers.

There is also indirect evidence of the resiliency of their parents, who are very hardworking and protective. Undocumented parents also draw from *familismo* for inspiration to try harder and do more for their children, according to a study by Parra-Cardona and colleagues (2006). The parents they interviewed expressed a belief that life in the United States, even with the barriers they and their children have to face, is better than the life they would have if they were to stay in the place they were born. The children expressed a strong enthusiasm for being in school.

Recommendations

There are a number of ways in which we can capitalize on the children's educational engagement, the optimism of their parents for their educational futures, and the willingness of teachers to be compassionate allies on their educational journeys. In this book, Alma Ruiz-Pohlert (Chapter 10) details specific pedagogical and institutional practices that benefit undocumented elementary school children and their families.

The data from my study demonstrate the teachers were compassionate, yet some were not correctly informed of laws and opportunities affecting undocumented students. Therefore, professional development for educators could include a yearly update on changes in immigration laws and policies. Cultural competency training that did not rely on color-blind discourse would deepen the teachers' pedagogical practice. The teachers relied on fairly superficial college-related connections (e.g., wearing their alma mater T-shirts). Although teachers have many responsibilities, there are many groups in the region willing to speak to students specifically about being undocumented and going to college.

At the school level, there are several ways in which administrators could transform the culture and ultimately the opportunities for the undocumented students featured in this chapter.

Administrators should understand the student population. It was surprising when the principal shared that she did not realize there were any undocumented students attending. She wanted to learn more from the research but was not taking an active role in conducting outreach with the families at the school in order to understand immigration issues. This is an essential first step in transforming the school in terms of an immigrant-friendly space because it could lead to specific, better-suited resources for the student population and inclusive language (e.g., "even though you don't have citizenship, you can still. . .") that could result in students further seeing their potential for going to college.

The students are already demonstrating a commitment to learning, engagement, and critical thinking. Their enthusiasm for being in school and for their teachers is already there. It is up to educators to take advantage of their positive energy and efforts.

Ultimately, teachers and administrators must foster an atmosphere of acceptance, security, and trust for undocumented children and their families. Instruction should reflect both a respect for home cultures and languages while simultaneously offering meaningful English development. Understanding that some children need more of a boost than others requires careful staffing, which is important in creating programs that can respond sensitively to the needs of undocumented students.

Conclusion

Although the undocumented students in this study seemed to know their status, they may not have realized the full implications their undocumented status might have for their futures until much later, as we will see in the following chapters. It has been posited that being undocumented, as an identity, becomes salient when matched with experiences of exclusion because "undocumented children move from protected to unprotected, from inclusion to exclusion, from de facto legal to illegal" (Gonzales 2011:602). In the case study presented here, the elementary school students are legally "included" in the educational system; yet in this community, the ultimate form of exclusion—deportation—was common. The elementary school students may not have been able to give a developmentally sophisticated account of their experiences of being undocumented, but they certainly lived in a context of hypervigilance and suspicion. I know families in the school's surrounding community who simply did not enroll their children in school for fear of detection and deportation. The structural impact of programs such as Secure Communities in this region (as discussed in Chapter 2) is influencing what we have known about the life course experience of undocumented students.

The children in this chapter were aware of their fragile status and the possibility that they or a parent could get deported. Still, they loved being at school, learning, and making friends. In refusing to succumb to life's circumstances, these students have found a resiliency from which we can all be inspired.

Notes

1. People often use the term *la migra*, the Spanish slang for the border patrol. The US Department of Homeland Security (DHS) has replaced the name Immigration and Naturalization Service (INS) with Immigration and Customs Enforcement (ICE).

2. An Internet meme is "the propagation of content items such as jokes, rumors, videos, or websites from one person to others via the Internet" (Shifman 2013:362).

3. As a reminder, the interview excerpts are verbatim. We wanted to honor the ways in which the participants talked in English, Spanish, and Spanglish (e.g., we did not correct the text when instead of saying "I took," a participant said, "I taked" (pronounced *tay-ked*).

4

Middle School: Creating New Paths

Since 2000, I have coordinated programs and services for the Gaining Early Awareness and Readiness Program (GEAR UP), which helps Latino/a students and parents understand the importance of education and prepares them early for college enrollment and completion. A unique feature of GEAR UP is that we recruit cohorts in middle school, support them through high school graduation, and encourage them to attend college. As a first-generation Chicana college graduate, I work with many families with backgrounds and histories similar to my own. I often see my own parents' faces in the parents of these new immigrant families. I am compelled to help them develop the necessary communication skills, increase their knowledge of the US educational system, and connect them to resources with the goal of producing more Latino/a college graduates of all immigration statuses.

In collaborating with Marisol Clark-Ibáñez to learn more about the general research on middle school, we realized that scholarship was concentrated in the areas of bullying, "deviance," and peer groups. Many articles conceptualized middle school students as troubled or as victims. Not a single peer-reviewed academic article focused on the undocumented students' experience in middle school. In this chapter, I attempt to provide an overview of how middle schools operate with regard to undocumented Latino/a students through the lens of GEAR UP, which is embedded in many middle school campuses in the North County region of San Diego.

Cecilia Rocha is the author of this chapter.

As I reflect on the enthusiasm demonstrated by the undocumented elementary school students in the previous chapter, I believe middle school may serve as a "cooling out" period for their educational aspirations. This chapter describes a variety of ways in which many middle school educators and administrators can make a crucial difference in the lives and futures of undocumented students.

The Middle School Context

Middle school is a hard time, developmentally, for youth. They are maturing into new identities and practicing new gender roles. Institutionally, middle schools are organized so that students are in new classrooms and interact with new sets of classmates up to seven times a day. New habits are being formed to prepare students for high school.[1] This process alone is overwhelming for most US-born students. Undocumented students must navigate additional challenges and circumstances in an already difficult developmental period.

The undocumented middle school students featured in this chapter were part of GEAR UP. I aim to present a compelling portrait of the diversity of undocumented middle school students' experiences and the ways in which GEAR UP has served to support their educational journey. Unlike programs such as Advancement Via Individual Determination (AVID) that have an academic screening process, any student can join GEAR UP.[2] We believe every child can be successful.

In general, middle school is a crucial (and often overlooked) period in the educational pipeline. According to Balfanz (2011), when a sixth-grade child attends school less than 80 percent of the time, fails math or English, or earns an unsatisfactory grade in a core course, *without intervention this leads to a 75 percent chance of dropping out of high school.* Many middle schools implement formal tracking; research has found that if students have difficulty in one area (e.g., English) then they are tracked "lower" in all other classes (Wells 1989).

Most states do not report or monitor middle school rates of completion. However, in 2011 California became the first state to publicly acknowledge middle school dropout rates. It reported that "17,257 eighth-grade students dropped out" before high school age, a 3.49 percent dropout rate (Bonsteel 2011).

For Latino/as, the rate of middle school students going on to enter high school is thought to be lower. For example, in San Diego County during the 2012–2013 school year, of the 210 students who dropped out of *seventh* grade, 115 (or about half the group) were Latino/as; out of the 272 students who dropped out of *eighth* grade, 135 were Latino/as. About half of the students leaving middle school were Latino/as: 250 of the 482 dropouts were Latino/as.[3] Although undocumented students are not tracked by the state, one might conservatively guess that they are among Latino/a students. It is also important to note that these are conservative numbers; the California Department of Education (2013) acknowledged that English learners, students with learning disabilities, migrant students, students in alternative schools, and socioeconomically disadvantaged students tend to be underreported. Again, undocumented students likely intersect with some of these underreported student populations (e.g., migrant, English learner, low socioeconomic status).

Behind the numbers, the middle schools in our region changed significantly for the worse over the first decade of the new millennium. In 2000, there were Spanish-language classes offered, honors courses in all core subject areas, five or more sections of AVID, and cultural classes such as Encuentros. AVID is a program designed to prepare underrepresented and low-income students for high school graduation and college admission. The Encuentros curriculum is based on California standards and focuses on teaching students the historical and cultural significance of Latino/a leaders and community figures. Students learned their historical background and learned to formulate their own identity as it related to their families, educational experiences, and college and career goals.

Fast forward to 2013. None of the current GEAR UP middle schools offered Spanish or honors courses, they had a limited number of AVID sections, and there were no Encuentros cultural courses. These changes have a large impact on Latino/a first-generation and undocumented students. The Spanish and Encuentros classes were a venue in which Latino/a students could feel comfortable speaking Spanish at school, and therefore their Latino/a background was accepted. The programs validated the students' cultural background, which we know is important for their academic success.

The absence of an honors program in middle school will have a profound effect on the educational pipeline for those attending underresourced schools. The honors program offered the opportunity to prepare early for the academic rigor of high school advanced courses. The lack of this program puts Latino/a students at a disadvantage because they are unable to compete in high school with students who had an honors program at their middle school. Moreover, the reduction of AVID classes leaves first-generation, college-bound Latino/a students with fewer resources to learn note-taking and studying skills and less access to writing and math tutorials. It also takes away an in-class support system. School counselors are already overwhelmed with their large student caseloads, so AVID teachers typically helped address students' college questions when the school counselors were unavailable.

Finally, middle school students know when they are not given the same resources and opportunities and held to the same high expectations as their counterparts in middle-class and upper-class schools. Storz (2008) conducted in-depth interviews with middle school students who were clear they did not experience the same schooling as others in more affluent middle schools. They felt left out and wondered why there was less investment in their futures. This caused them to feel not only that their school was a low priority to the city, but they were too. I have spent more than a decade in low-resource middle schools and can attest to the unequal ways in which schools are funded and the low expectations that plague some middle schools' cultures.

Undocumented Middle School Students

In this chapter I present representative undocumented middle school students involved with GEAR UP: highly motivated students, students who already experienced "trouble" in and out of school, good students who went about their school life "under the radar," and newcomers. The description of these students, whose names are pseudonyms, will show the diversity of undocumented students' experiences in middle school.

The Achievers: Dulce and José

Most middle school students have a difficult time verbalizing and expressing their thoughts and desires. Dulce and José broke this mold from the very start of middle school. These students knew what they wanted to achieve and were willing to do what was necessary to meet their personal and educational goals. They seemed to have an edge over many other undocumented students in that they came to this country at a very early age and attended US elementary schools. Consequently, their English was just like any other fluent English speaker.

Dulce started GEAR UP in seventh grade and was always one of the first students to sign up for programs and services. Dulce and her mother, Doña Marta, were open about Dulce not being a US citizen. However, neither let this circumstance stop Dulce from excelling academically or her mother from being involved at school. In fact, Doña Marta was an active participant in a Latino/a immigrant parent school group (see below for more discussion of this program). Dulce's family had limited resources, and the adults did not drive. I would frequently see them walking on the local streets. Despite their lack of transportation, Dulce and her mom rarely missed a GEAR UP student trip or parent information workshop.

They both were a source of inspiration to other students and parents. Doña Marta was illiterate. She took care of her young children at home and did not speak English. Despite her language and financial issues, Doña Marta was determined to see her daughter achieve more educationally and financially than she had. She stepped out of her comfort zone to help facilitate new opportunities for her daughter. For example, Doña Marta would often seek my assistance to fill out various forms and documents for additional support programs and attend all school award ceremonies, back-to-school nights, and parent-teacher conferences. She would accompany her daughter on GEAR UP college campus visits in and out of the county. In my experience, I have witnessed parents with similar backgrounds who are not able to surpass their limited educational and language skills and consequently avoid contact with teachers, counselors, and other school groups. Dulce was willing to do whatever was necessary to excel in school. Her mother served as a strong role model. Doña Marta refused to accept outcomes related to a life of poverty such as a poor education. She believed her daughter could take full advantage of the "American dream."

Dulce's extra efforts to stay after school for tutoring, along with her initiative to join the middle school AVID program, led to Dulce's teachers recognizing her academic and leadership talent. As an eighth grader, Dulce earned a $4,000 AVID scholarship from the San Diego Padres baseball organization. Dulce is an example of how personal determination and support from involved parents, teachers, and programs such as GEAR UP prevail over the obstacles related to being an undocumented student.

José is another example of an "achiever." He joined GEAR UP as a seventh grader at a middle school in Escondido. His parents also participated in the parent institute. José was a well-rounded student who maintained a high grade-point average (GPA), had advanced test scores, and participated in many student activities. He was involved in his school's Associated Student Body (ASB) and had helped organize many school spirit functions. José was a natural born student-leader, well liked by his peers, teachers, counselors, and GEAR UP staff members. This young man had everything going for him, but the fact that he was undocumented hung over his head like a dark cloud. He and his family knew that he had the opportunity to accomplish many great things. José's parents did not complete high school in their home country and strongly valued the educational opportunities their son was receiving. Regrettably, they feared his citizenship status would hold him back from achieving his educational goals. José's parents both worked to provide for the family but made every effort to attend parent-teacher conferences, GEAR UP activities, and other school-sponsored activities. It was amazing to witness the sacrifices José's parents made to support their son's leadership and academic commitments.

Unlike me and other parents with relatively flexible schedules, José's parents did not have jobs with paid time off. They could not leave work at a moment's notice to attend school functions. In 2013, José asked that the family forgo the expenses of giving him a birthday party and instead pleaded they use that money to start his petition for legal residency.

José and his parents are an example of a hardworking and dedicated team, aware of their challenges, who openly communicate with each other to resolve immigration-related challenges. Over the years, I have witnessed GEAR UP students discover they are undocumented only at the time of completing their college or financial aid (FAFSA) applications. (These applications have required Social Security numbers.) These students' discoveries have resulted in travesties that led to families separating and students too devastated to continue with the college admission process. For me, it has been difficult to witness parents hiding the truth of their children's legal status, especially when there is so much information available to help DREAMers. However, I also understand the role of the fear, misinformation, and anti-immigrant sentiments that lead parents to protect their children from knowing their undocumented status. The strain of secrecy and shame often prevents developing long-term plans to pursue a college education or obtain legal status.

Dulce and José acknowledged their families' sacrifice of coming to this country with very little in order to search for a better way of life. Additionally, they were extremely fortunate that their parents were a source of constant support and motivation. Humble and amiable personalities made Dulce and José teacher favorites and well liked by their peers. Moreover, they were considered leaders by peers and adults alike. Their maturity, acceptance of their undocumented situation, and pride of being both Mexican and American impressed me. Ojeda and colleagues (2012) found that for Latino/a middle school students, self-efficacy and conscientiousness (as displayed by Dulce and José) are strong predictors of academic success in high school.

Rising Above: Carlos and Joaquin

A difficult home life and an unstable family have taken a toll on students such as Carlos and Joaquin. The effects unfortunately surfaced at school as "bad" behaviors, increased absences, and low self-esteem. Their teachers could not see past the hardened façade. Our staff did not perform a miracle to change their perceptions or behaviors. The key was creating a bond of trust and listening to their stories. They had to emotionally process their family experiences but lacked the capacity to speak their minds.

Carlos joined GEAR UP in seventh grade at a middle school in Escondido. He came from a single-parent home; his father was incarcerated. Carlos was regarded as a "troubled" student because he had discipline and attendance issues. Some teachers were ready to write him off as a failure. Then along came two Latino male GEAR UP staffers who connected with Carlos by taking the time to listen and learn more about his story. Carlos was undocumented, and his mother worked multiple jobs to provide for her children. He admitted to making bad choices, but acknowledged he would like more out of life than a bad reputation. After a review of his transcript, the GEAR UP staff discovered Carlos had high test scores, and his grades did not reflect his ability. The staff worked with him, his teachers, and his counselor throughout the seventh grade to help him realize his potential. Carlos improved his GPA and participated in the eighth-grade promotion ceremony in June 2014, an accomplishment some thought impossible. Carlos deserved a lot of credit for turning his life around. His story had a positive outcome because adults rallied behind him and helped him form a vision of success.

Joaquin joined GEAR UP as a seventh grader at a middle school in Escondido. At that time, he had low grades and was known to exhibit aggressive behaviors in the classroom. His teachers often recommended him to the school counselor and social worker for further intervention. GEAR UP staff also found out his parents were not actively involved at school in traditional ways. Staff members were asked by the school counselor to talk with Joaquin to see if there was something GEAR UP could do to help him in school. After talking to Joaquin, the GEAR UP team realized he had the potential to do well in school with some extra academic and emotional support. As an "at-promise" student, Joaquin was eligible to apply for another program called Educational Talent Search (ETS).[4] GEAR UP staff met with Joaquin and his mother to complete the ETS application. However, during the appointment, the staff discovered he was undocumented. This made him ineligible for ETS because it is a federal program requirement that each participating student be a legal resident/citizen with a Social Security number. It was devastating news to him and his mother, but the staff let them know there were other programs available for undocumented students.

College connections have been very important to Joaquin's journey. First, the GEAR UP team at Joaquin's school had the California State University, San Marcos (CSUSM) student organization Standing Together As oNe Dream (STAND) make in-class presentations about undocumented students' pathways to college.[5] After the presentation, Joaquin went up to speak to the STAND students to learn more about their stories about how they made it to college. However, the turning point for Joaquin and his mother was a GEAR UP trip to the University of California, Los Angeles (UCLA) campus. During this campus visit, students heard the testimony of a current UCLA medical school student who was undocumented. Joaquin immediately gravitated to the speaker and had a long conversation with him. After this trip, Joaquin became more involved in after-school programs, such as the dance troupe. He participated in more GEAR UP activities. Most impressively, he stopped having teacher discipline referrals. Joaquin's increased involvement had a domino effect: his mom attended a parenting leadership program and the GEAR UP technology workshops. Joaquin continued to seek more information from other undocumented students and was motivated by their stories and successes. He hoped to one day be an engineer.

For years to come, Carlos and Joaquin will have to battle to rise above their personal circumstances and resist lowered expectations by educators and peers. Carlos and Joaquin both had single mothers who had to work multiple jobs. Consequently, limited parental supervision left them vulnerable to associating with gang members and breaking other school policies. It was not possible for either of them to change their home life or switch families to lessen the destructive impact these external influences had on them individually. The GEAR UP team helped Carlos and Joaquin as best it could to keep them on a path of academic success and personal growth. GEAR UP aims to increase students' confidence in themselves and positive connections with their communities and other social worlds (e.g., school, peers, and neighborhood).

Under the Radar: Jenny, Hector, and Jesse

Most of the undocumented students who GEAR UP staff members see in middle school avoid attention from teachers, counselors, and school administrators. They are decent students more than willing to learn and work, and yet they are extremely quiet. We come across many of these students because our outreach staff members are representative of the students' family, ethnic, and language backgrounds and live and study in their neighborhoods and communities. These factors help facilitate student-staff bonds and visually demonstrate a supportive and informed understanding of their undocumented situations.

The GEAR UP program motto is "Success for ALL, Whatever It Takes!" The outreach efforts included making presentations in almost every middle school classroom, where staff members explain our program and educate all the students about college opportunities. Staff first met Jenny while making a presentation in her English-language development (ELD) classroom. This particular presentation was made in Spanish and provided all the same information GEAR UP staff did in the English mainstream classrooms. Immediately following the presentation, we had a group of ELD students come to our office for more information. Jenny was included in this group, and we subsequently made a positive connection with her. It was motivating to know that speaking to the students in their native tongue with a message of hope was an effective means to reach them.

Jenny arrived in the United States in fourth grade and was still working diligently to learn English. As her language skills were developing, she was quite reserved and purposefully diverted attention from herself. None of her teachers knew Jenny was staying after school every day to get help on homework and striving to excel in academic subjects in addition to English. Jenny never missed a GEAR UP college visit or after-school activity. She maintained steady focus and dedication to her studies. She moved into mainstream math and science sooner than the average ELD student did. This was a great accomplishment; however, she never made a big deal out of it and always played down her success. I feel that her reluctance to be recognized deprived her of the teacher attention and intervention that could have propelled her to the level of the achiever.

Jesse and Hector are twin brothers who joined GEAR UP in sixth grade at a middle school in Vista. We learned Jesse and Hector were both born in Mexico and were undocumented. They had great attitudes toward school and life. Jesse and Hector considered GEAR UP a safe haven. They both actively participated in our trips and activities; they "hung out" at the GEAR UP office at their school. They could be easily dismissed because, in their classrooms, they did not draw attention to themselves academically or socially.

When I think of these students, I believe they represented the majority of the undocumented students in middle school: they never wanted to draw any attention to themselves and were content with "lying low." This didn't mean they lacked goals or perseverance; it just was a survival strategy. Jesse, Hector, and Jenny became essential members of our program. Many of our programmatic ideas stemmed from their high frequency of participation. We did not repeat visits to the same colleges so that we could keep them interested in attending, we recruited more bilingual tutors to help in the ELD classrooms, and we sought their input for workshops and activities.

These "under the radar" students became our target audience. We knew high achievers were likely to make it to college, with or without us. Our program is designed to change the school culture by opening up pathways for underidentified potential achievers and underserved students by providing college information and increasing college readiness skills. I believe we changed the life courses of students such as Jesse, Hector, and Jenny. We served as cheerleaders and advocates, roles that unfortunately their parents could not fulfill. These students' parents, like their children, did not call attention to themselves. They did not establish regular communication or contact with teachers, counselors, and other school personnel. The parents showed their support by signing permission slips for field trips and summer residential programs, many of which risked passing through immigration checkpoints. Without parental support, these students would not have been able to participate. We were honored to know these parents trusted us with the well-being and safety of their children.

Newcomers: The Chaparrito Crew

The GEAR UP team works to recruit, hire, and train a workforce reflective of the student population with which we work at each school. Staff is matched to schools based on previous educational and work experience. In 2013, we took on a middle school with a high percentage of English learners and new immigrants. Consequently, I assigned one staff member with experience working with youth in Latin American countries and a second staff member who was a former ESL student. Both were male and instrumental in creating a welcoming environment for all students at this middle school. Again, we used a strategy of incorporating native language and cultural connections into our programming. For example, we provided written and oral information in English and Spanish, we arranged for *baile folklórico* dancers from a local college to perform at lunch, and we made it a point to let students know that we came from similar backgrounds.

As a result, a particular group of eighth-grade boys began to gravitate toward our office. Every day this group would come in, sit at our tables, and talk up a storm during lunch or after school. The conversations usually started with which Mexican soccer team was better. Then it turned into a discussion on class assignments and asking for help with translations. The conversation usually ended with a joke or two. This scene would happen day in and day out.

They were some of the shortest eighth-grade boys around, but they had big personalities and charisma. The GEAR UP team named them the "Chaparrito Crew," indicating their short stature but also invoking a term of endearment. Most of the Chaparrito members were recent immigrants who had very little education in their homelands. We explained the differences in the grading system and the importance of state exams such as the state's English proficiency exam. We shared examples of other college students and professionals who came to this country at a young age. We witnessed the Chaparrito Crew become more confident and incorporated into the fabric of the school.

The Chaparrito Crew grew larger, and we noticed that every few weeks new students from all grade levels would join them in GEAR UP tutoring, events, and activities. Thus, at this middle school, we informally became the welcome center for new immigrants. By the end of the year, not all of them remained with the Chaparrito Crew; some students found their niche at the school with other peer groups, but it all started with banter about soccer with two Latino male staff members. There is no doubt that the Chaparrito Crew uniquely identified with the two male staff members and that this connection opened a pathway of positive communication. We finished the year knowing the students were more interested in their academic performance because they were completing homework. Also, it was apparent they felt more connected to school because their teachers were regularly informed of the help the students were seeking, and the students turned in more homework assignments.

The following school year, those two staff members moved out of state to attend graduate schools. Because of limited staffing resources, I promoted a white female GEAR UP program assistant working at that middle school for the previous two years as the program lead. I honestly did not expect a disruption in services or a decrease in participation of newcomers, especially given that the staff member was very familiar with the students and teachers. However, that is exactly what happened. The Chaparrito Crew stopped its frequent lunchtime and after-school visits. The white female lead was compassionate and sensitive. However, the special connection the young men in the Chaparrito Crew had with GEAR UP receded with the new team. I realized the lack of young Latino male educators and mentors is leaving some students underserved and disconnected from school (Saenz and Ponjuan 2009).

Middle School Intervention

By sharing the work of GEAR UP, we hope it inspires educators to adopt some of its practices, activities, and inclusive ideology. GEAR UP is a federally funded initiative designed to work with schools to create or enhance a college-going culture for *all* students regardless of race, socioeconomic status, or citizenship status. The US Department of Education has tasked us to increase students' awareness of college opportunities and academic preparation in the *lowest-performing middle schools*. Contreras (2011) has written about the effectiveness of GEAR UP (and other programs) to help promote underrepresented student access to higher education.

The middle and high schools with which GEAR UP works in the North County of San Diego have a majority of Latino/a, first-generation, college-bound, low-income students and families. Within this population, we have students who recently immigrated to the United States and undocumented immigrants. Over the course of each six-year grant cycle, we see children become young adults, observe their emotional and personal development, and many times witness the completion of their K–12 educational journey. Additionally, because GEAR UP tends to work with students and parents outside of school time, we see more of the realities they live with daily.

I have found students curious to learn more about how to improve their lives through education, Spanish-speaking parents anxious to be more involved in their children's education, and teachers willing to increase their expectations of students. These discoveries dispelled all the misconceptions that existed in the larger community. At the time I began coordinating GEAR UP, there was a high pregnancy and high school dropout rate among Latino/a students. While there is a national trend for both rates improving for the better, I believe our region has positively been impacted by the efforts of GEAR UP, due to the volume of students and the quality of our programs. As the schools and staff we work with change from grant cycle to grant cycle, the one thing that remains constant about our GEAR UP program is our commitment to *creating and enhancing a college-going culture.*

In middle school, GEAR UP coordinates college visits, in-class college and career presentations, after-school homework assistance/tutoring programs, and summer programs. We also offer parent trainings through the Parent Institute for Quality Education (PIQE), a national organization that developed a nine-week parent engagement education program to teach parents how to foster a positive educational environment for their children at home and school. The program helps parents understand the US educational system and provides concrete techniques to improve their students' grades, test scores, and attitudes toward school. Through this extensive and varied collective of services, we help empower Latino/a students and parents to realize that going to college is achievable. As a GEAR UP team, we are creative and willing to coordinate a variety of services to help increase Latino/a and first-generation students' college knowledge.

GEAR UP Best Practices

In our local middle schools, we have only three years to prepare students for high school. In the first year of middle school, sixth-grade students are sheltered and somewhat separated from the general population. The primary focus of sixth grade is to help students acclimate to the middle school setting, reteach subject matter covered in fifth grade, and scaffold subject matter/concepts for seventh grade. If you think about it, the middle school years only equate to two academic school years: seventh and eighth grades. It is no wonder students struggle to successfully transition to high school. The second and third years of middle school provide little time to master grade-level competency, mature emotionally, and gain the noncognitive skills (e.g., an academic mindset, empathy, cooperation) needed to move on to high school. To complicate matters, all of our schools have experienced some of the toughest budget cuts in California history. This crisis has forced administrators to funnel money away from arts, music, sports, field trips, and other extracurricular programs to core academic instruction.

The success of students today largely depends on the ability of adults to collaborate at all levels of education, from the curriculum delivered in the classroom to the academic support and social services provided outside of the school day. In fourteen years of working as an external college access program provider in middle schools, I have witnessed great people working together to improve academic outcomes for all Latino/a students and help minimize the gaps in a school setting that so often stunt the growth of this population's social capital. We offer five successful partnerships proven to help documented and undocumented Latino/a, first-generation students.

Teacher and Tutor Collaboration. One of the biggest components of GEAR UP is the college tutor-mentor program. Each middle school has between fifteen and twenty tutor-mentors. These tutors are in the classroom with the teachers, who incorporate them into their lesson plans to lead reading groups, math study sessions, and individual tutoring. Most of the tutor-mentors are Latino/a, first in their family to attend college, and most importantly live in the school's surrounding communities. The predominately Latino/a tutor-mentor staff members serve as role models who validate the students' aspirations to be educated, bilingual, and multicultural.

The tutor-mentors are placed in math and English-language development classes. In the latter, tutors help students new to the country adjust to school and help teachers translate and often times reteach content to students in Spanish. This is a great partnership devised to help students excel in and feel connected to school. At lunchtime and after school ELD students often come to the GEAR UP office for tutoring and homework assistance. This quality time allows students to practice their English and get help with their homework. The ELD teachers are also quick to update the GEAR UP staff on student issues and inform us of any academic difficulties. In many instances, GEAR UP staff members follow up with parents and teachers to ensure ELD students are supported at home. Jointly, teachers and GEAR UP staff have designed Saturday and summer programs for ELD students to build math, reading, and writing skills.

Bilingual Communications and Delivery of Services. There is often a misperception that Latino/a parents do not want to be involved in their children's schools. However, when schools generate mailings and phone calls in English only, they exclude a large group of middle school parents. The digital divide is still very present in the homes of the low-income, Latino/a, middle school families. Yet, schools are increasingly moving to online portals for parents to check their students' grades and homework assignments, along with teacher websites where they post tutorials, additional instruction materials, or support resources.

A language issue remains because many of the teachers are non-Spanish speakers and parents are non-English speakers. Schools are doing a better job now of providing bilingual materials and events. Teachers, counselors, and administrators work closely with GEAR UP staff to translate documents into Spanish. We help teachers translate during parent-teacher conferences. We make presentations in both languages, and we have offered technology workshops for parents to learn the basics of using a computer and familiarize themselves with the portals. We have seen attendance increase at parent and family events as a result of catering to the needs of both non-English and non-Spanish speakers. We feel strongly that these bilingual services will continue to provide a welcoming environment and empower parents with the knowledge and information to help improve their children's education.

Early College and Career Exposure. The world of middle school students who have newly immigrated and are from low-income families is fairly limited. This is absolutely no fault of theirs but is a result of the circumstances they have experienced or the fact that they know very little of their surroundings. We have found that students do not usually leave the boundaries of their neighborhood or city limits because they and their parents are undocumented.

GEAR UP conducts on average one college or career trip *a month*. On the bus ride, we often hear students asking their tutor/mentor what certain landmarks are or trying to figure out how far we are from their school. As we coordinate these trips, we are sure to arrange discussions/panels with Latino/a college student organizations, meet multicultural professors and professionals, and allow opportunities for students to express their views. This component of GEAR UP is probably the most memorable for students. Stepping onto a college campus or into a science laboratory provides a background to build goals and dreams, especially when they see people who look like them in those roles.

Teachers at the GEAR UP middle schools are extremely supportive of our trips and encourage their students to take advantage of these services. For example, during a previous spring semester, all the eighth-grade teachers worked closely with the GEAR UP team to take all eighth graders in the program to the University of California, San Diego, campus.

The school counselors have also collaborated with the GEAR UP staff to coordinate grade-level career days. Local businesses and organizations have sent volunteers from various career fields to speak with our students. During the career talks, students are then able to ask questions about the speakers' day-to-day jobs, educational backgrounds, and future availability of jobs in their fields. We also ask students to "dress for success" on the career days so that they feel they can one day walk, talk, and be the professionals they meet in their classrooms. After these career days, students often talk about how they now want to be veterinarians, nurses, CEOs, firefighters, and more. They are truly inspired.

We bring resources for undocumented students right to their school. GEAR UP regularly arranges for the CSUSM student organization called STAND to make in-class presentations to seventh- and eighth-grade students. The STAND students explained what the AB 540 law is and how it relates to college opportunities. Students also hear various stories of how undocumented students made it to college, powerful *testimonios* of resilience. The STAND students are great role models, giving back to their community by conducting this type of early outreach.

Working in partnership with teachers, counselors, and college student organizations, GEAR UP has delivered unique and high-quality college and career activities. Students deserve to have more of these opportunities inside and outside of school. These are the types of experiences that leave footprints in the hearts and minds of youth. I can attest to the change in behavior, attitudes, and academics as a result of one or more of these types of positive adult-to-student interactions.

Increasing Student Expectations. The middle school promotion requirements are few, and there are no mandated requirements. The existing requirements actually only pertain to participation in the schoolwide promotion ceremony. Basically, students need a 2.0 or higher GPA and no consecutive Ds or Fs during the previous two grading periods. At one of our GEAR UP schools, the principal instituted a 2.5 minimum GPA. This new policy challenged the students daily to raise their grades to meet the new minimum GPA. Both students and teachers feared that the majority of students would not meet the goal. Jointly, the school and GEAR UP conducted before-school, lunch, after-school, and Saturday interventions to help students meet this goal. It was amazing to hear students be excited about increasing their GPA on a daily and weekly basis. When it came time for promotion, more students met the promotion ceremony requirements than in previous years. The following year, the same school principal challenged students to raise their GPAs to a 3.0. GEAR UP was there again to help provide the interventions necessary to meet the new goal. It is not enough to make a bold proclamation; it is critical to secure resources for students to support and motivate them.

Parent Programs. GEAR UP has had a long-term relationship with PIQE. This program explains the US educational system and teaches parents to ask questions and advocate for their children. We have offered this program at all of our GEAR UP middle schools and have graduated more than 400 parents. The program's success is attributed to the partnership between teachers, counselors, and administrators. We work together to provide an environment in which this program can operate with minimal disruptions. Teachers let us use their classrooms, counselors and administrators welcome the influx of parents at their schools, and GEAR UP provides funds for the instructors and child care. It is amazing to see how parents sacrifice 2.5 hours a week to learn how to communicate educational knowledge and support their children at home. These weekly meetings allow for the exchange of dialogue on topics ranging from low test scores to concerns about being undocumented.

Interestingly, a decade or more ago, it was taboo for educators and/or families to discuss the legal status of students. Rarely did one hear families or parents vocalizing the fact that their children were not US citizens. It was also rare for teachers or counselors to bring this topic to light. It was not something youth and adults wanted to discuss for fear of ostracizing individuals. Now middle and high schools in our region offer regular student workshops and parent nights to talk to families about AB 540 and the availability of scholarships and grants for undocumented students.

The PIQE curriculum often includes topics related to undocumented students. One session included a student panel comprised of DREAMers who helped parents understand student perspectives such as having to live between two cultures and gaining access to resources at the college level. Panel members also shared stories of how they overcame language and other academic deficiencies. The PIQE program has given hundreds of GEAR UP parents a platform to share with *confianza* (trust) their family's legal status and educational goals. The duration of the PIQE program allows parents to get to know other parents on various levels. I have seen and heard many parents express that they no longer feel alone or embarrassed for having little or no formal education, for being undocumented, or for their initial lack of understanding of the US educational system.

It has been a great honor to help create a venue in which parents can talk with other parents and have a safe place to seek information and support. Working with the middle schools and PIQE has created a movement of documented and undocumented Latino/a parents prepared to advocate for and protect their children's educational and career goals.

Reflections

Through the lens of GEAR UP, we could see the social worlds of middle schools and undocumented families coexist, collide, and become bridges to success. Families support many of their children's aspirations to study and even go to college. Yet, at times families reflect traditional gender norms (e.g., girls are told they must marry instead of going to college; boys are told to work instead of going to college) and racist views that discourage their children from forming bonds with other GEAR UP classmates of color. If gang activity is part of a family's culture and tradition, there is sometimes pressure to associate and eventually belong to the gang, which detracts from the children's educational goals. We found this particularly true for the students not feeling accepted by teachers at school; students find a group who will accept and support them.

The undocumented students in our program rarely venture outside the world of their apartment complexes. They travel from home to school and sometimes the store. (This finding is similar for the high school students in Chapter 5.) In this community context, when I do home visits, I ask residents about the various students who wrote down their street addresses but not apartment numbers. The members of the complex know where everyone lives and frequently the last known location (e.g., they have gone to the laundry room or mailboxes). It is within this relatively safe, small space that undocumented students feel free to roam around and play. Yet, for the teachers and school personnel, certain addresses or neighborhoods carry a stigma for the students and families who live there.

Sporting events become a way for students to have fun and even show off their skills. Soccer in particular is a unifying activity in which language is not an issue. GEAR UP organized *fútbolito* tournaments among middle school (mostly male) participants, and it brought families together to cheer on the students. Those students involved in formal school sports also seem to feel more connected to school, although sometimes the cost of uniforms and other fees are prohibitive.

As parents become familiar with the goals and staff members of GEAR UP, they are less fearful of letting their middle school children travel. College visits, especially beyond the highway immigration checkpoints that surround our region, are a bit worrisome, but no parent has denied his or her child the opportunity because of deportation fears. However, I notice that as cohorts enter high school, and especially by tenth grade, parents are less likely to grant permission for their undocumented teenagers to travel by van or bus beyond checkpoints. I have observed that fear of arrests and deportations have more serious consequences as students get older and closer to being eighteen years old. Therefore, parents are reluctant to expose their children to situations that put them at risk for detainment by Immigration and Customs Enforcement (ICE) agents. Yet, although the undocumented students and families might not travel outside of the county, they continue to participate in other program components and services at their schools or surrounding communities.

Recommendations

Over the years, I can see the progress some middle schools have made, such as higher test scores and reduction of the achievement gap. More should be done to achieve equal access and opportunity for Latino/a students, documented or undocumented. Adults ought to be willing to go outside the box (school day) to help all students achieve and succeed academically, emotionally, and socially.

First, overcome limitations that prevent parental involvement because of school operating hours and traditional methods of communication used with Spanish-speaking parents. Traditional school office hours limit the interactions parents have at their children's school. Most working families have more than one job or find it difficult to ask for time off because it can become a financial burden. Schools usually stay open late only a couple of times a year for back-to-school night or parent conferences. The middle schools have great community resources such as computer labs; if they were open late in the evenings or on Saturday, parents and students would use them to learn more about the school or work on school projects together.

GEAR UP staff reflects the community's regional immigration origins. Programs such as ours and Migrant Education often have staff from the same town and states as the students' parents. Hiring from a pool of qualified community members and offering bilingual communication support is critical to increasing parental involvement. Conversations and discussions become easier when you have something in common, especially stories of back home.

Over the years, I have seen each school with which GEAR UP worked experience an increase in parent traffic to the school and participation in school-sponsored activities while we were active there. Parents feel comfortable seeking out GEAR UP personnel for support in answering questions or discussing family matters affecting their children. School personnel generally appreciate GEAR UP and its partners fulfilling the needs of their students and parents. Community program–school partnerships would be beneficial to students and their families.

However, this inclusive, nontraditional approach can be met with skepticism. For example, we held a parent information series in a middle school where, for school-sponsored parent nights, there was minimal participation by Spanish-speaking parents. Our GEAR UP parent series attracted more than 200 parents who came to learn more about college and community resources. The principal was uncomfortable with such an outcome and directly expressed to me suspicion about how such high levels of participation were achieved, especially after his staff had tried various times to invite parents to other workshops. Dissatisfied with our explanation about the methods we used to invite and retain parent participation, the principal made it clear this specific parent series was not welcome. We were no longer allowed to hold parent resource nights at the school. The principal did not respond to the parents' positive feedback about the series or their requests for the school to offer more. For me, it was personally and professionally demoralizing to realize my efforts to advocate for families had failed.

Second, increase funding for extracurricular activities and to sustain projects over the long run. First-generation, college-bound, Latino/a students need to feel connected to school. Of course it is mandated by law that students attend school on a daily basis. However, there should be an incentive that keeps them engaged in and out of the classroom. Currently, the GEAR UP middle schools lack varied and sustainable programs in sports, arts, drama, and other extracurricular interest clubs. Sometimes the schools are able to offer extracurricular activities through external grant sources. We have found that after students find a club or activity they like at school, it is easier to get them to participate in our GEAR UP events and programs.

Third, increase Latino/a adult mentors, staff, and faculty. Most school staff and faculty are white, and often they do not have similar family backgrounds to those of their students. This is not to say they are not supportive of Latino/a students; however, some are not always able to relate on a personal level with students or parents. Parents and students develop a sense of *confianza,* or trust, with people who have similar backgrounds, can speak their native language, or simply just have the same skin tone or ethnic features. My staff and I have the honor of listening to parents and students reveal their deepest thoughts and concerns; knowing this information has helped us develop new programs and services that better meet their needs.

Fourth, provide more family-oriented and cultural activities at school. Very simple activities have enhanced students' sense of pride and understanding of their cultural background. *Baile folklórico* dancers have performed at the GEAR UP middle schools during student assemblies, special lunch activities, and parent workshops. At one middle school, an *Arte Para Todos* (Art for All) program brought students and parents together to create art pieces, which are now displayed throughout the school. Some of our middle school principals host a monthly family lunch or *cafecito* (coffee) with the principal. These events open the school for parents to visit informally and spend time with their children and the teachers, counselors, and administrators. These activities truly create a stronger sense of community, collaboration, and understanding.

Fifth, increase student expectations and simultaneously provide interventions. Teachers have the prime opportunity to increase academic rigor in their expectations of *all* students. With large class sizes, it is challenging enough to deliver instruction as it is, but in partnership with others, the sky is the limit. It should be okay for students to know they need to work hard to move up a test level and/or increase their GPA. Teachers can and should help students form individual goals in each class and then hold them accountable to reach them. Goals help develop vision and increase intrinsic drive and motivation. Programs such as GEAR UP and other student support programs provide resources to help teachers in the classroom, develop interventions to extend learning, and further develop skills beyond those used during the school day. Students and parents are willing to work hard, but they need a vision and an understanding of why that work is needed to improve the quality of life of their children and that of our society.

Notes

1. Established in 1909, junior high schools, also known as middle schools, perform as a transition period between elementary school and high school (Wiles 2009).

2. Advancement Via Individual Determination (AVID) is a program that identifies academically promising students in noncollege tracks and provides them the academic and social support to help them succeed in a college track. It also offers intensive support and mentoring for applying to college. AVID was created in 1980 by Mary Catherine Swanson, a San Diego high school English teacher; the program has expanded nationally and internationally.

3. Data were from the California Department of Education Data Reporting Office. We conducted a query for dropout rates by ethnicity for San Diego County in 2012–2013 for seventh and eighth grades.

4. Educational Talent Search (ETS) prepares academically qualified, limited-income, first-generation youth to complete secondary school and enroll in and complete a program of postsecondary education. It provides academic, career, and college advising and financial literacy and aid information. It is one of eight federally funded TRIO programs designed to identify and provide services for individuals from disadvantaged backgrounds to progress through the academic pipeline from middle school to postbaccalaureate programs. (Note, TRIO refers to the initial three programs funded in the 1960s.)

5. For more on Standing Together As oNe Dream (STAND), see Chapter 9.

5

High School: Aspirations with Uncertainty

I, Yeraldín Montiel, wanted to write this chapter because the high school experience for undocumented immigrants was something I knew very well. I came to the United States at seven years old, and we moved around quite a bit because of my parents' changing jobs. I enjoyed school and did fairly well. After moving to the North County of San Diego, I encountered bias about being bilingual and was even mistakenly placed in English learners' courses until I was finally allowed to "test out" of that track. Like some of the high school students in our study, I had no idea I was undocumented until it came time to apply for college. I am now a college graduate and recently earned my teaching certificate. I can attest to the long journey it takes to graduate high school, and I witnessed many others not graduate. Therefore, as a researcher on this project, I find it amazing to learn that the undocumented high school students in the study lacked support and still received incorrect information from counselors. We found that even though they aspired to attend college, many faced challenges and uncertainty.

The Social Location of DREAMer High School Students

The intersection of being in high school, from a low-income family, Latino/a, and undocumented brings together powerful social forces related

---

Yeraldín Montiel and Marisol Clark-Ibáñez wrote this chapter together.

to schooling and life chances. There is a romantic narrative of undocumented Latino/a high school students who go on to attend elite universities and/or to be "super achievers," despite little opportunity to capitalize on their intelligence or talents. Scholars and activists frequently describe undocumented high school students at the top of their class or exceptional in leadership. Indeed, undocumented students frequently participate in more civic engagement and community service than other groups (Perez et al. 2010; Suárez-Orozco, Hernández, and Casanova 2015). We commend the students, their families, and the schools that support such excellence, but what about those working hard and pursuing their education under the radar of public accolades? Nicholls and Fiorito (2015) warn about relying on a "deservingness" model for political change. We did not recruit specific types of undocumented students, but we felt the eight students featured in this chapter might be more representative of *everyday* undocumented Latino/a high school students.

None of the students interviewed for this chapter were politically active, and the majority had not heard of laws that could help them as undocumented students. Their stories contrast with media focus on visible, active DREAMers, relatively small and powerful groups of undocumented student activists fighting for immigration reform. We join Covarrubias and Lara (2013) in cautioning against a narrow image of undocumented students.

Although the students we interviewed were less politicized, they were *exceptional.* In addition to their perseverance as undocumented students in an anti-immigration culture, these eight high school students were not experiencing the top three issues many Latino/as face in high school: teenage pregnancy, dropping out of school, and incarceration.

Although the pregnancy rate of all teenagers has decreased, it is still among the highest in Latinas. Regarding Latinas under the age of nineteen, 56 out of 1,000 will have a baby (Centers for Disease Control and Prevention 2013a). The Centers for Disease Control and Prevention (2013b) found that for more than one in five Latinas under nineteen, this will be not be the first birth—also the highest rate for all groups. One of the eight high school students in this chapter had a romantic partner, and all of them led fairly restricted lives that could make it harder to engage in sexual activity.

None of the students interviewed for this chapter were in danger of dropping out. Even those who may have come close were taking night and weekend classes to catch up on their studies. In 2010, 15 percent of Latino/as in the United States between the ages of sixteen and twenty-four years old were not attending high school, had not graduated, or had not earned their general educational development (GED) certificate (US

Department of Education 2014). Additionally, low-income students are five times more likely to drop out than are students from higher-income families, at a rate of 7.4 percent compared with 1.4 percent (Chapman et al. 2011). In this region, high school completion rates were as low as 50 percent (Nuñez-Alvárez and Ardón 2012).

Our study group's college aspirations were higher than the averages reported in a national study of Latino/as and college. Ross and colleagues (2012) found that 53 percent of Latino males and 67 percent of Latina females planned to enroll in a certificate program, pursue an associate's degree (community college), or attend four-year schools for a bachelor's degree. In contrast, all eight of our participants—100 percent—planned to enroll in university or college after high school.

Despite some close calls with immigration law enforcement, none of the students participated in any crimes or dangerous behavior. In fact, they actively avoided people and choices that could have led them into trouble. According to a report cosponsored by the Campaign for Youth Justice and National Council of La Raza: "Everyday, any given day close to 18,000 Latino youth are incarcerated in America. The majority of these youth are [*sic*] incarcerated for non-violent offenses. Most Latino youth are held in juvenile detention facilities (41%) and juvenile long-term secure facilities (34%)" (Arya et al. 2009).

Many scholars argue Latino/a youth are unfairly profiled, and evidence demonstrates that they are disproportionately punished (Aranda and Vaquera 2015; Arya et al. 2009; Solis, Portillos, and Brunson 2009). Thus, it is a small miracle the students in this study have not been stopped for *suspicion* of criminal activity. These high school students—low-income, Latino/a, and undocumented—are truly exceptional because they are literally beating the odds. They have been navigating their lives so as not to get pregnant, leave school, or become caught up in the criminal justice system.

As high school students, the teenagers in our study navigated challenging social and physical worlds. Some felt discrimination at school and from other Latino/as who were citizens. Their communities (physical space) endured the constant presence of the border patrol, which generated fear and stress. Their families supported their goals but were unsure of how to guide them. Our eight interviewees lived in conditions of poverty and felt education was the best option for a better life. As much as they aspired to finish high school, incomplete information and economic constraints threatened their college goals. Still, they were highly motivated teenagers. Every interviewee uttered the phrase, "*échale ganas*" (have determination) to describe how they motivated themselves or how their parents affectionately encouraged them not to give up.

The Study Participants

Ana María, Daniela, Carmen, Patricia, Joel, Yadira, Diana, and Alfredo attended different high schools throughout the North County of San Diego—in San Marcos, Escondido, Vista, and Oceanside—where the overall Latino/a population is about 50 percent. They came from various states in Mexico. Two students came when they were relatively young, and the others came as teenagers. All but one of the students had a family member who supported them to continue their education. (See Table C.1 in Appendix C for a summary of participants, including their immigration background.)

In this chapter, we present the themes that emerged from our analysis of the eight interviews. The high school students' responses were transcribed and used here verbatim in Spanish, English, and/or Spanglish; we did not correct their grammar in any of these languages.

Parental and Family Educational Support

Most of the students enjoyed some level of support from their families to pursue their educational goals. All but two had parents who explicitly told them they should go to college. In general, the high school students had parents who encouraged them never to give up; in the interviews they repeated, "*No me de por vencida*" ("Never give up").

Ana María was seventeen years old and lived with her parents and two brothers who were eight and thirteen years old. She came to the United States at eleven years old from Mexico City. She entered the US educational pipeline in the seventh grade (middle school). Her father worked in the local agricultural fields, and her mother cleaned houses. Both her parents finished high school in Mexico and encouraged her to move forward in her education: "*Aprovecha lo que ellos no pudieron tener*" ("Take advantage of what they could not have"). Her cousin was helping her because at the time he was attending college and discussed all the related issues with her. Her whole family supported her attending college. Her parents were always telling her to put in the effort: "*Me dicen que le eche ganas y que no me de por vencida*" ("They told me to have determination and never give up.")

Carmen was seventeen years old. At fourteen years old, she came from Guanajuato, Mexico, with her parents, two sisters, and a brother. Her father worked in the agricultural fields, and her mother helped package and sell the products of harvest at the same farm. Carmen's parents had a sixth-grade education, and they were very supportive of her education and wanted her to learn English. Carmen said they always told her, "*No me de por vencida para seguir adelante*" ("Never give up so you can move forward").

Patricia was fourteen years old when she came to the United States from Jalisco, Mexico. She migrated with her parents and her siblings, a fifteen-year-old brother, eleven-year-old sister, ten-year-old brother, and six-year-old brother. She laughed as she tried to remember all their ages. Her parents worked in the agricultural fields and had a seventh-grade education from Mexico. They were also very supportive of her schooling, telling her "*Es importante la educación para un buen futuro*" ("Education is important for a good future").

Although these students felt support from their parents, their parents were not sure about how to guide their children through the process of applying for and attending college. The students themselves, as discussed later in this chapter, were not sure either.

Lack of Support

Of the eight participants, two siblings from Jalisco, Mexico, named Joel and Daniela, explained that their father was not supportive of them obtaining any education.

When Joel first arrived at the age of sixteen, his father did not allow him to attend high school because he thought it was just a waste of time and wanted Joel to work. Yet, Joel never gave up on his hopes. All he wanted to do was go to school and become a geometry teacher. He went on to dream about engineering because he is really good at math. Still, it has been difficult for Joel to stay on the right path. He has been presented with the opportunity to join gangs and take drugs. One of his reasons for keeping focused on his dreams is his grandmother. When she was dying, she told him, "Don't you ever cry when I'm gone, because I will be in a better place. I will be taking care of you. But, I want you to promise that you will go to school and become a good man." His grandmother served as an important inspiration to him.

Joel and Daniela's father was also not supportive of her attending high school, much less college. Yet, she seemed to carry a bigger burden than Joel, from their time in Mexico on into the United States. She explained that her parents had minimal education back in Mexico. Daniela arrived in the United States at seventeen years old. The first year after she arrived, her father didn't allow her to go to school because he believed she did not need education: "*Me dijo, si no tienes papeles, p'que vas a la escuela?*" ("He said to me, 'If you don't have papers, why go to school?'"). He felt that because she was undocumented, she was not going to do anything with her education. For a year, she stayed home and helped her mother work. Finally, she was able to convince her father to allow her to attend high school, but she had to rush through everything in order to graduate on time.

For Daniela, being so far behind was a significant predictor of dropping out of school, but she was extremely determined to complete her high school degree and go on to college.

Daniela's story revealed the challenges of parents leaving the children in Mexico when they immigrated. From a very young age, Daniela and Joel lived in Jalisco with their elderly grandparents while their parents worked in the United States. Daniela and Joel took care of their grandparents, whose health and ability diminished dramatically after their parents left.

Daniela described having to "*hacer de todo*" (do everything) for her grandparents: cook for them, bathe them, hand-feed them, and change their adult diapers. She attended school sporadically, when she could; she did not want to fall behind in her education. In addition, Daniela would find any work possible, but money was not enough. Her parents sent her money, but instead she wanted to be with them, explaining, "*El dinero no compra la felicidad*" ("Money does not buy happiness").

To this day, she has not told her mother of the sexual abuse she endured at the hands of the adult, male members of her family and their friends. Her mother was not aware that all the scars on Daniela's back are from her *tía* (aunt) dragging her by her hair around the house. No one knew she had been cutting herself; she felt she had to do it because her pain was so great that she wanted to "get it out" in some way or another. Daniela wondered "*Dónde estaba mi madre cuando más la ocupaba?*" ("Where was my mother when I need her most?"). Some undocumented children and youth left behind come to the United States with scars, both physical and emotional, kept secret in addition to their immigration status.

The case of these siblings also points to the gendered experience of migration, which many scholars have examined with a focus on adult women (see Hondagneu-Sotelo 1994 on transnational motherhood and Salazar Parreñas 2005 on transnational childhood). For Joel and Daniela, the gendered story of migration began when they were children. Joel seemed at least partially excused from much of the elder care and housework; during his interview, he described focusing on his passion for math in Jalisco and appreciating that his grandmother encouraged him not to give up on his education. In fact, she pledged to support him *after* she passed away. In contrast, Daniela's experience is characterized by oppressive work conditions at home, limited educational participation, sexual violence, and trauma.

The Support of Educators

Teachers and counselors were crucial in providing the educational information these students needed to consider going to college. Programs such as Advancement Via Individual Determination (AVID) and Migrant Education provided meaningful staff and teachers who mentored the high school students interviewed for this chapter. Contreras (2011) argues that these programs are pivotal for moving students of color from high school to college. Every student featured in this chapter had at least one educational ally who motivated her or him not to give up on the educational dream (Gonzales 2010; Stanton-Salazar 2011).

Ana María relied on one of her ninth-grade teachers, who helped her with ideas and with revisions of personal essays she wrote for scholarships. This teacher always took the time to help Ana María and was extremely kind to her. Her AVID teachers and counselors helped her with the college application process.

Daniela received a lot of support from her high school English teacher, who reminded her each day not to give up and to work harder in order to get where she wanted to go. The teacher told her that if she got good grades, she would get a lot of financial help with scholarships.

Carmen had positive experiences with her teachers and counselors. Regarding her counselors, she explained, "*Me ayudan en cosas que tengo dudas. Les pregunto y ellos me ayudan.*" ("They help me when I have doubts. I ask them, and they help me.")

Joel credits his English teacher for all her help. She became his "angel in life" and opened many doors for Joel. He explained that even though some "shut right in front" of him, he turns "to the next door" with her support.

When Yadira transferred to a new high school, she felt lonely and started to go to the library during lunch to do her homework. After completing her homework, she would find herself reading books. She "really hated" English-language development (ELD) classes because she felt like she was "back in elementary school." One day she was reading in the library, and her ELD teacher approached her, saying, "If you are reading your book in less than a week, you shouldn't be in my class. I will make sure you get moved up to regular English." That same year she was placed with a teacher who also taught several advanced-placement (AP) English classes. Even though Yadira was now in regular English, her teacher taught it as if it were an AP class.

After this important intervention, Yadira excelled academically and volunteered for community service for her AVID class. "Getting good grades is easier than getting in trouble," she explained. By the time she was a senior she started to apply to several universities. Her AVID teacher told her to apply for several scholarships. He would print them out for her so that she could write the essay and complete the personal information.

Yadira, after finding out she was undocumented, went up to her AVID teacher and told him about her undocumented status with tears in her eyes. "I know you are. I knew it all along," he replied and then asked her, "That is not going to stop you, is it?" She felt that the last year all of a sudden made sense, such as her AVID teacher encouraging her to apply for so many of those scholarships. That teacher was the only one who helped her. Yadira was the only student out of the eight interviewed for this chapter accepted to a four-year university.

Diana's high school counselors were supportive. They knew about her status, as she described it, "not being really legal here." The counselors "tell you not to give up, that you still have a chance. It's not for you to just give up. People still make it even without being legal here." Diana also described teachers who supported her. "They really take focus, like, in kids who actually want to achieve so I have a couple of teachers who help me. They are really supportive toward the situation that I am in and me wanting to achieve and graduate from high school." She was excited to be "on track" but admitted, "It's kinda disappointing that I don't have the same chance as others, even though I want it." She explained that her undocumented status prevented her from future professions because she does not have a Social Security number. In Diana's case, she had the best support of the eight students interviewed but was still worried about her future because of her immigration status.

Alfredo, whose border patrol experiences were featured in Chapter 1, came to the United States at the age of fifteen by himself. He was motivated to study to improve his life, yet he had many fears about how and when he would continue on to college. He reflected, "*Pues, me da un poco de miedo porque quisiera seguir estudiando y creo que ahorita es un poco difícil, pero, pues, ganas le voy a echar y a ver que pasa.*" ("Well, I am a little bit afraid because I would like to keep studying but I think that it's a little hard to do right now. But, I am going to put in a lot of effort and see what happens.") His initial plan was to go to community college and then transfer. His teachers, his girlfriend, and her family were telling him to keep going forward and helping him think of a plan for college.

In particular, Alfredo shared that educators (teachers and counselors) in the Migrant Education program at the high school were most supportive. Alfredo and two friends had a serious discussion with one of his Migrant Education teachers about all that he had gone through. They listened and did not judge him: "*Les estaba contando como pasó todo. Se puede decir paso por paso. Estuvimos placticando y, pues, sí me entendieron y todo y me comprendieron y no me juzgaron.*" ("I was telling them how it all happened. I was telling them, bit by bit. We were talking, and, well, they could understand me and comprehend my situation and they did not judge me.") This type of support was essential for Alfredo's long-term success. Mejía and McCarthy (2010) found that migrant students experience high levels of depressive and anxiety symptoms, which can "lead to more serious mental health disorders, such as major depression, generalized anxiety, and post-traumatic stress disorder" (17).

Patricia was the only one who mentioned *partial* support from an educator. She reported seeing her counselor several times, who informed her about college choices. However, her counselor also told her that she could *wait* to go to college because of finances and her immigration status. The notion of "waiting" was not unbridled support of her dreams. Patricia was not totally deterred. The advice gave her pause and therefore resulted in a slight dampening of her aspirations.

Personal Motivation to Continue Education

In their interviews, all eight of the students reported many forms of self-motivation. Several directly stated that education was "something that cannot be taken away" from them despite immigration status or deportation. Some mentioned that family motivated them, as found in previous studies about undocumented and Latino/a students (Clark-Ibáñez, García-Alvardín, and Alva 2011; Easley, Bianco, and Leech 2012). Ana María revealed she was scared to go to college. She anticipated it would be difficult and different from high school: "*Me siento como con miedo . . . porque sé que va a ser más difícil el colegio y va a ser más diferente.*" ("I feel afraid . . . because I know that college is going to be more difficult, and it's going to be different.") She wants to go because her parents have sacrificed so much for her: "*No tuvieron la oportunidad de seguir estudiando*" ("They did not have the opportunity to continue their education.")

In addition, Ana María felt working hard was important to *challenge* the stereotypes that undocumented people are lazy: "*[Tengo] más ganas de seguir estudiando para demonstrar que no todos los indocumentados son flojos, como muchos los consideran.*" ("I want to continue studying so that I can show that not all of us who are undocumented are lazy, as many consider them.")

Some drew comparisons with those with citizenship. Diana tried to keep a positive attitude. "I try to not pull myself down because I know that I have achieved, I've [pause], I've achieved more than people who are legal here. So, that helps me feel stronger." Her undocumented friends "try not to be negative about it but when we all talk about it, we give each other support." Diana boldly stated, "Being legal here or not doesn't make you better than me. It doesn't always mean you will have a better chance than me. Things could happen. I could achieve *more* than somebody who is here, who is from here and has a Social Security [number] and is allowed to be here." The use of comparison highlights all they have accomplished without the privilege of a permanent immigration status. The students also find ways to manage their identities, playing against stereotypes to empower themselves; similar to what Goffman (1959) called "defining the situation." The undocumented high school students are "redefining" what it means to be undocumented.

Additionally, research finds that positive self-talk and positive reframing leads to higher grades (Cavazos, Johnson, and Sparrow 2010).

Education and Economic Challenges: Various Pathways Ahead

As most research on undocumented students notes, their navigating financial stress and hardship is significant. For instance, merely the fees for college applications could influence students toward deciding on community college instead of a four-year university. For example, Ana María applied to the local state university but said she probably will not submit the $55 application fee; the cost has made her consider going to the local community college. "*Apliqué para Cal State San Marcos pero tengo que pagar los cincuenta y cinco de la application, y como soy indocumentada, pues la verdad no sé si ir allá porque en el Palomar es más barato so es más seguro que vaya al Palomar.*" ("I applied to California State University San Marcos, but I have to pay $55 for the application, and, because I am undocumented, well, the truth is that I don't know if I will go there because at Palomar it is cheaper, and so I am pretty sure that I will go to Palomar.")

For others, such as siblings Daniela and Joel, entering high school late resulted in taking additional night and weekend classes to graduate. Daniela was eighteen years old and a junior in high school. She explained that she was trying really hard to keep up her grades. At the time of the interview, she was taking two English summer classes at Palomar College. At night, she helped her mother work cleaning restaurants. Daniela aspired to be an immigration attorney.

Joel wondered why he was working so hard if, in the end, he would still be an undocumented student. He described feeling different from everyone else. There were times when he did not want to keep going: "Just give up, find a job, and drop out of school." When those thoughts ran inside his head, Joel told himself he had gone through too much struggle to give up. He believed "all of the pain will soon transform into strength" to keep his dreams alive. "Education is the only tool that I have. Once you are educated, no one can take that away from you."

Yadira explained that because of her immigration status she did not want to get good grades and she did not care about school anymore. She did not see the point of studying because all that awaited her was working like her parents: "*Para qué estudio? De todas maneras voy a trabajar en el futuro!*" ("Why should I study? At any rate I am just going to work in the future.") She kept moving around schools because her parents had very unstable jobs, and they were frequently evicted. Interestingly, moving allowed her to make new friends and gain new educational motivation. On one of the moves in her last year of middle school, she encountered two other new girls: one was a "nerd," and the other was really good at sports. Yadira decided to talk to them because they were all new at the school. Diana, the "nerd," got A's in all her classes, and Sandy, the sporty one, got A's and B's. One day, Yadira and the girls were comparing their grades; she was the only one with all D's. That day, she asked herself, "Why is she getting good grades, and I'm not?" After that, Yadira kept a 3.0 GPA or higher: "*Si ella puede, yo tambien*!" ("If she can do it, so can I!")

Alfredo was in the most economically challenged condition. He worked in order to pay his rent and phone bill and buy food and clothing. He described his work as a little bit of everything agriculture- or garden-related: "*piscando naranjas, aguacates, limpiando las huertas, arreglando jardines, limpiando jardines, y, eh, todo lo que tenga que ver casi con jardineria*" ("picking oranges, avocados, cleaning orchards, fixing up gardens, cleaning gardens, and, uh, everything related to gardening.") He said that if he could graduate high school, he would only be able to afford community college. Alfredo also aspired to be an immigration lawyer.

(Lack of) Awareness of Laws and Educational Opportunities

Despite their motivation and their parents' and educators' support, undocumented Latino/a high school students had much misinformation. We gained major insight from the interviews in realizing that *none* of the eight students had a correct, comprehensive understanding of financial aid and college admissions; most had not heard of legislation that could enhance their lives.

For example, Ana María thought it was unfair that they charged white students less at the university than they did Latinos: "*Ves que los semestres les cobran menos a los güeros más barato y a los Latinos más caro. Deberían cobrarles igual.*" ("See, they charge white students less per semester; it's cheaper, and [for] the Latino students it is more expensive. They should charge us all equally.") She may have interpreted the in-state tuition versus nonresident tuition as a differential fee based on race/ethnicity. Ana María had never heard of AB 540 and the process for applying for in-state tuition for many undocumented students in California.

Similarly, Diana believed only *some* community colleges accepted students without a Social Security number. Her teachers told her there was a chance she *could* be accepted without the Social Security card and should try. In California, in contrast to other states, undocumented students are eligible to attend all institutions of public higher education.

Daniela strongly felt education was the only way to achieve a better life. However, she was unaware of AB 540 and what that could mean for her college tuition. In addition, she was unaware of the (at the time) proposed federal Development, Relief, and Education for Alien Minors

(DREAM) Act or Deferred Action for Childhood Arrivals (DACA). She eventually received help from Migrant Education with her educational goals.

Carmen was excited to be graduating with good grades. She had thought about college, and her parents wanted her to go, but she did not have any plans to apply nor did she know about the application process.

At the time of the interview, Patricia was only fourteen years old and had arrived in the United States the previous year. She knew she wanted to go to college; however, she did not know about AB 540 or the California or proposed federal DREAM Act.

Similarly, Joel did not know that identifying as an AB 540 student could allow him to pay in-state tuition fees at community college or a four-year university. He was unaware of the possible federal DREAM Act or DACA. Even though he was still in high school, he dreamed of going to a university and making his parents proud of him. He exclaimed, "Giving up is not an option!" Joel earnestly said that in fifteen years, he would look back and say, "The struggle was worth it."

Diana had heard of a possible law that could "give documentation to students who graduate from high school." She adds, "If that would happen, it would be a good thing. But, I try not to put so . . . [pause] . . . so much . . . [pause] . . . hope." She concluded, "It's not so hard not to be legal here because if you put effort anything can happen."

For our researchers recruiting and conducting the interviews, it became important to give all *interested* participants in the study the resource guide and to talk to each person about the various avenues for financial aid and college admissions. This many times prompted invitations for the researcher to talk with others in the participants' social network, including their parents. For this reason alone, the public sociology and activist nature of this project was crucial to pursuing social justice and educational goals for the community.

Thinking (or Not) About Status

We were curious as to how these undocumented high school students thought of their immigration status. They reported to us that they mostly tried not to think about it because it was too stressful and sad. However, when they really paused in the interview to reflect on their respective statuses, they collectively revealed a deep sense of lost opportunity and lost connection to family in Mexico.

Ana María explained that she did not think of her undocumented status too often nor did she get upset about it. She had several friends who were also undocumented, and they did not discuss their status (or feelings about their status) with each other. She initially revealed that she did not feel sad, hopeless, or depressed about her immigration status. Then, after pausing to think, Ana María expressed that she got sad thinking she could not visit her family in Mexico: "*Pues a veces me siento triste porque no puedes ir a tu país a visitar tu familia.*" ("Well, sometimes I feel sad because you cannot go to your country to visit your family.") Then, deeper in her interview, she became upset that her immigration status was holding her back because she did not have the same opportunities citizens did: "*Pues, sí se siente feo, como que detienen un poco porque no tienes las mismas oportunidades y privilegios que las personas que son legales aquí.*" ("Well, yes, it feels bad that it holds you back a bit because you don't have the same opportunities and privileges that others do who are here legally.")

Patricia did not directly experience any negative interactions with teachers based on her immigration status, but she admitted that people at school and in the larger community thought negatively of those who are undocumented, and it made her sad: "*Me da tristeza porque las personas, um, es mejor aquí porque tienes a sus hijos y tienen un buen futuro. Como son indocumentados pasan el riesgo de ser deportados.*" ("It makes me sad because the people who, um, it's better here because you have your kids and it's a better future. Because they are undocumented, they took the risk of being deported.") She drew strength in reflecting on everything her family (and others) had gone through for a better life.

Diana's parents informed her of her undocumented status when she was in middle school. Her parents told her when she was "more capable of understanding." She realized her status made it "a little harder for me to do certain things like get a job or go to a higher education, higher than high school." She admitted she did feel sad when she thought her status would "stop me from certain things that I would like to do. . . . I can see what other people do, and I can't because of it."

Yadira explained that when she was a junior, she "dragged" her mother to a college financial aid parents' workshop. At the end of the workshop, she was completing the form and asked her mom for her Social Security number. Her mother did not reply and just looked down. They left the workshop and, in the school parking lot, her mother told her that she did not have a valid Social Security number, so they could not complete the financial aid form. Since then, she had felt "different" from everyone else but also tried not to think of her status every day. Gonzales (2011) found that when students realize the meaning of their status it can undermine their college-going motivation.

Alfredo, in contrast, described that he was constantly thinking about his status and how to do better: "*Qué voy hacer? Cómo le voy hacer? Cómo voy a salir adelante? Trato de hacer las cosas con calma y despacio pero . . . necesito algo más y es un poco difícil de conseguirlo.*" ("What am I going to do? How am I going to do it? How can I be successful? I try to do things calmly and slowly, but . . . I need something more, and it's hard to get.") His undocumented status made him feel sad and depressed because he wanted to accomplish so much but had so little means to do so. He had people telling him not to give up, and this was very helpful: "*Me dicen, 'Sí puedes!' y '¡Animo!' y 'Qué te puedo ayudar para échale ganas.' La verdad, sí me ayuda bastante.*" ("They tell me, 'You can do it!' 'Hang in there!' and 'What can I do to help you?' The truth is that it really helps me a lot.")

Unlike the younger undocumented students, most discovered and fully understood the ramifications of their immigration status in high school. They began to feel different, and it caused them stress. Limited contact with their grandparents was particularly hard on the students and may have longer-lasting effects. Moorman and Stokes (2013) found that grandparents and adult grandchildren who give and receive support are much less likely to experience depression. With the border preventing this type of reciprocal and tangible support, these high school students also experienced yet another loss of support that could enhance their mental health.

Unequal Treatment in High School

Students navigated through negative dynamics at school. It is well documented that various structural forms of inequality, such as tracking, can serve as mechanisms of inequality (Gonzales 2010; Oakes 1985; Ochoa 2013). The students interviewed for this chapter were mainly viewed at their high school as Latino/a students, and very few people knew their immigration status. The students mostly reported instances of school officials applying rules unjustly to Latino/as (as compared with white students). Several also shared that their high schools had a chilly campus climate for new or undocumented immigrants. Yet, many still believed school was fair, and they were treated as if they had individual merit.

A few students discussed inappropriate or biased placement in courses. Yadira, who came to the United States with her mother as a young child, had mostly been through the US public school educational pipeline and was "barely holding on" when she entered high school. After years of moving around, her family settled in Oceanside, California. She spoke English well but was dismayed when her new high school placed her in English learner courses in which "the teachers told us, 'Apple is *manzana*!'" She was discouraged, reflecting, "You learn this in high school?" It took a chance encounter at the school library for Yadira to leave the ELD track for the regular courses.

Alfredo recalled the effort it took to be placed in a more advanced math class. He was originally placed in a geometry class that would not count for going to college. His counselor advised him against changing, saying the advanced class would be much too hard for him: "*El consejero primero que no me ayudó. El me dijo que era muy difícil y que no la iba hacer y que era imposible que me cambiaran. . . . Con unos maestros, fuimos a hablar con el consejero y esa fue la forma que me cambiararon de clase.*" ("The counselor at first did not help me. He told me the class would be much too difficult and he would not do it and that it was impossible to transfer me. With some teachers, we went to talk with him, and that is the way they changed my class.") It took several of his other teachers (associated with the Migrant Education program) to convince the counselor to transfer him into a more advanced math class. Alfredo felt he was being "put in his place" by the counselor: "*Sabes qué? Tú quédate allí y allí estate*" (as if the counselor had said to him, "You know what? You stay right there in your place and stay there!") Without the help of his teachers, he felt powerless. Unfortunately, among his friends, he had not heard any positive stories—"*la verdad, no*" ("the truth, no")—about their experiences with teachers in school, only negative ones—"*malas, sí*" ("bad, yes").

The undocumented students were confronting the larger issue of Latino/as not being placed in college preparatory courses. In California, the public four-year universities require students to complete a specific set of classes in order to enroll. As noted in Chapter 1, in this region, as few as 20 percent of Latino/as graduate with college prerequisites completed, which is lower than the state average. In 2012, in California, only 28 percent of Latino/a high school graduates completed these requirements; in the same year, 25 percent of Native American/Alaskan Native, 29 percent of African American, 32 percent of Pacific Islander, 45 percent of white, and 63 of percent Asian American graduates completed basic college prerequisites (University of California, Berkeley 2013). Thus, course placement and completion represents a massive leak in the high school to college educational pipeline; students can graduate high school without these requirements, but then they can attend only community college.

Campus Climate

Alfredo shared that one teacher was explicitly anti-"illegal" immigration. One day this teacher began raising his voice, saying to the class, "You all are the same. None of you have papers in here. You are all the same!" The class got very upset and began talking back to the teacher. Alfredo joined in—one of the first and only times—to say, "Not all of us." He did not shout but stood up and said again, "*No todos somos.*" At that point, the teacher got very angry and kicked Alfredo out of the room. Alfredo reflected and wondered why the teacher was so angry at the mostly Latino/a class for defending themselves from the accusation that they were "without papers," and all "illegals" were alike.

Ana María believed most students in her high school were treated fairly, but she did realize that sometimes white students were treated with preference: "*Te tratan igual, aunque en algunos casos tienen más preferencia con la gente güera que con los Latinos.*" ("They treat you the same, but in some cases they give preference to the white students and not the Latinos.") She gave an example: "*A veces las muchachas güeras llevan blusas que no deben y pues no les dicen nada y no se las quitan. Pero, cuando ven a una Latina con una playera que no deben, se las quitan.*" ("Lots of times white girls wear shirts that they should not, and no one says anything, and they don't remove them. But, when they see a Latina student with the same kind of T-shirt, she has to change it.") She admitted these issues were not major, but that she *did* notice them: "*Me doy cuenta*" ("I realized it.") She reiterated, "We are all humans" and did not take too much offense at these small inequalities. Ana María was adamant that she has never heard a teacher speak negatively about undocumented immigration or immigrants nor has anyone ever directly discriminated against her at her high school.

Alfredo believed school officials and especially parents of white students had a negative attitude toward Mexican students. He felt if there was a problem caused by a *güero* (white student), these people always blamed it on "*pinche Mexicanos*" (damn Mexicans). Alfredo admitted it hurt if he took it personally, but he tried to just ignore those comments.

Patricia reported that her Latino/a peers were the most harsh by saying little things to her, such as asking why she did not speak English and calling her "*paisita*" (country girl; a derogatory term akin to "wetback" or "fresh off the boat" to indicate newly immigrated person). In the interview, she was tearful when she did not understand why not knowing English was so offensive to other Latino/as. In Pérez Huber's (2010) study on racist nativism using *testimonios*, an undocumented participant recalled her Latino/a peers teasing her in elementary school for being a newcomer, having undocumented status, and not speaking English well.

In contrast to all of the other high school participants, Diana believed race and immigration status were not a basis for unequal treatment. She felt that her peers were valued on the basis of effort put into their studies. "I think they don't treat anybody by whether they are documented or not. They treat you more by whether you give effort or not, whether you show them that you care and that you wanna learn and [are] taking advantage of the education that you are being given." Diana tried not to think of her status when she was in the classroom and instead focused on what "they are teaching" her. Important to note, Diana described a comprehensive support system of counselors, teachers, and peers as she navigated high school. She was also the youngest arrival of all the participants, having come to the

United States at three years old. Covarrubias and Lara (2013) found that the age of entry for undocumented immigrants made a significant difference in educational attainment; for example, the longer undocumented students were educated in the United States, the better they performed in community college.[1] Diana seemed the most wedded to the US notion of meritocracy and efficacy.

Although few students experienced discrimination directly, all agreed a negative stereotype about undocumented immigrants exists. Steele (1997, 2010), an African American social psychologist at Stanford University, wrote about the "stereotype threat," a theory that knowing others have a negative image of the racial group to which one belongs can negatively affect one's academic performance because that awareness causes heightened anxiety and stress. Students in our study may have been affected by this reverse version of high expectations and self-fulfilling prophecy.

Deportation Fears

All of the high school students shared their fears about deportation. Navigating through the physical space of their communities was extremely stressful. There was cause for fear. In 2012, the US Border Patrol apprehended 6,548 accompanied and 24,481 unaccompanied children.[2] According to Amnesty International's 2009 report, *Jailed Without Justice*, more than 30,000 are detained *every day*, which includes both citizens and undocumented youth. The rate of deportation has increased, with 2012 having the highest levels of deportation in the US history. Fear of deportation, researchers find, disrupts learning routines and results in high levels of stress (Jefferies 2014).

Fear of deportation affected the students in two main ways. First, some students described their routine as school to home and back. Second, others were more active and participated in community service and student clubs. We argue that this distinction is important because students can develop important forms of social capital through expanding their social networks that lead to increased educational success and outcomes (Dika and Singh 2002; Ryabov 2009). For most of the students, Immigration and Customs Enforcement (ICE) could "freeze" students' mobility and participation in groups, therefore preventing traditional forms of social capital accumulation. Students interviewed for this chapter felt the presence of ICE prohibited their participation in civic engagement, in and out of school.

Her life as an undocumented teenager, as Carmen described it, was fairly happy-go-lucky. She giggled and made little jokes throughout the interview. Carmen was more serious when she discussed the reality of deportation. She was scared to walk on the streets and felt safe only when she was at school or home. She did not participate in any clubs or activities after or during school. Rather than share her fears with adults, she and her friends discussed the issue of deportation and safety "*muchas veces*" ("many times").

Patricia, the fourteen-year-old, described her major fear about deportation: "*Como susto que te agarren y te echan para allá. Que te separan de tu familia o así que no puedas estudiar.*" ("That they grab you and throw you over. That they separate you from your family and that you could no longer be in school.") If she were deported, she explained that she would stay in Mexico to work, "*Haría la lucha para entrar a un trabajo*" ("I would do the hard work to begin a job"). As a consequence, her life revolved around going to school and coming home. Sometimes she and her family would stop at a park, but rarely. She did not work, and she did not go to friends' houses. She did not do any school-related activities or after-school programs.

Joel also described his life as "the same every day." He went to school, stayed after school to get extra help with homework, went home and did more of it, and at night went to work with his mother. He said most of his classmates spent time "doing sports, going out with friends, having parties on the weekends, getting new shoes every month." Joel wondered, "Why did I grow up without my parents for fifteen years?" He was not sure if all the sacrifice had been worth it.

Diana explained that she basically went from home to school and back home. She mainly "hung out" and spent time with her family. She wished she could work: "Since I don't have a chance to work, I don't have a job, but, I would like to, if I could." The fear of deportation prevented these students, much like the elementary school children in Chapter 3, from participating in extracurricular activities and enrichment programs.

Ana María also feared deportation but was involved in many activities. She reflected that if she were deported, she would call her parents to bring her home to the United States. She would not want to be in Mexico because of all the violence and "*delincuencia*" ("delinquency"), but she would have to leave it up to her parents. She knew that upon her return, she would work even harder to go to college. In Ana María's case, her fears did not prevent her from being involved with AVID, traditional Mexican folk dancing (*baile folklórico*), and some after-school activities at her church. At the Catholic Church, she helped with all the events and assisted the teachers as they prepared "the little ones for their first communion."

Alfredo had actual close calls with *la migra* (the border patrol) and fear of possibly being apprehended. He lived alone and worked in the agricultural fields on the outskirts of town; he had witnessed (and successfully ran from) ICE raids twice. His third encounter involved a high-speed chase followed by a canine "on foot" pursuit when his friend tried to save them from being apprehended at a driving under the influence (DUI) checkpoint (which serves as a de facto immigration checkpoint within the city limits). Each time, Alfredo escaped and hours later would find the courage to safely walk home or to work. He described a basic routine each week: he walked to school, he worked hard while at school, he stayed after school with tutors in the Migrant Education program who helped him with his homework, he returned home to finish his homework, he talked on the phone with his girlfriend each evening, and he worked Saturdays and Sundays.

When Alfredo reflected on what would happen if he were deported, he explained that he would cross again. "*No trataría de quedarme en México. Yo trataría de volver a pasar. La verdad, yo en México, no.*" ("I would not try to stay in Mexico. I would try to come back over. The truth, me stay in Mexico, no.") Even though all of his family members are physically in Mexico, he reiterates that he would have *no one* in Mexico. "*La verdad, allá, yo no tengo a nadien, a nadien, a absolutamente a nadien.*"[3] ("The truth is that over there I have no one, no one, absolutely no one.")

The idea of getting deported stayed in his head during classes. He shared that out of nowhere, he thought about what would happen if he were deported that day, the next, or in two days. He brainstormed ideas for how not to get caught. "*Me a tocado ocasiones en la que sí estado en la clase y, no sé porque, pero se me viene a la mente, 'Qué pasaría si me sacaron hoy, mañana, o en un par de días? Qué voy hacer?' O 'Cómo lo hago para que no me saquen*?'" ("I have had occasions that I have been in class and, I don't know why, but these thoughts come to mind. 'What would happen if they picked me up and deported me today, tomorrow, or in a pair of days? What would I do?' Or, 'What do I do for them not to pick me up?'") Based on these worries, Alfredo tries to leave his house as little as possible. He does not drive, and he walks only to the most basic places, such as the store and school.

Still, Alfredo recently joined a club in high school called Club Futuros. Members have done field trips, social gatherings, and an assembly at which they danced. In the community, Alfredo signed up to volunteer for a tutoring program that helps young people (eight to fourteen years old) in a nearby large complex of low-income apartments. He helped them with math and taught a class about computers. He credited his girlfriend and teachers for connecting him to these activities. Alfredo commented on surviving in the United States: "*La verdad, no es fácil pero tampoco es imposible.*" ("It's not easy, but neither is it impossible.")

Reflections

The voices from these eight undocumented Latino/a students demonstrated the diversity of their experiences in high school. The students challenge the notion of a monolithic idea of "undocumented." Yet, two strong themes emerged from their interviews. They are committed to the American dream, and they have the idea that hard work will pay off in the end. The students felt that, on most days, their struggles and continued efforts would be worthwhile. Although each had moments of doubt, their belief in the role of their education in the American dream resonated for each student (see also Perez 2009). One of the main sources for their educational aspirations was their parents' support and sacrifices. This can be conceptualized as a form of "cultural wealth," a set of beliefs and practices from home that helped them advance their goals (Yosso 2005).

Yet only one student, Yadira, was actually college bound. For example, Carmen was doing well in her classes but had no plan of action to apply. All of the students aspired to attend college but had very little information and, in some cases, *misinformation,* such as Ana María thinking that the university charged whites less tuition than it did Latino/as. Again, we emphasize the importance of our researchers giving the AB 540 resource guide to anyone even remotely interested in participating in an interview, whether he or she completed one or not.

Social capital is gained through rich social networks and the resources garnered through the members of one's networks. The undocumented high school students interviewed for this chapter seemed to lose access to traditional forms of social capital because of limited networks and exposure in the community. They lived relatively low-key lifestyles and were fearful of deportation. Most of the students, such as Patricia, described a home-school-home routine, with nighttime and weekends for working. Although some researchers reported that undocumented students have high levels of civic engagement (Perez et al. 2010), only two of our eight students were moderately involved in one or two clubs or activities. All of our high school students stressed living life quietly and sticking close to home because of their fears of deportation.

When students described the importance of a mentor or advocate, these educators were typically related to AVID or Migrant Education. Contreras (2009), Gonzales (2010), and Stanton-Salazar (2011) have discussed the importance of institutional agents who help students bridge institutional structures of oppression, such as tracking. Some teachers and counselors were unsupportive of the students, but *having at least one educator there to help them* seemed to make all of the difference for the students.

Overall, the students were fairly optimistic that at school they were being treated equally in terms of their status. Yet, they noted small injustices they experienced and observed that specifically targeted undocumented students and Latino/a students in general. Although the students in these interviews downplayed the significance, we know that micro-level inequalities can make a significant impact in a classroom or school climate (Clark-Ibáñez 2005), which can then negatively affect outcomes for marginalized students. The students were much more clear that they were aware of negative sentiments about undocumented immigrants and Latino/as in the community. Yet, some students, such as Diana, cited these negative stereotypes as motivation for them to succeed beyond a high school education. Yosso (2005) described this approach as drawing on "resistance capital," whereby "knowledge and skills are fostered through oppositional behavior that challenges inequality" (80). Rather than taking on self-defeating forms of oppositional behavior, students such as Diana believed that doing well in school was the best way to fight stereotypes.

The students were extremely motivated. They felt they had gone through so much in their short lives that they could not give up on their dreams and their parents' hopes for them to have a better future. For example, Alfredo's journey and near misses with ICE officials speak to the commitment the students have to remain *and thrive* in the United States. Many students wanted to take their experiences and make careers based on helping others.

Finally, for most, their parents were important sources of inspiration. In Joel's case, his grandmother's dying wishes kept him motivated to stay out of trouble. All the students acknowledged the sacrifice made by their parents to bring them to the United States to have a better chance at life. Yet, the students also acknowledged they had been given unequal chances at achieving these dreams. Diana's comments encompass this complexity in explaining what she knew about legislation for undocumented students: "I try not to put so . . . [pause] . . . so much . . . [pause] . . . hope." They wanted to and needed to believe immigration reform is coming soon.

Recommendations

The undocumented high school students in this chapter felt dismissed and unwanted in the general high school climate. They found community and support with specific AVID teachers and Migrant Education counselors. As with the culture at Hillside Elementary School, featured in Chapter 3, some teachers cared about their students; however, the counselors and administrative leadership did not have sufficient resources for undocumented immigrant students. To this end, our recommendations are geared for high school teachers, administrators, and especially for general counselors: high schools can become sites of social change and transform the lives of undocumented youth (Jefferies 2014).

Creating Space

School personnel cannot officially ask students or their parents about immigration status. They must create a safe space for these conversations to occur. Nonverbal ways to indicate support of undocumented students are college posters on counselors' office walls or handouts freely available on college options for undocumented students. I collect information from health-care providers in the area that will serve undocumented families and have them in plain sight in my office. When meeting with students, counselors and teachers can indicate awareness of undocumented immigration issues by not assuming everyone has a Social Security number. Some may not know they are undocumented, especially when they begin high school.

Cuing in General Presentations

As teachers and counselors work with classrooms or groups of students about college options, "cue" the audience about including undocumented students by always having additional information for them. Speakers should not exclude (either verbally or physically) those students "without Social Security numbers" from college presentations. If appropriate, speakers can clearly state that undocumented status does not prevent students from attending college in their state. If the state does have anti-immigrant policies, the speaker should explain what they are; students will be well served if they investigate nearby private or out-of-state college options.

Understanding Consequences

For undocumented students, advice that helps students in the short term can have consequences for the long term. Knowing that students are living in poverty, counselors and teachers sometimes encourage students to finish high school early with the idea that they can work. Students themselves might also consider this option. However, this could jeopardize future access to college in terms of affordability. In many states that have in-state tuition waivers for undocumented students, students must show they attended high school for *three years* in order to avoid paying out-of-state fees, which can be up to three times the amount of an in-state rate.

No Legal Advice

Immigration law is tricky and always changing. Students have reported to me that when dealing with immigration court, innocent omissions of information had dire consequences. Also, what might work for one student may not work for another—myriad factors are considered in legal decisions regarding immigration. Teachers and counselors should have resources to which to refer students if they need legal assistance. Local immigration advocacy groups and national groups, such as Legal Aid and Jewish Family Services, typically have lists of free or reduced-cost legal options for undocumented immigrants.

Culturally Competent Financial Aid

School counselors and teachers should provide financial aid workshops in the language(s) spoken by parents of undocumented students. Evening and weekend workshops would be especially accommodating. Invite local colleges and universities, along with college students, to participate in these sessions. If a state-level DREAM Act exists, this is particularly important. If no such legislation exists, speakers can explain that the FAFSA requires legal residency or US citizenship without asking anyone about his or her status. Presenters should find the scholarships that do not require citizenship.

Scholarship Audit

If the school or district has scholarships, administrators should do an audit to check for unnecessary requirements regarding citizenship or Social Security numbers. Scholarship applications sometimes use boilerplate language that may not be needed but that excludes qualified undocumented students.

Continual Self-Education

Finally, counselors, teachers, and administrators can consult the websites for the College Board and Educators 4 Fair Consideration for current policies on college-related issues for undocumented high school students. Continual professional development and resource-sharing make an impact on the climates of schools and the educational outcomes for the undocumented students.

Leaps of Faith

Teachers, counselors, and administrators should consider assuming college could be within *every* student's reach. As Ochoa (2013) found in *Academic Profiling*, teachers and counselors tend to invest more resources and support in students already in the college track or honors courses. An example to remember is Fredi García Alverdín, author of Chapter 2 in this book, who after graduating high school worked as a night janitor and believed college was not for him. One night, while cleaning a trash can in a mall, he came across the MiraCosta College catalog. He put it in his back pocket and two weeks later enrolled in college. He completed multiple associate's degrees, finished his bachelor's degree, earned his master's degree, and was accepted to doctoral study.

Notes

1. Covarrubias and Lara (2013) also found that *undocumented, US-educated immigrants* had lower rates of bachelor's-level and graduate school achievement compared with noncitizens and citizens. Noncitizens likely migrated to the United States with their college degrees.

2. Based on the US Border Patrol Juvenile and Adult Apprehensions website (http://www.cbp.gov/linkhandler/cgov/border_security/border_patrol/usbp_statistics/usbp_fy12_stats/usbp_juv_adult_appr.ctt/usbp_juv_adult_appr.pdf).

3. "Nadien" is how Alfredo pronounced the word *nadie* (nobody or no one).

6

Community College: A Gateway

In comparison with the compulsory nature of K–12 schooling, higher education is voluntary. Choosing to attend community college might be the first time a person directs his or her own education. According to the California Community College Chancellor's Office, there are more than 6 million community college students in the United States and 2.1 million in California. In states where undocumented students are granted access, many begin their journey to higher education at a community college because of its open access and relative affordability (Jauregui, Slate, and Brown 2008).

Debates about the role of community college center on whether it serves as a gateway to higher education or a gatekeeper that causes students' aspirations to cool beyond the point of transferring to a four-year college or university (Brint and Karabel 1989). Dowd (2007) argues that community college is indeed both. She writes, "It is becoming clear that community colleges have both a democratization effect and a diversion effect, but that these effects are experienced inequitably by students of different backgrounds" (415). For example, 80 percent of community college students state they want to transfer to a four-year university; however, only 12 percent actually do (Brand, Pfeffer, and Goldrick-Rab 2014). Community college was the gateway for the undocumented students in this study, yet many reported aspects of community college curricula, staffing, and policies that made it more of a gatekeeper institution. Undocumented stu-

Bettina Serna and Marisol Clark-Ibáñez wrote this chapter together.

dents stop attending community college at a disproportionately higher rate than do other immigrant students (Terriquez 2014).

A sociological perspective is useful to understand the micro level (interactions), meso level (institutional practices), and macro level (policies, laws) that shape students' educational experiences at community college. Examining these interconnected layers will help us better understand how to improve the conditions for undocumented community college students on and off campus.

The Participants

The community college students featured in this chapter were determined, at times frustrated, and fighting for their educational opportunities. They made it from high school to higher education in the form of community college. The undocumented Latino/a students interviewed for this study attended community colleges in Southern California: North County San Diego (fifty miles north of the US-Mexican border), Riverside (east of Los Angeles), and the Coachella Valley (in Palm Desert). The complete list of community college participants can be found in Appendix C (Table C.2).

These interviews were frequently emotional; the students had just achieved one huge educational milestone by graduating high school and now were in community college with hopes of transferring to a four-year university. The undocumented community college students in our study were high achievers and first-generation college students. They witnessed their parents, without education, work hard for little money, and they wanted to improve life for themselves as well as their families.

Like many other undocumented students, those in community college believed in giving back to their own community and helping those coming along a similar path (Contreras 2009; Perez et al. 2009). The participants in this study were students involved in school—they joined clubs and organizations that supported their educational goals, such as Movimiento Estudiantil Chicano/a de Aztlán (MEChA; founded in 1969 during the Chicano movement and currently the largest educational-empowerment organization of Raza or Chicano/a youth in the United States). Most of the students in this study were enrolled in school full time and also worked fifteen to thirty hours a week, often at two or more jobs. They paid all of their school expenses and helped their families with bills. All of the students aspired to obtaining degrees, and the stories of the students "represent sacrifice, selflessness, and the *ganas* (will) to persist despite the uncertainty of their ability to work legally once they complete their degrees" (Contreras 2009:611).

We have a small subset of the community college population. The overall transfer rate for community college students is about 10 percent (Shapiro et al. 2012). Among students with goals of transferring, only about 20 percent transfer to a four-year university within five years (Altstadt, Schmidt, and Couturier 2014). Our sample did not include those taking community college courses in technical or vocational programs, child-care provider certificates, English as a second language, and noncredit courses.

External Factors

A number of external factors shaped students' community college experiences. The students were very low income, so finances affected their aspirations and ability to take courses. Additionally, legislation prevented some students from attaining comprehensive financial aid. Being undocumented still translates to "unlawful presence" in the United States; therefore, fears of deportation loom. Even the students awarded Deferred Action for Child Arrival (DACA) status, who are protected from deportation, worry about their parents or siblings who do not have protection. Yet, the participants resisted these structural forces in a variety of ways.

Affordability and Legislation: The Tale of Two Sisters

Although affordability is touted as the top reason so many aspiring students attend community college, for undocumented youth who do not qualify for the AB 540 benefits, the expenses are exorbitant. State-level decisions on tuition related to immigration make a significant impact on undocumented students (Nguyen and Serna 2014). Four of our participants were not AB 540 students. We share the story of two sisters to illustrate the practical and psychological differences shaped by legislative decisions.

Deysi was nineteen years old and in her first year at the local community college. Her older sister, Aracely, was twenty and in her second year. Both of them excelled at college, took on a full load of classes, and participated in a college club that supports undocumented students called Alas con Futuro, translated as wings soaring to the future. Deysi was an AB 540 student, and Aracely was not. Their stories illustrate the important role financial resources and legislation play in achieving their educational goals.

The sisters came to the United States as teenagers. They enrolled in high school in Desert Hot Springs, California. Aracely was placed in the eleventh grade, and Deysi was placed in tenth grade. Aracely excelled in school, getting honors and good grades while taking English-language development (ELD) classes. She was able to pass the California high school exit exam on her first try. Deysi also did very well academically and enjoyed learning. During her senior year, she took a class called Senior Studies to help her prepare for college and scholarship applications.

Aracely was not aware that, if she wanted to afford college after graduation, she needed to be in high school for at least three years to qualify for AB 540 status. In her mind, she was glad to have successfully completed high school quickly and looked forward to college. Her high school counselor did not discuss college, ask about plans after high school graduation, or give her information about AB 540 and its eligibility requirements. Like the high school students in Chapter 5, Aracely was not informed about opportunities and advised how to proceed with her education. Yet, going to high school for only two years instead of three would make all of the difference for the rest of Aracely's college career. In 2014, in-state tuition at a California community college was $46 per unit, and out-of-state tuition was $190 per unit. There is almost a $2,000 difference for full-time enrollment for one semester between AB 540 and non–AB 540 students.

A year after she graduated high school, Aracely researched the laws regarding undocumented immigrants on her own. Deysi, her younger sister, was able to benefit from this information. At the time of the interviews, both sisters were in community college together. Deysi paid about $300 per semester, and Aracely was paying almost $2,000 a semester for a full load of classes. The sisters were both awarded the College of the Desert's "Pathways" scholarships, which helped pay their fees. They made up the difference through their parents' contributions and their jobs. Most of the family's money, however, was used for Aracely because she had to pay out-of-state tuition.

Even though both sisters came to the country at the same time, were undocumented, and graduated high school, they experienced the educational journey differently because of status differences. Aracely felt more of an outsider than Deysi, who was eligible for AB 540 status. Abrego (2008) found that those with AB 540 status experienced much more political, educational, and social empowerment than those before the legislation. In this case, the meaning of status is significant in "real time" and shows the power of labeling along with how the legislation structures opportunities.

The sisters shared a passion for education and believed it was their only way to have any kind of future for themselves. Yet Deysi likened Aracely's situation to someone invisible to the larger society. She sadly described her older sister in this way: "She's part of the group, but she's not anything. She doesn't exist. She's [like] an imaginary friend." Aracely herself felt much more alienated than those with AB 540 status. Current laws, such as AB 540, are partially helpful but exclude others just by a matter of a year or more. In this case, it created a divide between undocumented students classified as AB 540 and those who were not. However, Aracely felt more empowered when her peers elected her club president of Alas con Futuro.

Financial Challenges

Despite the relative affordability of fees at community college compared with those at four-year universities, the community college students in this study still struggled to pay for college.

For most of our participants, attending community college was their default because they could not afford attending a four-year college. Ariana, for example, was hesitant to talk about her immigration status, but she explained during our interview that she wanted to tell her story because she believed it was important. When asked about how far she would like to continue her education, she said she wanted to transfer and go to a four-year university but did not think it was going to be a possibility for her. She had been accepted to four-year colleges during her time in high school, but because of the cost, she was not able to attend and decided to head to a community college. Ariana described her situation: "I am very confident about my . . . academically I do pretty well. But my . . . yeah . . . what holds me back is the money. I was proud of me. I was like, 'Oh, look, I got into these schools.' . . . And, I mean, I don't have the money to go, but I got accepted. So . . . [trails off]."

Students wondered whether their financial and time investments in college were worth it because they might not be able to work in their chosen professions. Currently, only piecemeal, selective, and temporary work permits, such as DACA, are available to this population. Students analyzed their time at the community college—and whether they would even continue with a two-year degree—by balancing the expenses with the future payoff. Martin, a student at MiraCosta College (MCC), also held onto hope that things would change within the school system and the political climate. He explained, "So I just had to take a break from everything just to see what I really wanted to do, if that was actually my last resort or not. So after this semester is over, I'm gonna go back to school, finish what I can. I don't know . . . if it's even worth it going to school anymore."

Christina arrived in the United States when she was seventeen. At the time of the interview, she was twenty-one years old and had been attending community college for one year. Christina was taking English and math classes, but she was more focused on her English class because she felt she needed the language to communicate with those around her. She expressed her desires to continue her education, but she was doubtful she would finish. Here she paused to wonder if it would be worth the struggle:

> *Pues, me siento frustrada porque pues no es justo de que uno estudie y le eche ganas y que sufra uno y todo. Y al fin de cuentas, no te sirve de nada, si me entiendes. . . . Que no puedes ejercer tu carrera pero a la misma vez dices si me servirá de algo, algo allá, no sé, la esperanza nunca uno la tiene siempre.* (I feel frustrated because it's not fair that someone can study and put in a lot of effort but then suffer because at the end of the day, it may not be worth it. Do you understand? I cannot work in my profession but they say it will benefit me somehow, sometime. I don't know. Sometimes you lose hope.)

Although only a few of our participants opted out of a semester of community college, the odds of finishing community college are not favorable. As will be discussed more below, Terriquez (2014) found that undocumented immigrants who had stopped attending community college did so because they experienced financial hardships, felt excessive stress, and/or had to work more hours because a family member had been deported.

The Role of the Family and Finances

Every community college participant had a close family member very supportive of his or her educational goals. However, the reality was that being in school or studying meant the student was not working to support his or her family. When conditions of poverty overlap with educational aspirations, tensions may result for undocumented students and their families (Gildersleeve 2010).

At the time of our interview, Maria was taking a break from school because her mother could not afford to continue to give her money to pay for school. Maria explained that education was less important to her family than the bills her mother had to pay. Throughout the interview, Maria verbalized that it was her own decision not to go to school that semester because she did not want to cause stress for her mother. She also said she was very private about her school life and did not talk about it much with her family. Maria stated that they knew she went to school, but it was not "like a family reunion" where they all got together and talked about how her life at school was going. The interview was filled with sadness and regret; it was a tough time for her.

Lupita had some family support. According to her, "My brothers are very supportive of me going back to school. My mom, not so much. I think she . . . she believes that I should just start working and bringing in an income to the home already, but my brothers have been willing to help me out with some of the stuff. They've been very supportive. They say that I should keep on studying and doing what I can to succeed."

Esperanza lived with her aunt and uncle, who wanted her to continue her education. She spoke about how she was the only one in her family who was undocumented, and that created some situations in which her extended family would forget she was not a citizen. "I'm like, the only one of my family members who is undocumented," she said. "Sometimes my other aunts and uncles are like, 'Oh, have you gotten a job?' And I'm like, 'No, I can't!' But then they will be like, 'Why haven't you gotten a job?' It's like, [shouting] 'I CAN'T GET A JOB, IT'S HARD TO GET A JOB!' [laughing]." Esperanza was good-natured, laughing about the times her family forgot she was undocumented. These experiences underscored, however, that some family members wanted to see her contribute financially to the family, but she was dedicated to her schooling and stayed focused on her education.

Deportation

One of the biggest fears among the students was the possibility of being deported. The difficulty of being in school was that when an individual registered for community college, he or she had to declare AB 540 status, and the students feared being discovered by their peers or even professors (Contreras 2009). It was hard for undocumented students to find new companions at school because they were living double lives. At times when they needed guidance from mentors, counselors, or professors, the students might not have asked for help for fear of having to reveal their status. As a Palomar College student, Elizabeth was scared to share her views (or her status) with a professor who spoke about "illegals" in his criminology class. She did not know whether, if she revealed her true self to the professor, he would report her as undocumented.

Teresa, who was twenty years old, was another student from a North County community college. She was still in the process of deciding if she wanted to continue her education because of her fears about her immigration status. She had taken a class but during our interview was taking the semester off to think about whether she wanted to return to school. One of her main concerns was that people would find out about her status. She was very scared of being detected. When she would have questions regarding school issues, she did not find counselors or mentors to confide in because she felt embarrassed about her situation, so she would find the information through other sources. While she had attended school, she did not have a driver's license and found it scary to travel to school and back in either a car or public transportation, especially at night, and she did not want to get caught.

Teresa elaborated, "It's hard for me to have transportation to school. I really can't. . . . I don't have a license to drive, and if I take any train transportation or anything, I'm afraid to do it; just the fact I'll go myself, so I . . . I don't like that, you know, to just take . . . the train and know who's there every time I go, and especially if it's at night. I work mornings, so if I were to go in the afternoon it would be, like, at nighttime, and going myself I would not like it. So, that's one of the reasons I kind of stopped going, and then the other one is just financial. I don't have that much money to actually become a full student; I just try to take it little by little, and, um, I think that's about it. That's why I stopped kind of going."

Teresa was also very afraid of what could happen next. She tried to think about her days as living them one day at a time, but sometimes it would be hard for her because she felt that so much could go wrong. She felt she could not change what would happen.

After January 1, 2015, Assembly Bill 60 allowed any California resident to obtain a driver's license, no matter his or her immigration status. Until 1994, undocumented immigrants were able to have a driver's license as well as obtain car insurance. Therefore, they could drive to work and conduct everyday activities. After the law changed, undocumented immigrants still had to drive to work, so being pulled over by law enforcement resulted in many vehicle impoundments, tickets, arrests, and sometimes eventual deportation (Drive California n.d.). Given that community colleges are by nature commuter schools, the change in the law for driver's licenses could signal a positive change for undocumented community college students.

Lupita described her feelings about her status: "It depresses me. . . . My situation depresses me a lot. It also makes me angry. I don't know, it's a lot of . . . I think it's something that should be fixed already because it's a lot of people need it right now. It's just depression and sadness 'cause you don't know what's going to happen to you. Uncertainty. You don't know . . . umm . . . if you'll be able to stay here forever. Like, how about work? And traveling? And you know . . . mmm . . . it's a lot of . . . mmm . . . getting health care." Lupita's depression was mixed with anxiety about her future.

Ariana spoke about how she felt during an event that made her realize anything could change within a couple of minutes: "I don't think about it every day. It just comes up when something makes it come up. Like last night, my mom! I was like, 'Oh my God.' Last night. Ok, so my mom usually gets home, like, at 6, 'cuz she works in the fields. So last night she got home at like 8:30. I was like, so worried, every time she gets home late. I am thinking . . . [tapping her fingers on the table] 'Fuck! The Border Patrol probably took her!' It's just, like, so many things. That's usually what triggers my . . . my . . . that triggers my . . . like, wow, I am illegal here, and so is my mom and my family. But usually, it's just a normal everyday life. So it doesn't really matter that much."

She was shocked out of her sense of security for a moment, and she realized there could come a day when something changed drastically, and if her mother—the main support of the family—was gone, she would have to try to make ends meet to take care of her brothers.

Maria's sense of "normalcy" was shattered when her brother was deported. Afterward, she was constantly on edge about her situation as an undocumented student. She thought education would be a way for her to help her brother, but at the time of the interviews, she was beginning to feel very hopeless about her situation, and it seemed she had lost her sense of determination. She explained, "Once I started turning eighteen, I started to realize that I'm an adult, and they have the right to, like, like, let's say, to take me. It's just way different now. That's when you start seeing a lot of things. I started seeing how, like, my brother, ever since he got deported, like, he's been through a lot now. It affects all of us emotionally but mostly me. I feel like, like, maybe I can do something about it but really can't. You know? I wish I could." She was consumed with worry about helping her brother in a difficult legal situation and also for herself. Previously she had been able to go about her educational journey with much less worry, but the deportation of her brother put the reality of being undocumented at the forefront. We see evidence for Gonzales's (2011) theory about how becoming an adult (i.e., older than eighteen) transforms undocumented students' perspectives.

Teresa also tried not to think about her status much, but at times it would "creep up" in her mind and make her think about what would happen if her parents ever got deported. She feared more for her brothers because of the uncertainty of who would take care of them if her family members got deported. She took each day as it came and counted it a blessing she was still here. She did not want to think about her legality constantly because it made her fear attending school and other functions.

Selena reported that her mother was scared because Selena was frequently in the community doing educational outreach for her club, Alas con Futuro. It made her mother nervous to know that, through her community work, her daughter was open about her status. Selena elaborated, "It's hard because she tries to support me in a way, but then again in a way she doesn't. In the way when I have to go to the club meetings or to the high schools, she will tell me, 'I don't want you to go because I am scared. I don't want you to do this because it's not for you' or whatever the case is. In that way, she is not that supportive as I would want her to be. But I try to explain to her and I try to talk to her and show her how I feel about it. And she's trying."

Not thinking about his status was a way Julio coped with his situation: "Just keep going to school, think positive that somehow you will be able to finish school and then legalize your status." Numerous studies have found that undocumented students are stressed and scared about their immigration status and that of their parents (Aranda and Vaquera 2015; Castellanos and Orozco, 2005; Gonzales, Suárez-Orozco, and Dedios-Sanguineti 2013; Hovey 2000; Jauregui and Slate 2009; Martinez 2014; Mejía and McCarthy

2010; Neff and Hoppe 1993). In our study, undocumented community college students had a sense of hope if they continued on their educational paths, but at times it seemed like an impossible goal.

Institutional Factors

The students interviewed for this chapter revealed that several institutional factors—conditions within their community colleges—had shaped their experiences there. Although some elements of campus climate and practices did not support undocumented students, we found that two main factors at the institutional level (a student club and a concerted approach by various departments) had a strong impact on student success, campus policies, and the region.

Lack of First-Generation College Support

Because our interviewees were first-generation college students, they recounted feeling isolated and not understanding how college worked. Because of their immigration status, they did not qualify for federal programs such as the Extended Opportunity Programs and Services (EOPS) or the College Assistance Migrant Program (CAMP). If college- or state-funded programs did not actively recruit low-income Latino/a students, they might have missed potential undocumented participants. For example, Maria, an eighteen-year-old, second-year student, shared her experience of registering for college classes and about the day of orientation. She felt out of place because she was the only student who did not have parent support at the orientation. She felt that she was alone, and if she had a question to ask, she was too scared because she did not have her parents there with her.

While in high school, Lupita took community college classes as part of a special outreach program. She became familiar with the college campus and passed along information to her friends who were not in the program. She completed some of her general education classes for an associate of arts (AA) degree before graduating from high school. However, after she arrived as a college student on campus, Lupita felt out of place and explained that she wished she had friends with her. She also shared frustration regarding how she was the only one on this path, and she wished others would be there with her. She said, "I have to admit that it . . . I did feel kinda lonely doing it. Like, I had another friend going to the community college so I wasn't *that* lonely, but when it came to family and other people doing it, I . . . it was kinda like, I just . . . People weren't there." (She was referring to "people" like her—Latina and undocumented.) Lupita points to how she felt about the lack of

Latino/as in community college. Additionally, as a first-generation college student, she was traveling in uncharted territory.

Julio came to the United States when he was twelve years old. The year he enrolled in elementary school, the school had stopped using a bilingual program for students who did not know English. He explained, "The classes were mainly in English so I couldn't understand. It was a struggle but after, in sixth grade, I started to understand English. I started doing my essays and stuff like that, so it became easier for me." During his high school career he had a counselor tell him that he should think about furthering his education, but the counselor did not follow up as to where he could find information regarding how he could pursue college. His parents and friends did not know how to help him. Julio independently found information on how to attend school. He did not look for scholarships because he did not believe he would be eligible. He completed FAFSA but was denied because of his undocumented status. He was wary of asking for help from non-Latino/a counselors or professors: "So, I guess what I am trying to say is that if it wasn't for the Latino presence at MiraCosta, I wouldn't ask for help from the faculty members." At his community college, the Latino/a professors were important institutional agents who connected him with resources.

Campus Policies and Awareness

At College of the Desert, a main factor in the lack of institutional support was that undocumented students were unable to obtain school identification (ID) cards because they did not have Social Security numbers. This was very troubling because students needed their cards to have access to other services at the school. In addition, College of the Desert required that students use Social Security numbers for many other activities. None of the interviewees had Social Security numbers. The students we interviewed at this school told us about their trouble receiving their IDs. Their responses were that because they could not get their school IDs, they could not get their library books, deal with admissions or the registrar, or access some of the health services available to other students. It was a hindrance for these students because they were part of the school but they were excluded. As one participant explained, "We pay for our education! We pay for school, and yet we are considered outsiders in our school."

When students did earn a scholarship, most students reported trouble picking up their scholarship checks without having their state IDs or Social Security cards. The students would have to find a counselor or some college staff member to advocate for them with the cashier's office. Ironically, several participants had taken a scholarship class at the community college that did not have any immigration status requirements. Esperanza discussed how it helped her to be able to find scholarships that catered to undocumented students and for which she would be eligible. "I am taking an Intro to Scholarship. . . . Yeah, which is like, a class that helps you, like, prepare yourself for like, to get. . . . How to prepare a portfolio to get scholarships. Like suppose you have to apply for a scholarship last minute, you have all your scholarship stuff ready. So you have everything you need for that specific scholarship. And you're like, ready to go." We believe it is wonderful that the scholarship class was offered, but the overall policy of the college discriminated against undocumented students.

One participant explained an argument he had with a student services staff member at MCC. He had previously dropped out of community college and then returned to have a more successful experience:

> I remember having an argument with a member from the registration office over the validity of my existence because she had told me that I owed the school out-of-state student fees because I did not exist in the state of California. She said, "Well, because you do not have a Social Security number; you are invisible." I could not believe it. I was so mad. I replied, "Lady, I have been in this state for ten years. You are staring right at me, and unless I somehow become transparent, I pretty much exist."

The staff member lacked essential knowledge about AB 540, which allows students without Social Security numbers to attend community college. Even more offensive was the outright acknowledgment of the student's invisibility. In addition to the major obstacles for first-generation college students, undocumented students must endure dehumanizing treatment to obtain basic service to enroll in college.

Classroom Interactions

This type of micro-level interaction also occurred in the classroom. Julio drew upon "passing" as a classroom strategy. He spoke about how he felt his community college professors thought all the students had a similar background and that they should all be performing at the same level: "I guess most white professors assume that we have the same background as white students. And we have the same opportunities. There are professors that think this way; you are in a community college—you have to be able to assimilate to white people." While this could be a problematic assumption, Julio appreciated being given the same expectations as peers with citizenship.

Elizabeth had taken a criminology class at Palomar College. She explained that the (white) professor, in general, seemed to have little regard for all the students and specifically used offensive language regarding immigration. Elizabeth detailed a classroom incident and what happened afterward:

> We were talking about immigration law and then he [says something] like, "Yeah, well you know, illegal this, illegal that."
>
> I don't remember what the conversation was, but "illegal blah blah illegal. . . . We should close our border because illegal this and illegal that."
>
> It was just always, "illegal aliens illegal aliens."
>
> So I just kinda felt like, "What? Dude, you know, you're a professor; you should know better!"
>
> I went to confront him. I went to his office. I told him, "You really hurt people, like, you really hurt people saying 'illegal alien.'"
>
> I'm like, "You don't know . . ."
>
> I didn't tell him my status, but I'm like, "You don't know who in the classroom . . . is an undocumented student."
>
> Then he says, "No, undocumented is not a word. Our law says illegal."
>
> Oh, my god!
>
> "It says illegal alien."
>
> It just brought my eyes, like, what? I mean I got watery eyes, like . . . I'm, . . . like, right now. [crying]
>
> I'm like, "I met so many wonderful people who are undocumented students, and I mean, they have so much to give, and I don't think they deserve to be called illegal aliens."
>
> "No, but that's what our law says so that's what we need to call them."
>
> So, ugh!
>
> Then he saw that my eyes were getting, like, teary and he's like, "Oh, you don't have to get upset. You know that's the law."
>
> And it made me feel like crap. Oh, my god! I can't believe there's professors like these! I can't believe this professor [begins sobbing] was being such a jerk!

Elizabeth was extremely upset recalling this interaction with her professor. Because of his insensitivity, she believed she could not share her status with him. When she went to speak to him during his office hours to share her thoughts, the professor stubbornly stuck to his interpretation of the law and did not acknowledge the dehumanizing nature of the term *illegal alien*.

However, in the case of College of the Desert, where undocumented student activists have made strides to improve campus services, students felt less fearful of discussing their immigration status. Georgina, the president of a student club formed to support undocumented students, shared that when she first began community college, she felt scared and ashamed of who she was. She would sit in the back of the classrooms and not say anything because she wanted to blend in. However, now that she has been part of the club and is also the club president, she feels empowered by her status.

Student Clubs: Alas con Futuro

The club mentioned above, Alas con Futuro, was created at College of the Desert. The sisters featured at the beginning of this chapter were active members in this club. It was founded by students and general counselor Jose Simo in 2008 and initially had seven members. It grew to about twenty members, but its numbers have fluctuated from seven to thirty members yearly. It has had two advisers, Jose Simo and Fred Sangiorgio, both of whom are general counselors. (We had the opportunity to meet and interact with the club members at various meetings from 2012 to 2013.)

Club members are continually doing outreach programs for parents, students, high schools, and anyone who wants information regarding how to get into college. It is one of their core strengths. The club wants undocumented students to know they are able to continue their education. Frequently, club members go back to their alma maters and talk with former teachers and counselors; they return to do assemblies at which they can inspire current students to consider going to college.

One of the most exciting things the club did for the first time in 2013 was to participate in the college's "club rush," during which student clubs recruit new members. They explained that they had never felt they could participate in club rush before, but that year they were actually part of the larger college scene promoting their club. They were a little apprehensive about it, but because the campus climate regarding undocumented students has changed, they felt better for doing it. The club rush event went well, and they will continue with it.

The strong bond, much like a close-knit family, strengthens the effectiveness of the club. They all know this and really believe their bond is what helps them move along with their education and any life problems in general. Studies have found that programs with "family-style" practices and norms lead to increased success for Latino/a and Chicano/a students (Irizarry 2011) along with American Indian students (Guillory and Wolverton 2008). The students report that it feels like home to them, because they know they all have one thing in common, and they can help each other. The students remembered 2012, when they were working together and relied on each other to complete the California Development, Relief, and Education for Alien Minors (DREAM) Act financial aid application, finding scholarships open to them.

They also seem to be making an impact in the region. Alas con Futuro members revealed that they had a better reception in the *southern* side of the Coachella Valley than in the north. The south side is comprised of Mecca, Coachella, Indio, and Thermal. The north side consists of La Quinta, Palm Desert, Palm Springs, and Desert Hot Springs. These areas are divided by the agricultural industry and socioeconomic differences. The south has more farmworkers, immigrants, and minorities than does the north side. Club members mentioned they were in the midst of preparing for their first assembly at Palm Springs High School. The school had asked them to come for a two-hour session exclusively devoted to AB 540 students. Previously, Palm Springs High School had not accepted their request to do a presentation. The requests to do outreach from southern schools had decreased, but they felt it was because so many more of the staff members—counselors and teachers—were more informed about AB 540 student issues.

The club also partakes in the yearly high school counselor conference held at College of the Desert. There is a specific session about the status of AB 540 students and how high school counselors can help these students. Many students in the club shared that they had been let down by counselors who did not think they were going to be able to make it in the United States; some were told to "move back to Mexico" because that was where they would be able to pursue a career. The yearly counselor session has helped many of the counselors see that they have been advising students in the wrong direction and have to rethink their strategy on helping undocumented students. This club also embraces an "ally" approach, such as with the Gay Straight Alliance, in which undocumented and documented students join to work toward social justice for immigrants.

Network of Resources

Unlike College of the Desert, MCC did not have a single club dedicated to the issues of undocumented students. However, the college supports a network of clubs and student services that work in overlapping ways to actively help undocumented Latino/a students.

Two clubs in particular, Puente and Encuentros, seemed to attract and support Latino/a undocumented students. The Puente Club stems from the Puente Project, a nationally acclaimed transfer preparation program that provides guidance and mentorship to underserved student populations. The program is co-coordinated by a counselor and an English instructor. Students take personal development and writing courses. In addition, students are paired with a community mentor. The curricular focus on Chicano/a literature and living experience in the United States, especially California, is attractive to Latino/a students and undocumented students. The Puente co-coordinators and program mentors provide much-needed guidance to these students to help them navigate the often-treacherous educational pipeline. The Puente Club acts as a mechanism to develop student leadership and conduct outreach at local area high schools.

The MCC Encuentros Leadership Club grew out of the Encuentros Leadership of North County San Diego's yearly Career Exploration Conference, directed at young, Latino males. MCC students inspired by the annual conference decided to create a club to promote higher education to community college and high school students. One of the original founding members of MCC Encuentros was undocumented and since received DACA status. The club hosted a highly successful motivational conference that 150 local area high school Latino/a students attended to become familiar with MCC.

MCC regularly hosts major workshops related to undocumented legislation for the larger North County community. For example, when DACA was announced, Yesenia Balcazar, then student services coordinator and now EOPS director, hosted a series of events that drew staff, students, and faculty from neighboring colleges and provided free legal services from local immigration attorneys. The three workshops were designed to help MCC students and community members receive (1) free information about DACA, (2) free consultation and legal assessment from attorneys, and (3) free assistance in completing the application packet. MCC partnered with the DREAMER Assistance Network, which helped with many of the legal resources.

MCC reached out to various student groups from the nearby colleges and universities and also helped with recruitment, advertising, and volunteering at the event: MEChA students from MCC, Palomar College, and California State University, San Marcos, Standing Together As oNe Dream (STAND; formed to support undocumented students). Importantly, through their networking with the various lawyers and immigration rights groups, many of these college students were trained to help others in the community with the DACA preliminary application process. Various units at MCC participated, in particular the offices of EOPS and Cooperative Agencies Resources for Education (EOPS/CARE) and CalWORKS (which offers work experience and support for students who are parents and receiving welfare). In the local community, the Human Rights Committee from Oceanside Club and Friends of EOPS Club also donated time and resources to the event. The series of workshops, which took place over two months and hosted about 1,000 participants, is just one example of how different departments on campus supported the undocumented community at MCC and in the North County San Diego region in general.

MCC is a model for how to coordinate, create, and support resources accessed by undocumented Latino/a community college students. The faculty, staff, and administrators work in concert to provide the access, opportunities, and experiences for undocumented students to thrive and for many to transfer.

At both MCC and College of the Desert, the counseling faculty, student services staff, and some faculty work to support the journey of the undocumented students. Many of these institutional agents are Latino/a. Contreras (2009) found that Latino/a educators or staff members were more likely to help undocumented students. For the students in this study, trust seemed more readily established with them. Just by being at the college or university, they served as role models for those students because they could see professional possibilities for educated Latino/as. Contreras (2011) adds that these key staff and faculty members often help academically promising, low-income, Latino/a students cultivate cultural capital to help them succeed.

Personal Level

Arriving at college, even if it was not a four-year college or university, was a major milestone for the students in this study. They were working hard to achieve the American dream and yet also finding many barriers to fulfilling their educational goals. Our participants expressed conflicting emotions about their role in society and how to persist when the future for professional goals or even paying for the next semester's tuition was uncertain.

Identity

Most of the students interviewed felt American at some level and had complicated feelings about their connections to their home countries (Perez 2009; Torresa and Wicks-Asbunb 2014). Culturally, they were firmly entrenched in their families' traditions and rituals. However, in terms of citizenship, they felt American. Simultaneously, their connection to the United States had to do with their belief in the American dream—that they could overcome obstacles with hard work and perseverance. Most felt betrayed by this myth because their immigration status and all the barriers that came with it were preventing them from realizing their full potential.

Ariana commented directly on her identity. She admitted that she looked like an "average young twenty-year-old that blends in with the crowd," but inside she knew she was different from her peers. As she explained, "Um . . . it's hard to define myself because um . . . I really don't want to go back to Mexico. . . . But, yet again, I am from Mexico, so I'm, like, in the between." It was hard for her to identify with a country she had not seen since she was a little girl.

Selena also felt she was at a crossroads with her identity: "I consider me as an American but also I don't. So, being an American is, like, being part of this country. Even though me being undocumented or . . . or . . . whatever they may call it. And it doesn't give me an identity in the US. . . . But I still consider myself American because of the fact that I am here, I am going to school, and trying as hard as I can to succeed." Selena believes in the United States credo: hard work will pay off in the end.

At seven years old, Esperanza was sent to the United States when her mother passed away in Mexico. She lived with her aunt and uncle, who were very supportive of her going to school and helped her pay for most of her educational expenses. Esperanza was majoring in psychology because she wanted "to know how people's minds work." We met during her first year at community college, and she was adjusting to her role as a student there. Her reflections on identity began with a discussion about national anthems:

> Over there in Mexico you have to learn the, like, the anthem. I don't even know it anymore. I don't know how it goes. Like, I knew it. But I just don't know it anymore. Like, I pretty much know the anthem for here. Like, the pledge of allegiance and [the] heart. Like, you just say it, and I will just go along with you. The Mexican one? I don't even know. So, like, I guess I've, like, grown up here. But I remember stuff from Mexico but not that much per se. So, I would pretty much consider myself an American, even though I don't have that many benefits.

A simple thing such as the pledge of allegiance along with the time spent in the country represented the connection she had to the United States. To Esperanza, it did not matter where she was born; what mattered was her allegiance to the country she called home.

Martin explained, "Just 'cause I don't have certain papers with me or, like, I'm not a citizen, that doesn't stop me to be a normal person, a normal student that's there to make a better future for myself, have a career, have a successful life. I don't need a paper to show that I am capable of being an American here in the US."

Resistance and Empowerment

Despite external and internal dynamics that presented challenges to their educational success, many students were not giving up on their college dreams. Deysi described her ability to keep going by using the metaphor of the bee:

> I think that nothing is impossible, it's just that if you believe it. But, no, since I don't believe that . . . no. Nothing is impossible for me. I feel like I am a bee. Because bees are impossible . . . because the scientist say[s] they . . . because their bodies are so big and their wings are so small that they are not supposed to fly. But they fly anyways. Because they don't listen to humans! So they do whatever they wanna do, because they have wings they fly! And that's how I feel. Even though someone is telling me, 'Oh, you cannot do that!' I know I am able to do that. I have two hands, two arms, two legs; I have everything I need. So, I just do it!

Selena was a first-year college student at College of the Desert. She was eighteen years old and had multiple sclerosis. She explained that many people had talked to her about college—some expressed optimism, and others were discouraging. However, Selena believed she was on the right path for her life and would not be "backing down" on getting her education. She explained her perspective on not giving up:

> Even though they say, "Oh, after college or after you get your degree or your doctorate or whatever . . . you're not going to be able to work in your career." But at least you're going to have the knowledge and you're going to try your best. So, mostly because I want to be a successful person in the future. And, well, even though they try to stop you, well, I am going to try to show them that they can't in a way. I'm trying to go for my doctorate. I know it's a lot of school, but at least it's worth it. I think it's going to pay off in the future.

Julio spoke frankly in his interview about what he described as his "place in the ladder of our society." One of his reasons to continue school was to prove to those that did not believe he should be in this country that he was a great student. He shared, "When I first started school that was the set of mind that I had, you know. Go to school and prove [to] other people or mainly prove [to] white students, 'Americans,' that I was smarter than them. I could get good grades and finish school. And take the same classes that they have or they are taking and do better than them. That is what I said in my mind." Julio navigated being a first-generation college student and decided how he was going to respond to perceived stereotypes about undocumented immigrants.

Conclusion

We return to the central question about the role of the community college for undocumented students. The role of the community college depends on the external (structural) factors facing the students as well as the students' experience within the community college setting (internal, or institutional, factors). Personal responses (identity formation, resistance) to structural and institutional challenges propelled students to think critically about their own education and organize for social justice. There were powerful effects when community colleges had administrators, students, and key staff members who took on college policies and interacted with other activists in the region. Participants noted and appreciated the Latino/a staff and faculty members who empathized with their situation. Based on students' accounts in this chapter, College of the Desert and MCC put the "community" back in community college with significant outreach efforts and resources directed at undocumented youth, adults, and families in the larger community.

For the students interviewed for this chapter, transferring to a four-year university was their goal. Students revealed that they attended community college because of its affordability and close proximity to home, but many had intended to apply to a university. Therefore our recommendations will be focused on this process. (The next chapter offers detailed suggestions that apply to both community colleges and four-year universities.)

Reflecting back on the interviews, we noticed that although students aimed to transfer, few mentioned an academic plan or other necessary tools to ensure their success at this goal. No one mentioned visiting or working with the transfer center. Instead, the students relied on each other, club advisers, or individual trusted allies, such as a counselor or a professor.

Thus, our specific recommendation is for community colleges to bolster their transfer center programs and outreach efforts for all students (to increase general transfer rates) and, in particular, to develop resources for undocumented students. Community colleges offer the fewest barriers and the most opportunities to enter higher education. Undocumented students' motivation should be encouraged. Although it is great to have an ally on the staff or faculty, the transfer process is complicated and requires specific knowledge from a transfer center counselor.

Similarly, other units on campus, such as admissions and financial aid, could have additional training and designated experts on undocumented students, AB 540 eligible or otherwise. Informally, students share with each other information about the best student services staff members and those to avoid. Therefore, student services unit managers and program directors could capitalize on the passion and expertise of staff members who are already the "go to" person for undocumented students. If lacking the proper authority, such a staff person could be trained to provide expert, compassionate service.

A comprehensive approach could result in a resource webpage listing for AB 540 or undocumented students through which these students and their parents could directly contact community college personnel. In the recent experience with Covered California, "research revealed that Latinos specifically were more interested in working with enrollment counselors and agents to get assistance with the application and health plan selection process" (Covered California 2014:42). This practice is aligned with a long, successful public health practice of using *promotoras*, or community health workers, trained to connect low-income clients and/or clients of color to services (Otiniano et al. 2012).

Community colleges have an enormous reach for diverse groups of undocumented students. Their impressive enrollment numbers, affordability, open access, and multiple programs (e.g., adult high school diplomas, English as a second language, vocational certificates, associate's degrees, and college transfer credit courses) make community colleges important sites for nurturing promising futures for students with a broad range of goals.

7

The University: A (Mostly) Safe Haven

Within the educational pipeline, undocumented university students constitute a very small group. Less than 2 percent of Latino/as who go on to any type of college are undocumented (National Conference of State Legislatures 2012). Of this group, just a small number attends a four-year university, whereas a significant number attends a two-year community college. There have been impressive publications about and by undocumented students at the University of California, Los Angeles (UCLA).[1] The students interviewed for this chapter were enrolled in a relatively less selective, more affordable public university. With these nineteen interviews, we hoped to capture their stories, struggles, and successes.

Our participants were near or at the end of the educational pipeline. They were still challenged by many of the conditions of poverty and stress about deportation described by undocumented students in previous chapters. The reality of attending university, despite being academically prepared, becomes an enormous challenge because of the financial barriers. In addition, undocumented students also confront sociolegal challenges in the greater community. Ultimately, we found that students in our study managed information about their status and identities in a variety of ways.

Gricelda Alva-Brito, Fredi García-Alverdín, and Marisol Clark-Ibáñez wrote this chapter. We published portions of this chapter in a different form in an edited volume (Clark-Ibáñez, García-Alverdín, and Alva 2011). With Gricelda Alva-Brito taking the lead, this chapter draws on the original interviews, and we focus on the management of self in the university context.

The Regional Context

We present a case study approach, similar to that in Chapter 3. All the students in this study attended a medium-sized, public university located about fifty miles from the US-Mexican border. The campus offers undergraduate and graduate programs. Diversity, multiculturalism, and academic excellence are some of the cornerstone values and principles of its founding. About one-fourth of the students are Latino/as along with smaller populations of black, Asian American, Pacific Islanders, and Native American students. The majority on campus is white.

The region surrounding the university, where most of the students and their families lived, could be described as having a "hyper-hate anti-immigrant climate" (Clark-Ibáñez, García-Alverdín, and Alva 2011), referring to the law-enforcement agencies, civil groups, and local legislative bodies that actively engage in anti-immigrant practices designed to intimidate, disenfranchise, and at times terrorize local communities. The region was plagued by police and sheriff checkpoints allegedly for driving under the influence of drugs or alcohol (DUI) yet orchestrated at all times of day and miles away from drinking establishments; the American Civil Liberties Union (ACLU) was investigating those conditions because the checkpoints disproportionately targeted immigrant communities. Additionally, community groups had protested the practice of local law enforcement calling Immigration and Customs Enforcement (ICE, or border patrol) to "translate" during minor traffic infractions, which could result in discovery and detention of undocumented immigrants. ICE also maintained a high profile on public transportation, which includes buses and trains.

Several anti-immigrant hate groups are active; for example, the Citizens Brigade, Friends of the Border Patrol, and Minutemen. These groups appear at day labor sites, churches, and organizations that give workshops or services to undocumented immigrants. For weeks in 2010, members of the Minutemen group distributed xenophobic, anti-immigrant, and generally derogatory flyers in the free speech area of the university our interviewees attended. Faculty members who supported undocumented students received threats via e-mail. The "hyper-hate anti-immigrant climate" caused this university to become unsafe for students, faculty, and staff.

As noted in Chapter 2, various cities in the region have passed "anti-immigrant" city ordinances that include requiring landlords to check for immigration verification and reducing the number of people allowed to live in a single dwelling (or limiting the number of cars they can park). The intersection of these hate groups and actions forms a hostile climate for the undergraduate students who make their way to school everyday on foot and by train, bus, or car. We will discuss how these dynamics affect students' learning later in the chapter.

The Students

Our sample consisted of nineteen undocumented Latino/a college students: sixteen females and three males. Our participants' ages ranged from eighteen to twenty-four years old. The students' majors included social sciences, business, biological sciences, and math. Their age at arrival in the United States spanned from two to thirteen. We conducted the in-depth interviews during the 2010–2011 academic year.

The undocumented Latino/a university students we interviewed were brought to the United States at an early age and have families of mixed status (some family members are citizens or legal residents, and others are not). Most excelled in high school and were granted admission to the university without consideration for special circumstances.

They generously gave one to three hours of their time to talk with us about their experiences as undocumented university students. We present the themes that emerged throughout the interviews in the sections that follow.

Navigating the Hyper-Hate Community Climate

All of the students discussed the difficulty of getting to campus and maneuvering in the surrounding community. This finding is reflected in recent qualitative studies on undocumented students' experiences (Martínez-Calderón 2009). For example, Laura expressed, "I do get very depressed. You think *que no afecta mucho pero sí afecta.* [You think that it does not affect you but it does.] School would have been much easier. Or driving. I can't [drive] here because there is a checkpoint. I wish that I could travel *pero no puedo* [but I can't]. Simple things like that." Andrea worries about shopping for groceries: "They can come into stores, *como El Tigre* [such as The Tiger, a supermarket], and they can actually ask you for your papers and that make[s] me feel, 'Wow.' You realize how bad things [could] get."

Vanessa described, "I live in a city that is very conservative, where checkpoints are almost routine." Fear of living as an undocumented person in this community was a very real emotion for these students. Monica shared, "What if my parents get deported? They do drive without a license. ICE has raided work. I fear that my family might be deported. I fear losing everything we have worked for."

Most participants explained that they were alerted about roadblocks and checkpoints via text messaging, the Internet, the news, and informal networks on and off campus. Thus, the key to navigating the hyper-hate community climate was social capital, which involves "personal connections that facilitate access to jobs, market tips, or loans" (Portes 2000:3). Social capital is based on trust, reciprocity, norms, and networks, which may translate into material goods (Adger 2003). Many researchers have used this concept to understand educational outcomes. We found that social capital is crucial to surviving the act of physically coming to and from the university, where it is presumed undocumented students will have a better educational outcome.

The regional political and anti-immigration climate shaped the experiences of students within the setting of the university. Because of the university's designated free speech spaces, anti-immigrant groups such as the Minutemen have come to campus to share their views. During these times, especially, students walking on campus from building to building felt it was dangerous. While sitting in a classroom with others who come from the same region as the Minutemen, the students in our study could be at times uncertain about the political affiliation or political conviction of their peers. The participants explained that the university itself offered a *relative* "safe haven" for them as students.

Managing Undocumented Status and Its Effect on Self at the University

The undocumented university students in our study drew on a variety of strategies to manage their immigration status, both on and off campus. A major theme that emerged from the interviews was whether students felt empowered to claim their "educational citizenship" or, more commonly, to "pass" by not revealing their immigration status. Our interviewees carefully considered when to deploy each of these strategies. These choices had both costs and benefits to the students' sense of self.

Educational Citizenship: Claiming Their Place at the University

Students drew upon the right to have an education as a form of empowerment. We borrowed this concept from Benmayor (2002), who has written extensively about cultural citizenship and the university. Specifically, she wrote that cultural citizenship affirms "the right for Mexican origin students to receive quality education, to be on college campuses in significant numbers, and to be appropriately supported in their academic and career development" (97).

A group of undocumented university students formed a club similar to the Alas con Futuro student club, discussed in the previous chapter. United for Education, a pseudonym, is devoted to supporting and advocating for undocumented students. The club is connected to a statewide activism network with the aim of passing legislation that would help undocumented students. The club's rallies, outreach efforts, and fund-raising activities may contribute to wider understanding of undocumented students' experiences, challenges, and contributions. (However, its membership does not reflect all the undocumented students on campus. For example, the club has had up to fifteen to thirty active members over the years, but there are more than two hundred AB 540 students on campus.) Ironically, this club creates visibility for undocumented students and their plight but also inadvertently increases the risk of exposure described by participants below.

Isabel, a leader in the club, cherished the opportunities to help others in her situation. She explained, "People that I know, who are in the same situation as me, are younger than me. They use me as a role model. When they tell me their difficulties about what's going on, I tell them my difficulties and what helped me out to keep on going." Clearly, peer support can be crucial to a student's success but is hard to develop when very few know each other.

The community context makes a difference in students' ability to reveal their status, seek help, and speak out for themselves and others. For example, in one study in a larger, more liberal region of Southern California, students may not be as protective of their status. Similar to the work of Menjívar (2006), Abrego (2008) conceptualized undocumented college students as having a liminal status: they are "illegal" by virtue of their presence in the country, but they have a legal right to attend the university. On campus, they can manipulate their identity and avoid questions about legal status. In her longitudinal qualitative study, Abrego found that the passage of the California AB 540 created a new, *neutral* identity of an *AB 540 student* rather than that of an *illegal alien*. She found that this empowered her participants to reveal their status and be more visible on campus. They were drawing upon an "educational citizenship" discourse.

However, few in our study felt so bold. To be sure, leaders of the advocacy student club were visible and outspoken about immigrant rights and education, but the hyper-hate anti-immigrant climate in the region dampened the empowering effects of the legislation. As we have witnessed with the passage and near passage of legislation that supports undocumented status, more activism is visible on the university campus and throughout the community, as seen in the "Undocumented and Unafraid" campaigns. (See Chapter 9 for more details on activism.) As with the "coming out" process of people who are gay, lesbian, bisexual, or transgender (Rivera-Silber 2013), there are costs and benefits to one's sense of self in revealing publicly one's status, and the stakes—for doing it or not—are contested. Both groups employ strategies regarding whether to be out or not that they consider carefully when to deploy.

"Passing": Immigration Status as Invisible

In their interviews, many of the students said they "passed" as a way to manage their undocumented immigrant identities. Goffman's (1963) concept of "passing" is crucial to understanding how students see themselves. Being undocumented carries a stigma in this society that requires them to manage their identity in a variety of ways. Many revealed that passing was a way not to be stigmatized (i.e., being "illegal" or "unlawfully present") by others.

Most undocumented students are required to reveal their status when they enroll in the university so that they can be considered AB 540 eligible and qualify for in-state tuition. Federal law protects their privacy, as it does that of all university students in the United States. Invisibility has its benefits: students navigating around the university by keeping their status private usually felt less fearful than other members of the undocumented community in terms of deportation. Monica explained, "I feel welcome on campus. *Since not everyone talks about [their legal status],* I don't feel any hostility towards AB 540 students. I feel that I am treated as any other student" [emphasis added]. Recently the campus decided to use student identification numbers, rather than Social Security numbers, in order to prevent identity theft. For undocumented students, this change has deep significance. Gisela explained, "I feel comfortable [at the university] because in here they don't ask you, like, for your Social Security number. All you use is your [student] ID. So, you get all over school with your ID, so that is like your passport for school." Leticia bluntly said, "We blend in with everyone."

Yet, this invisibility, or passing, has several shadow sides. The social isolation students felt forced them to be less reliant on peers, thereby losing out on potential gains from social capital and putting them at greater risk for depression and dropping out. The secrecy also caused them to be less likely to speak out in the classroom in debates or discussion about immigration. The students interviewed for this chapter were frustrated because many of the debates and discussions centered on misconceptions about immigration, but participation could risk revealing their immigration status.

Social Isolation. The first, most prevalent shadow side is that all the students in our study felt socially and academically isolated at various points in their schooling. As mentioned previously, having social capital is one way students succeeded in school. However, because of their hidden identity, some students could not capitalize on their social ties because they kept their status a secret. Also, this type of isolation could lead to depression and leaving school (Tinto 1993).

As Mercedes stated, "Most students are not aware that we are here. There is not enough awareness. I don't feel comfortable talking about my legal status because I don't know others' [status]." In fact, the undocumented students themselves were sometimes not sure who else was undocumented. Laura expressed, "I don't know who doesn't have papers here, so everyone I see is born here."

Most participants kept their status to themselves and rarely shared it with their friends. José explained, "[My friends] ask me, 'Why don't you have an ID? Why don't you have a driver's license? Why don't you do this and that?' I would be, like, 'Man, I am busy!' I did not tell them because I did not want them to consider me a charity case or anything. I guess I don't really trust them. I would feel more secure if they did not know because . . . they could tell someone and . . . I could be deported."

Maritza said she did not know anyone with her status, adding, "I don't feel comfortable to tell anyone." She regretted the few times she revealed her status and explained that friends "were just like, 'Wow, can't you just fix it?'" She went on to explain, "They were trying to tell me I was dumb and that I didn't know [how to get out of the situation] but it's really hard [for others] to understand." Vanessa shared that it took her two years to reveal her status to her best friend because "you need to know who you can tell and who you can't." We noted that in many of the interviews the issue of who to trust and who not to trust was crucial to the participants.

A few participants in our study informally found social support in others in similar situations. Gisela remembered, "When I was doing my credential, I had . . . two friends who did not have a green card as well. We just kind of, you know, [said to each other] 'Let's just go for it, just go for it. We can't give up now because we are almost done.'" As mentioned previously, social capital can be crucial for undocumented students to continue their education and not fall through the cracks of the educational pipeline.

Navigating Classroom Dynamics: Invisibility Could Become Silencing. Another shadow side of being "invisible" (in terms of their immigration status) is that it may have had a chilling effect on classroom learning for undocumented students. Students noted that hostility and therefore fear for safety arose in classroom discussions on immigration.

In terms of learning, most felt they could not speak up in debates as much as they would like to because they feared retaliation. Gisela explained, "I kind of keep everything to myself. . . . Like, if we are having a class argument, I might say stuff about it. I feel like [saying], 'Oh, you have no idea what it's like to be illegal.' [However] I just think that to myself because I don't express it." Mercedes described a recent incident: "In my history class, the topic of immigration was brought up. I tend to hold back and do not want to let them know my point of view. Afterwards, I would feel bad." Students participated but did so cautiously and at their own peril. They knew they were expected to participate, and they wanted to. However, they "held back," as seen in Mercedes's comments.

Research on the chilly climate in the classroom has traditionally focused on gender, and these studies can give us additional insight into its effects. Hall and Sandler (1982) found that college professors treated female and male students differently in the classroom, giving preferential treatment to men, which could discourage women from pursuing certain careers. The authors indicated that a chilly classroom climate created disadvantages for women by allowing "disparaging remarks" toward women, making them feel unwelcome, and not expecting them to engage in class discussions. Such a chilly classroom climate affected the learning process in a negative way because the value input in class discussion was not expected of women, and students missed out from learning a different perspective. Fassinger (1995) found that gender played a role in class discussion, in which men tended to make more comments or participate in class. She argued that the chilly classroom climate might have been created by students themselves rather than by faculty. Therefore both faculty and peers might have been involved in creating an unfriendly climate in the classroom. However, more risk is involved for undocumented students than for women citizens in terms of revealing their opinions

Most of the students were similar to Cecilia, who expressed, "You know when you are in the classroom? You can't really say your point of view. Like you know someone who is in the classroom might disagree with your opinion, but what if someone disagrees *badly*?" She echoed the fear of a peer going to an extreme (e.g., reporting the student to immigration because of her undocumented status). Gender (being female) and immigration collide. Martínez-Calderón (2009) also found that students are "pushed into the shadows" because of fear of visibility leading to their discovery as undocumented. Disagreements occur in most classrooms, but for these students the stakes are too high if a student who is conservative or against "illegal" immigration decides to report them to ICE. De Genova (2002) reports that this is a common and real fear for most undocumented people. Because students are hesitant to fully reveal their ideas for fear of being discovered, they remain less actively involved in discussions about social policy regarding immigration.

Managing Their Identities Caused Stress. A final shadow side of passing was that the students in this study actively managed their identities, which caused some stress in their lives. It should be noted that because of racism and unequal treatment, Latino/as, regardless of status, experience more stress and depression than do non-Latino/as (Araújo Dawson 2009). In our sample, the status of the participants negatively shaped how they experienced their classes and the opportunity to learn. Mercedes summarized her feelings: "I have felt overwhelmed and stressed out. Being in this situation, it is so easy to give up." Vanessa revealed, "I have cried a lot. I know my situation, and I know I can go away easily. It just sucks because I work so hard, and I think I deserve to be here."

Isabel, similar to the other students, was visibly upset in the interview when she explained her feelings regarding her status: "I just feel hopeless right now. A couple of days ago, I broke down [she begins to cry] in the car with my brother because I felt hopeless. I told my brother, 'You are seventeen, you are working and giving me money to pay for gas.' I felt dumb. I am the older one, and I am supposed to help you out and not *al revés. . . . Me siento tan inutil* [not the reverse. . . . I feel so useless]." Isabel was managing role conflict: as an older sister, she was supposed to be supporting her little brother, but as an undocumented young person, she was the one who needed his support. Families such as Isabel's with mixed-immigration status are becoming more common with increases in deportation; see Fix and Zimmermann (1999) for more details. These students felt acute anguish about their status and the related economic and social limitations.

Students bolstered their spirits by firmly believing their predicament was not fair and was not their fault. They identified the adverse conditions they faced as a result of their status—such as the types of jobs they must have and their lack of mobility in the community—and expressed bitterness. Recall, these were exceptional and academically talented students who made it through the leaky educational pipeline for Latino/as in the United States, as discussed previously.

Although all the participants spoke about managing their negative emotions because of their status, Maritza was one of the most descriptive. For example, she mourned not having a "regular job" and admitted, "I hate my job 'cause I had to go clean houses with my mom, like, Friday, Saturday, and Sunday to pay for my tuition and . . . babysit at night." She also reflected on the relative privilege that she noticed when she babysat: "I babysit Caucasian kids, and they have everything. I keep asking myself: 'I have been here. I've been getting an education. They have rights that I don't, and I have been here all my life.' I don't understand that." Maritza became very emotional in an interview when she recalled that she was awarded a scholarship, but then it was taken away because she did not have a Social Security number. To make matters worse, the scholarship was then granted to her friend, but "he didn't use it because he was not motivated [to apply for college]." The condition of being undocumented and its ramifications result in students feeling hopeless, as found in other studies on undocumented college students (e.g., Abrego and Gonzales 2010; Aranda and Vaquera 2015).

The students had diverse ways in which they coped with this frustration. Several discussed journaling and exercising as a way to manage their emotions. All the participants explained how they gave themselves positive talks to continue with their education as a way of combating depression and hopelessness. For example, Martha shared how she repeated to herself, "I have to be strong. I have to be strong." Others spoke of an inner strength such as Aurora described: "I just have this thing within me that I'm not going to give up, you know. . . . I know that in the future everything will change, and I will be ok, but I just cannot give up because, I mean, I have been here all my life, and I don't know why they won't give me an opportunity." The students did not internalize their lack of future opportunities. Although they sometimes felt like giving up, they persevered.

Political involvement was again mentioned as a way to stay motivated. Most cited their participation in the AB 540 college club. José described what was helpful to him: "We just talk about . . . you know . . . even though *con nuestro* [with our] status how it is, so we can keep going maybe. . . . Right now, we are encouraging [each other] to finish our education so when the [DREAM Act] passes, we'll be ready to go. I guess that's a way to keep motivated."

In fact, most of our students decided on additional schooling as a way to cope with not being able to join the workforce in their chosen professions. Paula described the next steps in her life: "PhD is next. I see myself working in the field of biomedical research to find a cure for cancer or diabetes." Maritza, Vanessa, and Mercedes also wanted to pursue a doctorate. Maritza explained her reasoning for wanting a doctorate degree: "I think that education—they can't take that away from you." Andrea and Cecilia aspired to obtain professional master's degrees. The students' goals of additional schooling reflect core values for the Latino/a families of achieving education and working hard (Glick and White 2004; Martínez-Calderón 2009).

Finally, all of the students were first-generation college students, meaning they were the first in their families to attend a four-year university. The main motivation to stay on their journeys came from their families. Laura excitedly explained, "I want to do this so I can help my entire family. Not just me, my dad, my mom, and my sister but *mis tíos, mis tías, todos* [my uncles, my aunts, everyone]! It's what keeps me going." Students such as these drew upon their social support and hope for a better future. Their collectivist attitude, as opposed to an individualist one, became a strength from which they derived their determination (Benmayor 2002).

The Role of Campus Actors

Just as the regional context shaped the students' management of their identities, the university campus had an important role in setting the tone and offering resources that directly affected the trust building and educational successes of these students.

We found that certain institutional actors were perceived as being advocates and mentors. Participants revealed that they were savvy in figuring out with whom they were "safe" to discuss their status. Vanessa explained, "I know who I can go to, which professors will be open and supportive of me." Most named specific counselors and staff members who worked in various programs related to student support services and who had specific social justice agendas. Stanton-Salazar (2001) has found that these institutional agents are crucial to the success of marginalized students. In contrast, other units of student services were reported as rarely used by the participants. In particular, participants repeatedly mentioned academic advising, financial aid, and the career center as services they felt did not support them or were not helpful. Although United for Education is making significant strides to help with educating staff and administrators about undocumented immigrants on campus, the institution must invest in the professional development of student affairs staff to best serve undocumented students.

Faculty awareness (or lack thereof) seemed to have a major impact on students' educational trajectory. We found that the two participants in the teacher credential program encountered the most trouble. Routine requirements for working or interning in schools, such as fingerprints and background checks, put undocumented students in a tricky situation. Students revealed their status to their professors, found ways to negotiate around the requirements (volunteering), or dropped out of the class. Maritza chose to reveal her status to her professor but was still deeply emotional about having to do so. She described learning about needing to be fingerprinted: "I was devastated inside of me because I was like, 'Oh, my God! Will I be able to continue?' Right after class I went to the professor and told the truth. I was like, 'I am in this situation. What can I do?' I worked with the professor, but every time I would cry after class. I had to just deal with it."

Another participant, Laura, recalled when she needed to be hired as a student teacher to obtain her credential but could not because of her undocumented status. Her professor told her to drop the class if she could not be a student teacher. Laura went through a stage of fearing that she would drop out of the program. However, she found a way to be a "guest teacher" to complete the obligations of the credential program. These are additional steps that other students who were citizens did not need to undertake or manage.

Did the campus explicitly work toward empowering and supporting undocumented students? Not exactly. Specific units and individuals seemed to do a good job of positively affecting the experiences of our participants. However, the very invisibility that allowed students to maneuver on campus with relative ease also meant that other important units and individuals, such as academic advising, financial aid, program coordinators, internship programs, and professors tended to be less informed, potentially harming the academic well-being of the students in our study.

Recommendations

Based on our research findings, we have various recommendations for universities and for improving the learning conditions for undocumented university students.

Institutional Commitment

The university must adopt a zero-tolerance policy for anti-immigration hate activities. The undocumented students in our study conceptualized the university as a safe haven. This was a result of their ability to negotiate their legal status. However, if the "hyper-hate community climate" encroaches any more upon the university setting, it could erode their sense of safety and threaten their legal right to attend college. The university can respond with swift and clear responses to anti-immigrant activities through public e-mail notifications and message from the university president. Relatedly, universities should support annual campus climate surveys that must include specific prompts addressing the safety of undocumented students.

Task Force

The university must be explicit about supporting undocumented students; a task force would be an important step to institutionalizing a positive climate. Up until recently, the university featured in this chapter mostly supported undocumented students through individual efforts. Because of the work of United for Education (discussed above), the administration invited key actors to form the AB 540 Task Force on the topic of undocumented students on campus. Members include representatives from financial aid, the Educational Opportunity Program (EOP), the College Assistant Migrant Program (CAMP), student affairs, admissions, the chief diversity officer, career center counselor, general counseling adviser, faculty members, recruitment-outreach coordinator, and students.

Resource Center

Universities and colleges should designate a space on campus that could serve as a one-stop shop for undocumented students' needs. In spring 2014, the president of California State University, Fullerton, Mildred Garcia, designated state funds (permanent dollars) to open the Titans Dreamers Resource Center (Nault 2014), with a full-time staff member who coordinates services. In 2012, the University of California, Berkeley, opened the Robert D. Haas Dreamers Resource Center with a private donation, which came after the university established the Undocumented Student Program with a half-time staff person housed in the EOP offices in 2010. The University of California, Davis, established its AB 540 and Undocumented Student Center in fall 2014 (Easley 2014).

Many California State University (CSU) and University of California (UC) campuses have followed in this direction by establishing permanent staff members to help coordinate responding to undocumented students' needs. For example, in the UC system, Chancellor Janet Napolitano designated funds for legal support through UC law schools (Swedback 2014), scholarships, and enhanced student services. These included establishing student affairs positions such as an AB 540 coordinator. (Many believe these initiatives responded to criticism of Napolitano becoming chancellor after serving as secretary of Homeland Security and overseeing programs that led to historically high deportation rates.) There are 900 AB 540 students accounted for in the UC system, which has well over 200,000 students enrolled full time (Swedback 2014).

Regular Training

The university should sponsor staff and faculty development regarding the issues faced by undocumented students. We created a one-day conference, funded by various units and departments in the university, that brought in lecturers on the history of undocumented students and current research. There were panels of undocumented student speakers from other institutions and a session on teaching.

We created the first campus Safe-Space Training for the Undocumented Student Population in spring 2014, attended by more than eighty students, staff and faculty members, and administrators. Other campuses, such as Loyola University, Chicago; California State University, Long Beach; California State University, Fullerton; and Arizona State University, have long-running ally trainings. The University of California, Berkeley, recently hosted a legal rights webinar for undocumented students and educators.

Based on our conference and safe-space training evaluations, students who attended reported (1) they learned they were not alone and/or (2) they learned more about the complexities of being undocumented. Faculty and staff felt the conference was a "master class" in undocumented student issues. In summary, the event raised awareness on campus, educated students who were not undocumented about the issues, and provided social support for those students who were undocumented. These types of events must be *institutionalized* and organized yearly.

Informed and Aware Pedagogy

Faculty members need to be aware of the presence of undocumented students, their rights, and the barriers they face. For example, when professors assign projects (e.g., service learning) or fieldtrips off campus, they should create alternatives for those who have limitations in transportation and physical movement in the region. Syllabi should address academic speech and writing expectations; this is a great place for explaining why the "i" word should not be used (i.e., illegal immigrant, illegal alien).

Also, the stress felt by students in classroom discussions of immigration was quite apparent in our interviews. We do not advocate less discussion, but we would advise faculty to include a format for some students to voice their opinions that would be confidential and/or anonymous; journaling, for example, is an effective pedagogical tool to deepen students' learning (Navarrete 2013).

Finally, participants in our study constantly assessed whether faculty members were "safe." Faculty members sympathetic to undocumented students' learning needs should be explicit about their knowledge of the issues and find low-risk ways for students to approach them about any trouble they are having in class because of their status. Ideally, much like the rainbow flag and "equality" sign used to show support of gay, lesbian, bisexual, and transgender students, faculty could use posters or stickers on their office doors to indicate understanding and support of undocumented students. At this campus, after attending the safe-space training, participants received a sticker with an image of a hummingbird with the words, "Education without Borders" and the university logo. An undocumented student designed the logo, and the Office of Diversity, Equity, and Educational Inclusion funded its creation.

Staff and Services Truly Serving Undocumented Students

Student support services currently underused by undocumented students should begin efforts to become more informed and sensitive to the needs of our participants. Undocumented students pay their tuition with jobs most students could not imagine undertaking; it is only fair that they benefit from the services their tuition supports, such as the career center and academic advising. Student affairs and other major divisions in the university should administer their own surveys to determine student usage and find ways to conduct culturally sensitive outreach to the diverse undocumented student population on campus.

The psychological counseling services at the university are crucial components in keeping students motivated and in school. Depression is a serious concern in this population (Aranda and Vaquera 2015; Gonzales, Suárez-Orozco, and Dedios-Sanguineti 2013; Martinez 2014). As a group, Latino/as do not routinely use the university's psychological counseling services (Constantine, Chen, and Ceesay 1997; Cruz and Littrell 1998). However, the counseling department should work with student clubs that attract Latino/as (and other students of color) to begin culturally sensitive outreach efforts and create peer-counseling programs.

Because of the efforts of the students and the passage of the state-mandated financial-aid legislation, the director of the Financial Aid Office for this campus appointed a staff member the expert "point person" for the undocumented or AB 540 students on campus and those who are incoming. This type of leadership has been essential to educational and cultural knowledge about financial aid for both the staff and the students.

Campus police officers also should be provided professional development regarding undocumented students and their families. The undocumented interviewees on the campus in this study did not have negative interactions with the campus police. However, other universities report having to do intensive professional development on why a student might not have a driver's license and, in some cases in which there are special licenses mandated by state legislation, why these versions look different than regular licenses. One of the Southern California state universities created a memorandum of understanding with the campus police that informed their procedures on, for example, what to do if an undocumented student is pulled over for a traffic violation. We would encourage extending procedures and understandings to encompass incidents when the undocumented parents of students drive to campus to pick up their daughters or sons. This type of collaboration would also improve campus police relations in terms of racial profiling of campus members.

Conclusion

This chapter demonstrates the ways in which undocumented students experienced learning in a region characterized by a "hyper-hate climate." The participants conceptualized the university as a safe haven because their legal status was not the focus of their identities and roles as students. However, students' "invisible status" negatively affected their learning experiences and how they sought social and academic support. Social support was essential for our participants when dealing with their status. Many found comfort with immigrant-friendly academic programs, faculty, and staff, which made it easier for them to have a positive campus experience. Furthermore, most of our participants' learning experiences were affected by not being able to fully engage in immigration discussions in the classrooms for fear of revealing their own status and the consequences that could come with that exposure. Despite the danger, some shared their status with others and took leadership positions on campus.

Undocumented students seemed to experience mental distress as a result of their status (Gonzales, Suárez-Orozco, and Dedios-Sanguineti 2013). Students were not able to legally work and as a consequence were economically constrained when financing their education. However, our undocumented students were resilient; they went above and beyond to persevere in their academic studies and their respective roles within their own families. They worked to make the region and country better places even when many laws, policies, and practices were actively working to eliminate their presence.

Passage of comprehensive immigration reform with a clear path to citizenship for all undocumented immigrants could change the lives of these students and those who come after them. Their efforts would not go to waste. Immigration has often taken center stage in the national political arena, and there is hope for comprehensive reform. Meanwhile, undocumented students deal with the reality of an unjust and unequal educational system and immigration laws. In the next chapter, we focus on the experiences of university students who have graduated; they poignantly shared about the heavy weight of unresolved immigration law on their lives.

Note

1. *Underground Undergrads* and *Undocumented and Unafraid* are reports published by the UCLA Center for Labor Research and Education (see http://www.labor.ucla.edu/).

8

After College Graduation: Bittersweet

In this chapter, we examine the last stage of the educational pipeline: What happens after graduating from college for undocumented students? The word "bittersweet" was used in most responses.

Unlike those interviewed for previous chapters, these participants shared their experiences via an online, open-ended, anonymous survey. The survey contained twenty-nine questions; nine of them were demographic and the rest were open-ended questions about their college graduation experiences, feelings and experiences after graduation, political activism, and future goals.

The participants were recruited from different social network sites and listservs in early fall 2012. The survey opened in October and closed in December. Earlier that year, on June 15, 2012, President Obama announced the Deferred Action for Childhood Arrivals (DACA). Several participants applied for DACA, and they shared their feelings about the process.

More than sixty people visited the online survey website, and thirty-four completed the survey. Twenty-four females and ten males became our sample. We created pseudonyms for each participant. Most of our participants were born in Mexico (twenty-seven) and others represented Guatemala (two), Costa Rica (one), Peru (one), Ghana (one), Trinidad (one), and the Philippines (one). Most participants went to college in California. Several attended college in New York or Texas, and a few individuals represented colleges in Wisconsin, Connecticut, and Washington

---

Omar Canseco and Marisol Clark-Ibáñez wrote this chapter.

State. The verbatim excerpts in this chapter are taken directly from their surveys. (Please see Table C.3 in Appendix C for a summary of these participants.)

We were most impressed with the broad representation of academic disciplines in this group: communications, psychology, political science, urban planning, social work, black studies, Chicano/a and Latino/a studies, religious studies, women's studies, education, sociology, criminology, music, business, accounting, health information technology, computer science, biotechnology, chemistry, biochemistry, electrical engineering, civil engineering, public health, and nursing. Most enjoyed their undergraduate experiences, and many found the university a safe space—safe from Immigration and Customs Enforcement (ICE)—after they arrived on campus (see Chapter 7 and Martínez-Calderón 2009 for examples).

The participants represented academic excellence: ten indicated they were in graduate programs at the time of the survey (e.g., chemistry, engineering, artificial intelligence, sociology, criminal justice administration, student affairs/educational leadership), and several others indicated they were preparing to apply to graduate programs such as law school, social work, medical school, and various doctoral programs. However, almost all were working in low-paid "under the table" jobs such as construction, house cleaning, babysitting, fast-food restaurants, and manufacturing factories. Perla, a participant who came from Mexico at the age of three and majored in Chicano/a studies, found a job at a factory where she was paid $4 per hour because of her undocumented status. The "takeaway" from these postgraduates is clear: long-term immigration reform is needed to capture this impressive human capital.

Bittersweet Transition

Graduation day is one of the biggest milestones and rites of passage for young people in this country. It is a time of celebration and happiness. Sociologist Sally Raskoff (2010) writes that rituals such as college graduation are more than just a way to commemorate milestones; they "affirm that our behaviors are socially acceptable and worth striving for, and they connect to important social norms." The "norm" for postcollege graduates is to begin (immediately or eventually) a career path. Yet, graduation for the participants led to a precipice characterized by uncertainty, fear, depression, and low-wage labor. The participants felt accomplishment, excitement, anxiousness, happiness, and sadness, all of which led to a bittersweet condition.

As Julio shared, "On graduation day, I was happy but also experienced moments of depression and had thoughts of suicide. I did walk in my graduation. I even delivered the commencement speech. What a glorious day." This participant, who graduated with a major in political science, had to think that day, as well, of his "parents being unemployed, fear of deportation for a minor traffic violation, and struggling against an exploitative employer." He added, "It was hell on earth, to say the least." This participant applied to graduate school in criminal justice administration and worked with his dad as a mechanic to help save tuition money.

Esperanza, who was brought to the United States from Mexico when she was four years old, shared: "As I was graduating it was bittersweet. I was extremely excited because I was going to be the first in my family to graduate from college, but I was also extremely sad. I knew I wouldn't be able to pursue any of my career goals. I felt hopeless and helpless most of the time. Being undocumented really loomed over my head, and it was hard for me to savor my graduation moment as I walked on stage."

She vividly details the feeling of accomplishment as the first college graduate in her family. Most of the online survey participants were the first in their families to attend college and complete their degree.

Unfortunately, they found themselves in a "catch 22" because they could not pursue their careers as a result of their legal status. Anabel, a participant who graduated in health information technology from a Texas university, explained: "Even though college was a great accomplishment, it was one of the hardest things that had happened to me." She explained that she had to hold back the tears at commencement because of her mixed feelings of "happiness and hopelessness." She shared that after graduation, "I have a part-time job, but with a degree, making $7.25, so I don't feel like I accomplished anything."

Although the participants may have found the moment of graduation a significant milestone, they were also reminded of what loomed over them in the years to come. *Every participant mentioned depression or sadness in his or her survey.* In their pathbreaking research, Gonzales and colleagues (2013) reported that undocumented status carries with it a number of stressors and daily conditions that result in a profound sense of hopelessness. Also, as with participants in their study, some of the postcollege graduates in our study chose to isolate themselves from their friends who were citizens, which may have actually compounded levels of depression and anxiety.

Flor, who came from Mexico at twenty years old and graduated with a communications degree, described the trajectory of her feelings in detail, "Two weeks after graduation, I was fine. I was working and resting, since I always worked full time while going to school. However, about four months after graduation, I got into a really bad depression because I found myself useless since I was not going to use my degree. Also, knowing that my legal status was going to take about nine more years or even more. I was very depressed for about five months, but the total depression lasted about a year and a half." With the help of her professors, she entered a graduate program but once again faced the daunting issue of what came afterward. She wrote, "I need to have a job where I do not have to work hard, physical labor."

Laura, who came from Mexico when she was six and graduated with a major in sociology, shared her graduation experience: "I was really excited to be graduating; I am the first one in my family to graduate college, so it's a pretty big deal. At the same time I was feeling hopeless. I would think that my dream of graduating college was finally coming true, but that I would be unable to use my degree because of my legal status." The excitement the participants felt during graduation quickly took on the form of hopelessness because they understood, and were reminded at that precise time, that after graduation their careers could not be fulfilled because they did not have a Social Security number or work permit to legally work in the country.

Several participants felt *less accomplished* because of the realization of how their immigration status would be limiting them. Some reported not walking in or not celebrating their graduation. Lupe, who came from Trinidad to the United States at age twelve and lived in New York, wrote, "Graduating was bittersweet for me. I felt accomplished being the first person on both my mom's and dad's [sides of the] family to graduate from college. This feeling of accomplishment was limited because as graduation drew closer, the reality that my options of advancing would be limited began to sink in. Even though I was the first to graduate, and my parents would have loved to see me walk, I did not attend the graduation ceremony. I was very depressed during that time." She recalled, "Around the time of graduating, I lashed out at my parents a lot. I blamed them for not thinking of my future. That was very immature of me, but I was depressed and had the most hopeless feeling in the world. Of course, I know that my parents were only trying to survive by moving here, but I wouldn't allow myself to see it that way at the time."

Gloria came to the United States at the age of ten and went to a prestigious private university in New York. She graduated with a major in computer science "in record time." She wrote, "I worked very hard and completed a four-year degree in three years, partly because . . . the cost of the school was great. I did not walk in my graduation ceremony. I did not see the point. There were no celebrations."

Luna, who came from Costa Rica at the age of eleven, did not want to walk in graduation but did anyway. She wrote on her graduation cap, "Now What? Undocumented Dreamer." In addition, she was unexpectedly faced with pregnancy and quickly found a job at a fast-food restaurant for $8 an hour. Luna illustrated the feeling of emptiness and uncertainty: "I was feeling empty. I didn't know what the future held."

All respondents felt at a loss. Lucia, who came from Mexico at the age of nine and later majored in biochemistry, explained: "I felt empty. I felt like I was not done. I wanted to go further in my education and could not do so. I was scared that that was the end for me, and like my parents, I would have to take underpaid, hard-labor jobs. I felt so restrained, like everywhere I turned there was an obstacle, and I could not move. I felt frustrated and cried a lot. It was like finishing high school all over again. The vivid feeling of being undocumented arose again." She was in graduate school in chemistry and planned to apply to doctoral programs. Although she was not politically active as an undergraduate, she became a student leader on campus advocating for undocumented students as a graduate student.

The feeling of emptiness and not knowing what the future will bring for undocumented people is very stressful. These participants' struggles and experiences were closely tied to what the future held for them. Their status does not let them fully participate in US society. Being reminded of this fact caused the majority of the participants to become depressed as graduation day approached. Another participant described the feelings of hopelessness that emerged upon graduation, "I think at a time when I was supposed to be celebrating the next step in my life to advance myself, I felt more hopeless and stuck than anything else." The hopelessness felt by the undocumented students was evident in their descriptions of graduating from the educational pipeline, such as from high school and college. In addition they were in a "catch 22" because they were very knowledgeable and excelled in their educational path, but they could not use their skills in the workforce. They were denied the right to participate in the very stage graduation beckoned them to begin.

Several participants wrote about family members who were not able to watch them graduate because of undocumented status, theirs or that of others. One young man in Texas, Santiago, who graduated with a major in criminal justice, explained that he and a classmate ordered pizza after graduation and quietly celebrated together. Although his mother was able to see him cross the stage, there was no party or celebration afterward. He had come from Mexico at the age of five and worked construction jobs during college ("they paid me cash") to pay for school. After he graduated, he helped his mother at her job as a maid at a resort. Despite this, like many other participants, Santiago explained, "I will never regret the experience, the education I obtained by going to college."

Another participant explained that her grandfather had died shortly before graduation: "It was hard on me and my family. He was loved dearly.

Frustration, anger, and sadness started building up in me since I was not able to go to his ceremony because he was buried in Oaxaca. I was also going through financial problems that I wanted to drop out of school that last semester, get my money, and come back. I was able to raise the money with my mom's help. She gave me all the share of our babysitting business."

Catarino, who came to the United States at age ten, shared that his father passed away in Mexico shortly after Catarino's graduation. He discussed the situation with his family, and they decided he should stay to apply for graduate school instead of returning to attend the funeral and risking the return across the border. Catarino went to college in the state of Washington and then entered a social work graduate program in Illinois.

The participants' efforts at school and in other social worlds were fueled by determination and resilience. Yet during each educational milestone, they faced severe hopelessness. Their undocumented status and lack of social opportunity became evident (or intensified) during the process of graduation. The bittersweet condition was grounded in a social reality of exclusion and disenfranchisement. It directly affected their psychological state, employment (or lack thereof), and professional development.

Isolation from Peers

Several participants explained that they removed themselves from social network sites and isolated themselves from others because they began feeling depressed with so many others asking about what they were going to do after graduation and learning about others' exciting career plans and opportunities.

Lupe, the communications major, wrote: "I was becoming more distant from friends as it became painful to watch them make plans and move on with their lives while I was literally stuck in the same place that I was before earning a degree. I deleted my Facebook profile in an attempt to escape questions about 'what r u up to?' or 'have you found a job yet?' and all those inquisitive questions that I just did not want to answer in fear of people becoming suspicious."

Gerardo, who came from Mexico at age ten and was a music major in California, shared that he avoided student clubs while in college. He reported, "People asked me about what was next, but I always dodged the question. I lost hope many times. I even cried. It wasn't fair. Psychologically, drained."

Elvia, from Guatemala, was an undocumented student in New York who graduated "with honors and in the top 3" percent of her class in computer science. She wrote, "I refused to keep in touch with my friends in college because I was embarrassed what I was working as. People think that you are being lazy or silly for having a degree and not finding a job in the field. They think you don't have the capability or skills, and that's why no company will hire you. I looked into going to graduate school but realized that I could not afford it." Elvia continued to share, "People expect you to be working in your field after you get a college degree, not working as a babysitter and cleaning houses, not that there is anything bad with taking care of children or cleaning houses, just that why does someone spend years getting a degree then?"

Rosa, who came to the United States from Mexico when she was fifteen and later earned a degree in business, described, "I cut off communication with some people from college. It became overwhelming having people ask me what I was doing with my degree. I obviously was not going to say I was a housekeeper. I clean houses for a living. People that are close to me know my legal situation but personally, I lie and let it be known to a few. I could count them on one hand."

A participant explained that for undocumented students after graduation, it was more of a passive process; others "drifted into their different paths which they could actually take—PhD programs and medical school—like they wanted" while she stayed behind. Esperanza, who graduated with a major in psychology, mentioned she had "extreme depression" when her friends left to travel and explore the world because she was unable to join them: "It tore us apart not to be able to enjoy so many of the dreams we wanted to share." She added that it was hard "having friends move to places I couldn't go visit, like Arizona." Manuel felt that because after graduation he was not driving or working—two things expected of college graduates and of men—it was very hard to initiate romantic relationships with women because he might not meet their expectations (since he was not able to drive on or pay for dates). He also feared women might be suspicious of him wanting a relationship so he could fix his undocumented legal status by marrying a citizen.

Professionally Qualified; Prevented from Doing So

After graduation, undocumented students felt trapped because going out into the workforce brought their legal status to the forefront. They reported the barriers they faced as they tried to look for employment knowing that they could not use their degrees to work in the United States. The most noticeable obstacle that loomed in front of most of the participants was not having the opportunity to find employment in their fields of study.

Ramon illustrated the result of not being allowed to work; he felt like a child excluded from social activities. He stated, "I felt like the little kid that was grounded and locked in his room, while he could hear all his friends playing and having fun outside in the park. It was horrible." Using an analogy of a child being punished, he described how his undocumented status acted as a social control. Ramon acknowledged that not being allowed to put his knowledge to practice through work felt like punishment. Not only denied access to participation in the workforce, he was also excluded from the social circles found in a profession. Like Ramon, other participants often felt socially limited and discriminated against in this fashion.

Manuel, who came to the United States at thirteen years old, graduated magna cum laude with a 3.92 grade-point average in civil engineering. He recalled his undergraduate experience: "I was always [so] busy doing [a] project, studying, and doing homework that I kind of forgot that I was undocumented. I was an overachiever with really high self-esteem." Then, he tried to find an unpaid internship in his field: "I was hoping to find an unpaid internship so that I could get experience. I already knew I could not get paid, so I was willing to work for free. I just wanted to get real life experience. Nevertheless, all the unpaid internships still required a Social Security number, which I lacked." After finishing his undergraduate degree, he spent time helping his family at home with chores, repairing friends' computers, and helping his siblings with homework. He chose not to drive or work illegally.

Without a Social Security number, undocumented graduates cannot participate in formal labor institutions; they are disenfranchised and discriminated against. For the participants this is a form of punishment, and they are angry that the United States will not pass comprehensive and progressive immigration legislation.

This situation has taken a toll on Manuel's self-worth: "Now, I have too much time on my hands and I am always thinking in this things that I could be doing if I was working." Manuel shared important insights on undocumented students' efforts to navigate undocumented life. Because he could not legally work, he made an effort to obtain professional experience in his field of study by doing volunteer work through internships. Unfortunately this was not possible as a result of the legal documentation requirements. He did not want to work "illegally" and avoided driving because he could not get a driver's license. Manuel found other ways to contribute to his family's well-being by helping with child care and housework. He had applied for DACA and was waiting for approval.

Laura described her postgraduation job search in the Orange County area of Southern California: "Since graduation, I went back home and reunited with old friends. It felt like I picked up where I left off. I was looking for work. . . . I always worked in restaurant service, so I started looking for jobs in restaurants. I remember applying to positions at a restaurant where they were going to start me a[t] minimum wage. I went and trained, but they said they would call me back. During the training I felt really frustrated, I would always think that I didn't go to college to do that. I would think that I went to college to get a better job. Finally, my aunt told me she knew of someone looking for a nanny. . . . Being a nanny is what I've been doing since I graduated in 2009." This participant also shared that she is "yearning" to learn and wants to return to school. She planned to apply for DACA status.

Low-wage work was one of the few options available to these students. They found that because of their legal status they could not obtain jobs in their fields of study and must opt to work in service-sector jobs that pay minimum or below minimum wage. Many were faced with working under hard conditions and often worked for people less educated than they were. They knew that they filled a labor pool seen as expendable. In addition they found themselves not meeting social expectations based on a career track; by not working in their fields of study, they might have been seen as "unsuccessful" among their peers who were documented residents or citizens of the United States. They also found themselves feeling hopeless because of all the time, money, energy, and passion put into their education that in the end was not providing them greater opportunities.

Noemi, brought to the United States from Mexico at the age of twelve, was enrolled in a master's program at a San Diego four-year university during the data collection stage of our study. She described how limited opportunities to work in her profession as a result of her undocumented status had become normalized. She lamented that it has become acceptable in society to have millions of people living under such conditions. Noemi explained, "Facing struggles in terms of work since my undocumented status prevents me to have job opportunities. These struggles have become a part of my life. In my own case, I see all struggles as normality, since it is all I know since the first day I came to this country. Unfortunately, obtaining a degree has not changed or eliminated struggles in terms of work and opportunities."

Gerardo, who studied music, explained the economic hardship he faced: "I have real bills and the wage I earn is not enough. At this pace living without a 'legal status' I feel like I will miss many experiences, life opportunities, and my 30s will be just like my 20s, without a 'legal status.'" He got married after graduation, fathered children, and found a full-time job in manufacturing: "Started as a bagger and worked my way up to supervisor." Gerardo brings to light how undocumented people feel trapped in low-wage work and struggle to make ends meet. As Gonzales (2011) found, some had "let go hopes for career mobility . . . opting instead for security and stability" (614).

Only one participant, Antonio, decided to move back to his home country for a graduate degree and begin a professional career. He described the process of obtaining a Mexican passport, applying for graduate school in artificial intelligence (a combination of robotics and electrical engineering) in Mexico. Antonio has been able to work and intern in different Latin American countries. He explained that after he was an undocumented college graduate in the United States, "I set up new goals for myself as an engineer and individual. The main goal was to become a citizen of the world by traveling globally." He was accepted into his graduate program and wrote that after he was done, "I want to travel to another country and work as an engineer while learning another language." He admitted, "I was afraid because I had decided to move back to Mexico and did not know what to expect." Antonio concluded, "I don't regret it, since I have come to realize that I can go anywhere in the world now." Most of the participants, however, did not have the financial resources to undertake such a highly adventurous and rewarding journey. For many, leaving their families in the United States—parents, siblings—was unthinkable, and in fact, their worst fear (deportation).

Importance of Legislation

All the participants stated that legislation was most important for the undocumented community. The undocumented students who participated in this study mentioned the two proposals important to them: the federal Development, Relief, and Education for Alien Minors (DREAM) Act and DACA. They viewed both as steps in the right direction. However, they were also cautious and furthermore remained uncertain on what will come, especially out of elections. They wrote about the positive ways they have been affected by both the California DREAM Act and DACA. They also discussed finding solutions to their undocumented legal status through comprehensive immigration reform and a path to citizenship.

Some participants were able to benefit from the California DREAM Act, and those outside of California described how their state policies affected them. For example, Pedro, who came from Peru at the age of fifteen and later majored in business, explained that in Wisconsin, "the in-state tuition was here before but was removed two years ago. It is extremely hard to make . . . [$8] an hour and pay $6,000 in tuition every semester." He worked sixteen-hour days after graduation as a roofer to begin saving for business graduate school. He reported that his family had a very unstable economic situation and that this increased the tension between him and his parents; he was frustrated that he could not use his degree to help them financially. Although Pedro applied for DACA, he admitted, "Graduate school is more expensive and at the moment, I am afraid I won't have enough money to pay for this semester."

Pedro's social reality threatens his lifestyle daily. At $8 an hour, if he worked full time, Pedro would have to pay close to five full months of his salary for one semester's tuition. On top of this he must find other ways to make ends meet to cover housing, food, and other necessities. In some ways DACA helps ease the affliction undocumented students face, yet our participants felt DACA has limitations and thus were uncertain about what would happen after President Obama completed his last term.

DACA: A Cautious Celebration

The participants had mixed feelings when it came to DACA. Indeed, it grants deferral for two years only, and they emphasized that this executive order was a *temporary* act (because the next administration could overturn it). In addition they see that it was only a partial solution because of its requirements and limitations. Gerardo, for example, stated, "DACA is a temporary Band-Aid on a gushing wound." Martinez (2014) also found that participants were cynical about the long-term prospects of their DACA benefits. He commented on the uncertainty of his journey through college as well as the limitations of DACA. He reiterated the need for comprehensive immigration reform: "I started college in the year 2000. The DREAM Act was introduced in 2001. I actually thought that by the time I finished college, the DREAM Act would have passed and I would of [*sic*] been fine. More than a decade later, I sure was wrong. DACA is temporary and its . . . [future] is unknown, especially after an election. The DREAM Act will follow and by then I won't qualify because of my age, but comprehensive reform is my last hope and hope to millions of others who were also brought as children and are now adults."

Furthermore, Gerardo speaks of the situation that many youth who were brought to this country as children must deal with as adults. They face uncertainty because of the complexity of the immigration laws, and they must navigate an unstable path. Their hopes were placed on the federal DREAM Act and comprehensive immigration reform, but they expressed many doubts. Yet, as in the previous chapters, the undocumented postgraduates maintained resilience and were hoping for change. As Gerardo also mentioned, the DREAM Act has been proposed but failed to pass for years, so after a decade of studying and staying in school, he and his fellow DREAMers had not seen the change they expected. Several participants in this study were postgraduates and no longer qualified for DACA because of their age—either they came to the United States "too old" or are now more than thirty years old. Thousands of other undocumented students face the same reality: they have aged out.

Still, the participants found both the California DREAM Act and DACA valuable. Both changes in the law provided them a sense of security; it took some pressure and stigma away from their everyday experiences. DACA provides a basic state identification card or a driver's license. Elvia, the Guatemalan computer scientist who came to the United States at the age of fifteen, reported that not having a New York identification card prevented her from using community services, even the local swimming pool. Her little brother always asked why they could not go, and she explained, "When we took him to the town pool and took our passports, consular IDs, college ID, utility bills with us to prove to the people that we lived here, they refused to let us in. My little brother cried so much. He was only five years old. He saw his friends swimming and having fun inside. He didn't understand why the people wouldn't let him in. It was so frustrating for me. Now, I hope to have the opportunity to be able to offer a more normal life, to have some freedom and the strength to fight for our rights."

Participants reported DACA inspired hope for the future. For the undocumented postgraduates, DACA provided a sense of security and freedom to participate in social activities taken for granted by documented residents and US citizens. Wong and Valdivia (2014) found that DACA awardees felt more incorporated into the United States, and most found their first jobs or changed to better jobs. Carla, who was brought to the United States when she was two years old, wrote, "I have a workers' permit and a Social [Security card]. I feel wanted and normal. I feel equal in the state that I grew up in." Luna described DACA as if she had "seen light at the end of the tunnel": a pathway to further education and access to better jobs. Julio explained, "My feelings have changed now with DACA. I am hopeful and feel free. . . . I am glad that hellish era of my life will finally come to an end with DACA. I do not wish the suffering that I experienced on anyone. The struggle is diminished and undocumented can actually dance for joy and gratitude for what is happening with DACA." Feeling hopeful was important for undocumented students because they were seeing some change they had long awaited.

DACA was a new beginning that provided them some basic options taken for granted by residents and citizens of the United States. In the following example, Rosa described some of the changes DACA provided for her and other undocumented students: "I have applied to DACA and have been approved and received [a] work permit that although temporary is something I am extremely grateful for. Only someone who has been undocumented for so long, knowing the endless possibilities out there, can understand what this means to me and to others in this situation." Yet, Rosa reiterated the importance of comprehensive immigration reform: "I am elated to get a Social Security [card] and driver's license accordingly. As far as the DREAM Act goes, not sure whether it would ever pass. I want to believe comprehensive immigration reform will be adequate for most, including DACA beneficiaries."

Legal documents, such as Social Security numbers and driver's licenses, are vital for thriving in the United States. These documents provide a sense of safety as well as opportunities for informal social and formal economic participation. Although it is not *permanent* legal status, the participants were hopeful and saw these changes as steps toward resolving people's undocumented status. Yet, every participant emphasized the importance of comprehensive immigration reform. Lucia, the chemistry graduate student, eloquently expressed what many others wrote about: "Comprehensive reform however is what I await the most. As I am happy that my options are broadening and new paths are becoming accessible, I cannot help by [*sic*] feel that I am leaving my parents behind. We must not forget about the people who also work and contribute to this society just as much as students. We must not forget about other people who came also with a dream that has not been fulfilled. They left everything behind for us, for a better life, and they deserve a part also." The accounts described in these pages remind us of the urgency for change, specifically in terms of immigration legislation and a path to citizenship—a pathway to further social justice in the United States.

Experiences in Graduate School

In our sample, many participants applied for graduate school and were in their first or second year of study at the time of our interviews. Frequently, they were the only ones in their program who were undocumented, and others wrote that they were the first undocumented students to be accepted. Blanca, who came from Mexico at the age of thirteen and was later in an educational leadership graduate program, described her feelings about graduate school: "I find that the higher level of education [we attain as] undocumented students, the more 'lonely' it gets." The participants wrote of three main experiences: economic uncertainty, inability to participate fully in their program, and hopefulness for change.

During graduate school, many opportunities open up for typical students who wish to gain experience in their respective fields of study. Unfortunately for undocumented students, these opportunities are limited because of their legal status; they cannot work through the university as researchers or teaching assistants. Noemi explained her experience during her first year of graduate school: "It was also tough getting used to the graduate experience as an undocumented student because although most of my peers knew about my status, I still felt I was getting a very different experience. For example, while they were all doing research or teaching assistantships, I couldn't because of my lack of legal status." Undocumented students' need of legal documentation prevents them from fully participating in their educational and career goals. In this example, the participant explained some of the career development activities undocumented students cannot practice during their graduate school experiences. Internships and teaching assistantships are essential to developing career experience while completing the graduate degree. However, many of these opportunities require legal documentation as a prerequisite to participate.

Furthermore the economic hardships for undocumented students continued into their graduate-level education, mainly because they could not find jobs or internships to help finance their studies. Noemi, who was in a graduate program for sociology, explained her situation as she tried to finance graduate school after the company she worked for went out of business, "By mid-summer I was able to find a job in babysitting to pay for graduate school. I was bummed out though because even with a degree not much had changed financially because of my inability to legally apply for jobs." Finding only low-wage work to finance graduate school added more pressure for these students and limited their opportunities to develop experience in their fields of study. Noemi acknowledged the importance of being employed and the hardship undocumented students face when they cannot find jobs that help them pay for school. She described the stress of becoming unemployed the summer before beginning graduate school, "I knew that no matter what I had to have a job to pay for school. At the same time, I know how difficult things were now with trying to get a job so I was worried of being unemployed and not being [able] to pay for grad school." If she did not find a job prior to the fall semester of graduate school, she would have been faced with postponing her education.

Many of the participants who continued to graduate school placed a lot of emphasis on staying hopeful and came to terms with their experiences. Noemi explained this process: "I accepted these differences though and still tried to make the most out of my grad school experience because I knew it was an amazing opportunity to be able to further pursue my educational and career goals." Managing the different challenges they faced in graduate school became a way of looking at positive opportunities they had simply by being part of the graduate student community. Their staying hopeful and making the best out of graduate school further demonstrates the resilience of these participants.

Resilience Through Networks

As previously mentioned, the undocumented students in our study overcame many barriers. Through these experiences they learned and developed determination, which included developing a strong support system. In addition, they had rich insights on how to navigate in a society that does not welcome them with open arms.

Antonio, who left the country for a graduate program in Mexico, described how being undocumented gave him practice in institutional survival: "As an undocumented student . . . I was able to develop vision and look for opportunities where others cannot. Today even though I am not undocumented anymore, I am always on the look[out] for new things to learn and improve." He is no longer "undocumented" because he left the United States and returned to his country of birth for graduate studies. Yet his experience of being undocumented since he was fifteen taught him crucial life lessons.

Many of the postgraduates in this study shared that they developed skills and an attitude that made them successful. Esperanza wrote, "I like to think I make opportunities for myself out of places where opportunities don't exist (or shouldn't exist)." Pedro, who is earning an MBA in Wisconsin, wrote that being undocumented made him miss out on many opportunities such as internships and study abroad. However, he adds, "The problems are so many and so hard to overcome that once you get a regular/normal problem that other people get, you just think 'Are you kidding me? You are worried about that?' Now I know how to deal with stress and I have a LOT of patience."

The opportunities of which the participants speak were found in the social networks they developed, which helped the students continue on the path they wanted to follow. Undocumented students looked for social support from the people closest to them. These people were their families, friends, and professors. These allies and role models helped students stay resilient in their struggle to achieve their educational and career goals. Many described how others helped them form and accomplish their goals. Noemi shared, "My friends, professors, and other people I meet have also shaped my future goals because they give me the energy to keep on going."

These social networks also contributed in more clear ways; another participant wrote, "I have a passion for learning and contributing to society, but that passion definitely needs the motivation, inspiration, and help I have gotten from friends, professors, and others." Providing support for the students meant that members of the support system were "there" for the students and that they were actively participating in shaping the students' futures by inspiring and motivating them.

Most participants described their social networks—friends, family—as the most important factor in their not giving up hope. Olga, a participant from California who graduated with a health education major, wrote that during graduation she was extremely discouraged about working in her area of study, which resulted in her being "so sad and depressed." She asked herself, "*De que me sirvio ir a la Universidad y todo el dinero, tiempo, y estrés si no puedo ejersir mi carera* [*sic*]. (How was it worth going to the university, all the money, time, and stress if I cannot be in my career?) I was going to clean house, work in the fields for the rest of my life and with a degree. . . . But I have surrounded myself with family and friends who never allowed me to give up." Since then, she volunteers at clinics, helps in a labor center that advocates for domestic workers' rights, and is exploring graduate school options.

Developing a strong support system was crucial for the participants in pushing forward and staying resilient in times of ambiguity. Noemi explained, "I have a stronger support system. I've found comfort in my school and in my graduate cohort. But regardless I still have moments where I feel depressed, anxious, and fearful, most of the time." Although these support systems have helped, students still faced many barriers. With the support of the allies they created, they further progressed. Antonio, the electrical engineer who left the United States to study and look for opportunities in Mexico, shares the ways in which his support network helped him, "I believe everyone who helped me and support[ed] me during my studying in the US gave me the courage to travel outside in order to face world issues." His support system helped him recognize a more global perspective on his situation and pushed him to seek new paths and forms of resilience.

Gerardo highlighted the complexity of staying resilient: "I am lucky to have an amazing family and great friends. Ironically, I wouldn't choose any other life than mine. I've had great moments in high school, college, and now [as] a parent. Sure it is hard, but one day, I will be free. Free to choose." Looking into what the future holds was worrisome for these students; nonetheless they positively viewed the support of their families and friends. The resilience of Gerardo and the other participants in this study is an amazing example of how undocumented people do not conform to a label or category. They fight and continue on the path to achieving their goals.

The students in this study became more open-minded to other forms of struggles people in society faced. Through their own experiences they developed more acceptance of other people. They came to own the power of knowledge they held. Stated Esperanza, "I've gained greater compassion and empathy for people of all races, legal status, identities. I've gained an education and that's empowering. They can keep me from traveling or from driving, but they can't take away the power I feel from learning and empowering myself. I believe in paying it forward. Right now I'm in this situation, but when I can, I will pay it forward for other generations."

The participants in this study know that they have limitations on their physical mobility and legal status, but when it comes to their knowledge and resilience, they feel that *no law can take those away*. Rosa, who lives in Northern California, applied for DACA, and was working as a house cleaner in a small town after obtaining her business degree, wrote: "My life is blessed as it is. It could be better, yes. I am at peace with being undocumented. . . . College is, for me, to raise [*sic*] above ignorance and oppression." Furthermore, they empowered themselves by reflecting on their experiences of existing and surviving in the margins of society. They are also agents of social change fighting for a better future from which perhaps they may not benefit, but the goal is that future generations from the undocumented community can benefit.

Political Participation and Activism

In this sample of postgraduates, participants were likely to receive notice of this online survey through politically oriented and activist websites, listservs, and peers. We were curious to know how politically active the college graduates were (or had been) on issues of immigration. We hypothesized that this survey could have a selection bias toward a more politically active group because of the recruitment sources. Yet, of the thirty-four participants, just fewer than half (fifteen) mentioned *something* about participating in political activity and, within this group, only five could be characterized as DREAMer activists (see Chapter 9 for more on this specific activism).

Five participants described *major leadership* positions in college or in the community in terms of undocumented immigration issues. For example, Catarino, a participant in the Northwest, took the lead helping his private, liberal arts university draft a statement of support for undocumented students, the first of its kind in the nation. He also founded a nonprofit organization and traveled around his state to advocate for DREAM legislation and community outreach. Others were presidents of college clubs and continued similar roles in their communities or graduate programs. Antonio, who returned to Mexico for engineering graduate studies, had been very involved in his university's AB 540 task force as an undergraduate. He now participates in "Dream in Mexico," an organization that "offers the opportunity to undocumented students in the US to start the process of application to Mexican well-known, qualified universities." Other participants organized immigration marches and rallies and gave their time to related issues, such as the California Domestic Workers Bill of Rights (vetoed by Governor Jerry Brown) and the Occupy movement rallies. Some of the leaders in the sample began their work with MEChA in high school and then became more aware of their status while in college, which resulted in, as one of the participants wrote, "finding my own voice to create change."

Four reported *mixed levels* of political participation. For two participants, undergraduate experiences included club leadership and events with legislators. Pedro, the business major who attended graduate school in accounting, explained, "I went to the capitol and talked to many representatives. I worked on getting in-state tuition for undocumented students in Wisconsin." He was not at the time of the survey involved in any form of community or political work. Another participant, a criminology major who struggled with the death of her grandfather at graduation, was president of the college club that supports AB 540 students and conducted numerous outreach events for undocumented youth, but she left behind her political activism.

Two others were not active in college but became very motivated postgraduates. Lucia, the chemistry major, did not participate in any groups while attending college in central California, explaining that she only visited the "cadreamactnetwork yahoo group online." However, after she began graduate school in Los Angeles, she became extremely active on her campus and conducted community outreach for undocumented youth. Esperanza came to the United States from Mexico when she was four and studied psychology as an undergraduate; she admitted that during college she "was too depressed to deal with more legal issues." Now, she reports, "I am able [to] share my story with others. I feel better speaking about undocumented people, going to rallys [*sic*], and holding events. I have a greater understanding of how I'm helping change my community and bettering it." At the time of the survey, Esperanza was enrolled in a counseling graduate program.

The majority in this sample did not respond to the questions about political activity; however, six participants elaborated on how and why they were *not* involved. Elvia, the New York computer science major from Guatemala, shared, "Unfortunately I wasn't politically active as an undergrad; I was trying not to call much attention. I was fearful." Three reported that they did not have time because they were working so much and going to school. Their jobs were extremely hard physical labor, long hours, and night shifts. One of the participants wrote that she worked too many hours but that although she was not directly active, she was politically informed and helped others in her community who could vote understand the elections. Another participant wrote, "Once I talk about politics, I feel so hopeless and become so depressed that I try to avoid [the] topic." For her, immigration activism brought up too many negative emotions.

Although more than half of the participants were not politically active, given the legal issues they faced and uncertainty of deportation, political participation and activism were of great interest to our participants. Those who were politically active explicitly aimed to better the social conditions for the undocumented population as a whole. Thanks to the DREAMer movement, described more in the next chapter, others have taken a stand and participated in national protests or are working in community grassroots organization.

Conclusion

Graduating college was simultaneously seen as a milestone and a failure. The participants discussed the ways in which they could not fulfill the promise of starting a new career as a way to positively contribute to society. Their status as "college student," where most excelled and found comfort, was behind them. Many reflected on the painful realization that their jobs were the same ones they could have gotten before college (e.g., fast-food server, babysitter, roofer). We borrow an idea from Gonzales and colleagues (2013), who wrote that after undocumented youth became adults, it was as if a "thick boundary created the need to reorganize, or retell, discourses they held about themselves and to reformulate the answers to the essential questions during adolescence about 'who am I?' and 'where am I going?'" (1182). The DACA status was just a temporary way to go from being college educated to being a gainfully employed professional—yet only a handful of participants could apply, and the benefits lasted for only two years at a time. The renewal process has been complicated and expensive.

Ultimately, the participants who graduated from college felt that they had only partially "done their part" to help their families and make up for the sacrifices of their parents. Laura explained, "My parents brought my siblings and I to give us a better life. I have obtained the college dream but haven't been able to help out much financially. I know they are proud of me. I want to show them that their hard work and effort to get me through college has not been in vain. It is me that wants to give them a better life. My parents work so much. My dad is 63 and holds two jobs as a factory worker in the garment district. My mom is 51 and cleans two houses a day. Yet they never complain."

These college graduates successfully completed the educational pipeline—they went from kindergarten to a four-year college. Yet, many anguished and languished. As reflected in the previous chapters, institutions of higher education can better prepare undocumented students by offering legal clinics, career counseling, and specialized mental health services. Until there is comprehensive immigration reform to give them permanent status or citizenship, they cannot complete the *promise* of education in the United States—not for themselves, their *familias*, or their *comunidades*.

9

DREAMer Activism: Challenges and Opportunities

On June 15, 2012, President Barack Obama took executive action on immigration and announced the Deferred Action for Childhood Arrivals (DACA) federal program. DACA provides an opportunity for eligible undocumented immigrant youth to receive temporary work authorization and relief from deportation. A few days prior to DACA, on June 5, 2012, undocumented organizers staged a sit-in at President Obama's campaign office in Denver, Colorado. This sit-in was one in a series of actions undocumented youth had organized across the nation in an effort to urge President Obama to issue an executive order to protect from deportation undocumented youth eligible for proposed Development, Relief, and Education for Alien Minors (DREAM) Act benefits (Ingold 2012).

Notably, June 15, 2012, marked a key success for a subset of the undocumented "1.5 generation," defined as those who migrated at early ages and reside in the United States (Abrego and Gonzales 2010). They have been at the forefront of immigrant rights organizing since 2006. What began as organizing for the passage of the DREAM Act, proposed federal legislation that would have provided a path to citizenship for eligible undocumented youth, has evolved into a movement that seeks to address issues affecting not just "DREAMers" but *all* immigrants. In order to create just social and political change, undocumented youth organizers hope to empower undocumented immigrants (first generation and beyond) to take action and be at the forefront of organizing with, and for, immigrant communities. Organizers have also created networks of undocumented-youth-

---

Carolina Valdivia Ordorica wrote this chapter.

led organizations at the state and local levels to strategically build a stronger foundation from which to organize. These networks have then, for example, organized to overturn unjust immigration laws.

Despite the legal, emotional, social, and financial challenges undocumented youth face, a subset of the undocumented 1.5 generation has sought to engage politically, online and offline. In fact, Negron-Gonzales (2013) posits that undocumented youth organizers come to their political activity from a place of "oppositional consciousness" stemming from exclusion and fear. As an undocumented immigrant myself, I am a part of the undocumented-youth-led networks fighting for social and political change. Chapter 2 of this book explained the overview of immigration policies past, present, and proposed; this chapter focuses on the political action involved in supporting, resisting, and/or shaping this legislation. I first discuss the emergence of undocumented-youth-led organizing in the context of the immigrant rights movement. I then transition into how undocumented youth began to be at the forefront of organizing around issues affecting their communities. Much of this stage initially took place, and continued to evolve, both in online and offline spaces. Thus, I hope to describe in great detail efforts to organize online and offline. I highlight key organizations (e.g., DreamACTivist.org and United We Dream) and campaigns (e.g., Not One More) to demonstrate the varying goals, tactics, challenges, and successes of undocumented-youth-led organizing.

Beginning of the DREAM

Undocumented youth face several challenges as they navigate the K–12 and postsecondary educational systems. Immigration policies that have largely sought to produce and sustain *illegality* (De Genova 2002) have rendered undocumented immigrants ineligible to legally work, drive, travel, or receive many federal benefits (e.g., federal financial aid). Undocumented youth often find out what it means to be undocumented during or after their senior year in high school. At this time, many undocumented youth realize that they do not have a Social Security number to enter on their college, driver's license, work, and scholarship applications. Upon this realization, many undocumented youth face psychological consequences, including feelings of sadness, frustration, confusion, depression, and stress. Undocumented youth grow up immersed in US culture and the educational system, only to find out later that they do not have the same rights as their documented peers. Although undocumented youth may persist in their studies and/or careers, they constantly live with the fear and risk of deportation. This leads to additional psychological challenges because undocumented youth do not have certainty they will eventually be able to use their higher education degrees and pursue their careers in the United States. To address these challenges, undocumented youth have organized to support the passage of the DREAM Act.

When the DREAM Act was introduced, undocumented youth who would potentially benefit from it collectively identified themselves as "DREAMers." The name "DREAMer" came from the bill, first introduced in 2001 by Senator Richard Durbin (D-IL) and Representative Howard Berman (D-CA). At the time, the DREAM Act promised to provide a pathway to legal status for eligible undocumented youth if they (1) came to the United States at age sixteen or younger, (2) resided in the United States for five years prior to the bill's enactment, (3) had good moral character, (4) were under the age of thirty, and (5) served in the military OR attended college for a minimum of two years (US Senate 2010a).

In 2006, the DREAM Act gained momentum and support after documented and undocumented youth participated in the May Day immigrant rights marches. In Southern California alone, an estimated 40,000 high school students walked out of their schools to protest the Border Protection, Antiterrorism, and Illegal Immigration Control Act of 2005, HR 4437 (Valle 2006). Under HR 4437, the number of border patrol agents would have increased significantly. HR 4437 also sought to increase prison penalties for undocumented immigrants. Anyone who assisted undocumented immigrants, regardless of his or her own immigration status, also would have been penalized. On December 16, 2006, the bill passed the House of Representatives; however, it ultimately failed to pass the Senate.

The passage of HR 4437 in the House of Representatives outraged many communities. In particular, immigrant youth across the nation organized walkouts via social media networks (e.g., Facebook and Myspace) and text messages. Immigrant youth were able to rapidly broadcast information about the details of the walkouts to dozens of others via these methods (Yang 2007). Joanna Perez, a documented sixteen-year-old, organized a walkout in California's Central Valley with her friends after hearing about HR 4437 and the subsequent walkouts taking place in Los Angeles. This legislation would have affected her undocumented mother, which ignited her to take action. Joanna and her friends used their cell phones to text message others about walking out. They also used Myspace.com to reach students quickly. On the day of the walkout, Joanna was getting calls on her cell phone for more information. Because Joanna and friends had disseminated the message along with Joanna's phone number, Joanna was able to answer calls and explain the purpose behind walking out. As a result of the organizing by youth such as Joanna, nearly a thousand students gathered in Fresno, California (Khokha 2006). The walkouts were largely a space for immigrant communities to voice their opposition to HR 4437 and urge Congress not to take further action against immigrants (Prengaman 2006; Turnbull 2006).

Online Activism Expands

Shortly after the 2006 marches, several undocumented young adults created the DREAM Act Portal (DAP), which is to date the largest online community for undocumented youth. A simple search for the word "DREAM Act" on engines such as Google yields the DAP as one of the first results. Thus, it gives the website visibility and easy access among online users interested in learning more about the DREAM Act. The DAP has largely focused on bringing the DREAM Act to a vote. On its home page, the DAP provides information about the DREAM Act and how to get involved.

To date, the DAP has more than 33,000 members, and the site is divided into three main sections. Under the DAP's "Today" section members provide updates about the DREAM Act. For example, one update was published on December 20, 2010, after the DREAM Act was introduced and fell short of passing by five congressional votes. Titled "Reflect and Regroup," the article by Nick, DAP activist, shared with all the news that Congress did not pass the DREAM Act. He also urged undocumented youth not to be discouraged. Nick stated that the fight for the DREAM Act was not over. This was the closest the DREAM Act had ever been to passing, and much of that was a result of the organizing efforts by youth across the nation. Nick called on undocumented youth to reflect, realize that the fight for immigrant rights continued, remain committed, and regroup.

The second section on the DAP is for "Advocacy." On this section, members are encouraged to join in creating a collective source of knowledge about the DREAM Act. Members can easily select a House of Representatives member or senator, research his or her position on the DREAM Act, and submit what they found to the portal. The third section, "Forum," has the following categories: (1) "The News Room," (2) "The Lounge," (3) "Taking Action," (4) "New Members," (5) "Other Topics," and (6) "Suggestions." Under "The News Room," for example, members can find information about DACA and a proposed comprehensive immigration reform bill. For example, in one active conversation, members discussed an article about the Senate's Gang of Eight plans to announce a comprehensive immigration reform legislative proposal in 2013. This alerted DAP members that Congress members were planning to discuss a comprehensive immigration reform bill soon.

The second category, "The Lounge," allows members to share their experiences, questions, and concerns as undocumented youth. For example, one post was in regards to states that provide in-state tuition exemptions for eligible undocumented students. Members were encouraged to post information about additional states that offer in-state tuition exemptions for undocumented students and to include the website where they found the information. Additional examples of posts under this category are: "DACA

Application Tips and Resources," "NJ Driver's License," and "Traveling Through Los Angeles, CA, to San Diego by Car." Posts under this category demonstrate that in being part of this online community, undocumented youth can receive guidance on navigating the legal and educational systems.

The "Taking Action" category allows members to find information on, and post about, petitions and organizing events. This category allows youth to learn how they can become politically active. For people already involved, it is an opportunity to connect with activists around the nation. For example, one post contained information about an upcoming offline organizing effort. DAP member "2Face" noted, "The following [is] taken straight from a flyer being distributed around Hartford. Now I'm not sure whether there are marches going on nationwide on this day but it seems very likely." The post then included detailed information about the event, such as the day, time, and meeting location as well as the destination and purpose for the march. This protest in particular was about urging members of Congress to pass a just and humane comprehensive immigration reform bill.

In "New Members," people introduce themselves to the online community. A majority of the posts came from members who had recently applied for DACA. From DACA approvals to waiting periods, undocumented youth share with the online community their stories, concerns, and questions about DACA; for example, a post titled, "Long wait is over!! I am APPROVED!!" by user "morena83." Similar to other posts about DACA approvals, morena83 briefly described her situation. She identified herself as a twenty-nine-year-old who was born in Mexico and came to the United States with a visa when she was thirteen years old. In addition to her brief personal description, she shared her DACA timeline—when she first submitted her DACA application, when the US Citizen and Immigration Service (CIS) received her application, when she received a letter in the mail for her scheduled biometrics, when her DACA was approved, and when her work permit card came in the mail. By posting their timelines, undocumented youth can get support from other undocumented and ally DAP members as they wait for or celebrate their DACA approvals. These timelines also help record waiting times among the DAP members, and they give undocumented youth still waiting for their approval an idea of how long the DACA process takes.

In addition to members sharing their experiences going through the DACA process, members introduce themselves. For example, user "trueblueLA" wrote a post in February 2013 stating, "Name is Mitch. I've been stalking the website and the threads for about a year now and just now decided to register and join in the fun. I just think it's simply amazing and a true statement to the power of our community that we can all come together and help one another through our hardship and these new opportunities that have arisen." Mitch represents a common scenario in which undocumented youth may explore the DAP without signing up as a member but eventually join in order to contribute to the discussions and be part of the online community. This example in particular demonstrates the power of the DAP to connect undocumented youth from across the nation. After undocumented youth and allies find this space, they are able to gather information, register as members, and connect in ways that allow them to be part of a support network and take action.

Growing Online Connections

While the DAP continued to provide the space for undocumented youth to connect regardless of where they live, in 2006, organizers created two of the largest immigrant-youth-led organizations in the nation. DreamACTivist.org and United We Dream continue to be at the forefront of undocumented-youth-led organizing. DreamACTivist.org is a "multicultural, migrant youth-led, social media hub for the movement to pass the DREAM Act and pursue the enactment of other forms of legislation that aim to mend the broken immigration system." At DreamACTivist.org, online users can find updates related to the DREAM Act, DACA, comprehensive immigration reform, in-state tuition bills, and more, such as one update posted in April 2013 titled "VICTORY: Oregon DreamACTivist pushes through in-state tuition." This post described the victory of Oregon in joining more than a dozen states that offer in-state tuition for eligible undocumented students. DreamACTivist.org offers an online space for undocumented youth and allies to organize, share their stories, and find resources. This online space includes its official website and social networking sites such as Facebook. Other social networking sites DreamACTivist.org uses to connect with youth across the nation include Google+, Twitter, YouTube, Tumblr, and Pinterest. Youth can support the efforts of DreamACTivist.org by following updates on some or all of its social networking sites or via its e-mail listserv. DreamACTivist.org also has "sister organizations" in states such as Florida and Oregon. These organizations are crucial for youth interested in becoming involved offline.

Like DreamACTivist.org, United We Dream (UWD) is a national organization advocating for immigrant rights via offline and online activism. UWD is "a network of youth-led immigrant organizations around the country [that] strives to achieve equal access to higher education for all people, regardless of immigration status. [UWD] aims to address the inequities and obstacles faced by immigrant youth and to develop a sustainable, grassroots movement, led by undocumented immigrant youth and their allies" (United We Dream 2015). UWD also has a Facebook page and a Twitter account. Through the UWD web page, Facebook, and Twitter, organizers disseminate information to their online community about upcoming events across the United States, campaigns regarding immigration issues, resources and information about DACA, ways to get involved, and much more. For example, UWD launched a campaign known as 11 Million Dreams in reference to the 11 million undocumented immigrants. This campaign included videos and pictures of undocumented youth with their parent(s), highlighting the reality that undocumented parents have dreams, too, and that the time for comprehensive immigration reform is now. This campaign entailed individuals sharing their stories on the official UWD website, Facebook page, and Twitter account to help raise awareness and spread the word. After UWD members have released a video and/or photo, it is up to the online community to spread the message by sharing it with family and friends. By simply clicking a "Share" button at the bottom of a post, for example, online organizers post the same message on Facebook.

Members of these organizations have become visible and vocal leaders at the national level. For example, in 2007, undocumented youth testified in front of Congress to urge its members to support the DREAM Act. In testifying, DREAMers shared their stories, which often included their names, ages at migration, educational experiences, goals, and reasons they believed the DREAM Act is necessary. Here, the story of Tam Tran, an undocumented graduate student at Brown University, comes to mind. Tam publicly disclosed her immigration status in front of Congress. In a post titled "Dreamie of the Week," DreamACTivist.org featured the story of Tam, who can "be as out as possible because she is stateless and has nowhere to be deported to." Because Tam's parents fled Vietnam and were picked up by a German boat, Tam was born in Germany. However, "since Germany does not confer birthright citizenship, and Tam is not a Vietnamese national, neither country would take her." After Tam testified in front of Congress, sharing her story and the importance of the DREAM Act, Immigration and Customs Enforcement (ICE) officers targeted Tam's parents and sought to deport them. However, because Tam had a strong support network online and offline, she was able to stop the deportation of her family.

Undocumented youth began to realize they have the power to fight back even with the risk of deportation. Following the successful campaign to stop the deportation of Tam's parents, DreamACTivist.org noted, "As undocumented migrant youth, we have come to realize that at this point, privacy and anonymity might be our biggest enemy. It's better to be 'connected' to the movement and to be at the center of it than to be isolated. There is incredible power in numbers, and empowerment in group solidarity. And we can build that through networking." Here, DreamACTivist.org emphasized the importance of undocumented youth coming to be "undocumented and unafraid" and joining the movement.

Coming Out of the Shadows

As undocumented youth organizers realized their power to collectively create social and political change, they escalated their efforts. Most notably, they organized to "Come Out of the Shadows." The Immigrant Youth Justice League (IYJL) in Chicago, Illinois, introduced on March 10, 2010, National Coming Out of the Shadows Week. During this week, undocumented youth proceeded to publicly disclose their immigration status in an effort to declare themselves undocumented and unafraid. At "Coming Out of the Shadows" events, undocumented youth shared their stories, one after another, and urged other undocumented youth to come out as well. Undocumented youth also shed light on the need for a path to citizenship. Additionally, they challenged anti-immigrant sentiment and public opinion by stating that they were not *illegal*. Undocumented youth know all too well that public media outlets have sought to dehumanize undocumented immigrants by labeling them *illegal*. Colorlines.com has created an effective campaign encouraging individuals, educators, and politicians to stop using the "i word" and has experienced notable success within media outlets after the Associated Press, *New York Times*, and *Los Angeles Times* agreed to stop using this derogatory term.

Since 2010, local and state organizations have followed the organizing efforts of IYJL and have organized their own week of actions, which often include a "Coming Out of the Shadows" rally, banner drop, and even a protest. In 2013, undocumented youth living in San Diego, California, held their first banner drop advocating for justice and immigrant rights. Undocumented youth from the San Diego DREAM Team (SDDT) participated in the "Coming Out of the Shadows" national week of action because they believed in the importance of making political statements to advance social, cultural, and political change on immigration (Guevara 2013).

The years 2007–2010 signaled a shift in identities within the movement. Undocumented youth went from self-identifying as DREAMers to declaring themselves "undocumented and unafraid." Thus, the movement began to represent the struggles not only of DREAM Act–eligible youth but of undocumented immigrants in general, whose dreams also matter.

Online Context and Direct Action

Undocumented-youth-led organizing continues to draw from offline and online tools. In my master's thesis research, I focused on exploring what motivated college students to become organizers for immigrant rights as well as their experiences as they incorporated offline and online methods into their organizing efforts (Valdivia Ordorica 2013). I found that organizers are creating online communities to meet, organize, raise awareness, take action, and disseminate information. More specifically, they are using the Internet to create petitions to stop deportations, spread the word about recent campaigns, share their stories, and raise awareness about immigration-related policies.

Most notably, online activists are able to hold virtual meetings via social networking sites such as Google+ and Facebook. To meet online, activists only need access to a computer and the Internet—or even just a smart phone. Virtual meetings provide an option to share in writing one's views or to use one's digital camera to connect and be able to see and speak to everyone directly. Meeting online to organize has been particularly helpful in instances when meeting in person is difficult. There are cases of youth who want to be involved but have work, personal, and school responsibilities or lack a means of transportation. They are thus not able to attend in-person meetings. Online tools provide a unique opportunity for organizations to include more people in their efforts by virtually connecting with them.

I also find that undocumented organizers face several limitations to being politically active. They are unable to legally drive, which may limit their ability to get to in-person meetings and events. The urgent need to earn money can also conflict with the hours needed for active political participation. Undocumented youth often work long hours in low-paying jobs or find themselves working in the informal economy. They are also affected by federal immigration checkpoints and local presence of immigration officers as well as by the constant risk and fear of deportation. As undocumented youth realize the extent to which they can be involved, they are able to choose between online and/or offline venues depending on their availability.

Using the Internet also allows youth to make connections with activists across the nation. Because much of the online activism involves disseminating information and spreading the word about relevant campaigns and stories, activists can learn about each other's work and respective organizations. This has provided activists the opportunity to connect via social networking sites with activists they have not yet met in person but whose work they know and admire. Online activists can find a virtual community, extend their friendships with other activists, spread the word, find information, organize events, meet, and disseminate information. Notably, most organizers who use Facebook to be active online begin because they already have a Facebook account and are already connected to their friends. Similarly, those who use text messages to spread the word about events are doing so because they already have access to a cell phone and text messaging service. Sharing information via the media that activists already have at their disposal is in some ways easier and faster.

It is critical to note, however, that online activism does not replace traditional forms of organizing (Valdivia Ordorica 2013). Youth are instead *strengthening* their activism by using both online tools and offline strategies. Offline activists are holding in-person meetings to organize and create safe and supportive spaces for undocumented youth. They are also organizing events such as rallies, sit-ins, film screenings, phone banks, and marches—more traditional forms of direct action. They are building community and empowering others to join in their efforts. Offline, those who are not yet involved are able to see that there is a group actively seeking to address the issues affecting the undocumented community. If one wants to become involved, it is helpful to have come across an in-person meeting or action where the support is visible and clear.

Offline and online activism interact with each other; youth use both forms to supplement each other. For example, offline events provide visibility and empowerment for nonactivists and activists alike. Community members can see the support for immigrants if they come across a march. Online activism informs people who may perhaps already know about the issue and are searching for additional information about the cause and how to get involved. Those who are already aware of immigration-related issues can search the Internet for more information about relevant state policies, organizations, and campaigns. One of the drawbacks of online activism is that not all youth have access to technology, however. It is then crucial to have offline organizations in which youth can become involved.

Offline and online activism provide spaces for undocumented youth to share their stories. Offline, activists organize events such as "Coming Out of the Shadows" rallies, which I discussed earlier in this chapter. Undocumented youth can also share their stories offline at in-person meetings. Online, undocumented youth can share their stories in spaces such as the DAP. Undocumented youth have also created their own personal blogs in which they talk about their experiences. For example, notable organizer Prerna Lal has taken on online activism not only by organizing on DreamACTivist.org but also by creating her own blog. In her blog, she includes posts about her multiple identities as queer, undocumented, unafraid, unapologetic, a law student, and an organizer. Among the topics she writes about are immigration, law school, education, ethnic studies, gender issues, and human rights. For example, under the immigration category, Lal wrote about the Associated Press announcement that it will no longer use the phrase *illegal immigrant* in news coverage. In "Moving Beyond the 'Illegal Immigrant,'" Lal discusses the importance of the public using language that does not dehumanize immigrants (www.prernalal.com). Using online and offline tools, undocumented youth have been able to empower themselves, organize, and mobilize others to create positive change with, and for, the undocumented community.

In the next section, I return to offline organizing. Increasingly, undocumented youth across the United States are engaging in activism at the local, state, and national levels that has led to key political and cultural changes.

Local, State, and National Activism

Undocumented youth most often gather to organize with their local community or student organizations. For example, in San Diego, undocumented youth and allies who want to become active in their community regarding the issue of immigration can do so through the SDDT. The SDDT is an immigrant-youth-led organization that "strives for a society in which all immigrant contributions are valued, and where immigrants are treated fairly, equally, and with dignity, therefore individuals and families live without fear within their communities" (www.sandiegoteam.org). Undocumented immigrant youth in San Diego first came together in 2010 to collectively organize regarding the DREAM Act. At the time, the SDDT only had about twelve members. When the DREAM Act fell short of passing by five congressional votes in late 2010, many SDDT members felt disillusioned. As a result, the SDDT lost the momentum it had gained leading up to the DREAM Act vote. Five years later, undocumented youth living in San Diego reorganized and formally established the SDDT. SDDT has about twenty-five community organizers and continues to grow. Membership includes both undocumented youth and allies. The SDDT continues to organize presentations at San Diego high schools, fund-raisers, meetings, and political events.

A student organization in San Diego accomplishing similar work is Standing Together As oNe Dream (STAND) at California State University, San Marcos (CSUSM). The primary purpose of STAND is to "provide support and networking opportunities to empower immigrant youth including AB 540 students." To do so, STAND organizes fund-raisers, film screenings, and workshops, among other actions. Undocumented students at CSUSM created STAND, formerly known as Espiritu de Nuestro Futuro (EdNF), after they met undocumented students who created their own organization at CSU Dominguez Hills. In 2011, STAND was able to successfully award its first scholarships to undocumented high school and college students. After organizing fund-raisers such as fruit-cup sales, school dances, and raffles, STAND had enough money to award three $500 scholarships to undocumented students to continue their education.

Each community and local student organization that advocates for issues affecting the undocumented community offers a critical space for undocumented youth to connect and build a support network. In addition, these organizations are effective in providing services such as DACA clinics that offer information and resources at no cost to eligible undocumented youth and their families. Organizations such as the SDDT are also active in putting together presentations and workshops about how to apply for college, receive financial aid, raise funds, organize, share one's story as an undocumented immigrant, and much more.

Organizations at the local level also work with state and national organizations to strengthen the efforts of the movement as a whole. The California Immigrant Youth Justice Alliance (CIYJA; formerly known as the California DREAM Team Alliance) was formed in 2011 when local-level "DREAM Teams" from all over California gathered to collectively organize after the federal DREAM Act failed to pass. CIYJA is led by a steering committee composed of one or two representatives of each local team. The steering committee is in charge of making decisions about whether to support various immigration policies and events. The alliance is also there to ensure that each team has the support of the others. For example, when making a decision to support a given comprehensive immigration reform amendment, the alliance takes into consideration the best interests of all of the teams. After the vote, if the decision requires an action, each local team will organize an event to hold in its city. In addition, CIYJA also holds annual retreats. In 2012, CIYJA for the first time met in San Diego. At this 2012 retreat, members gathered at the Centro Cultural de la Raza to brainstorm about the alliance's messages and actions in 2013.

Youth have become involved in activism at the local, state, and national levels. In addition to DreamACTivist.org and United We Dream, they can join the National Immigrant Youth Alliance (NIYA), which came together in 2010. NIYA's core values include empowering youth, educating the community, and escalating social action in order to achieve equality for all undocumented youth. Notably, NIYA was the first activist group to infiltrate a detention center. In July of 2012, seven undocumented activists intentionally sought to be taken into the Broward Detention Center in Florida to demonstrate the contradictions between reality and what President Barack Obama had announced in June 2012. President Obama had called for discretionary prosecution, stating that ICE officers should not focus on low-priority cases. That is, DREAM Act–eligible youth and undocumented immigrants without a criminal record, for example, would not be high priority for the administration to deport. However, the reality even after the memorandum of June 2012 is that undocumented immigrants are still being detained and deported even if they are low priority.

The infiltration by NIYA demonstrated that inside the Broward Detention Center, there were undocumented immigrants who in fact qualified for the DREAM Act or a U visa (Nonimmigrant Status for Victims of Criminal Activity) and in some instances required urgent medical care. NIYA activists were released from the center after ICE officers learned about their intentions, and the activists successfully helped stop the deportation of a few of the detainees by organizing hunger strikes, online petitions, and phone banks. In addition, NIYA activists in Illinois laid down on the road, trying to prevent the detention center's buses from taking detained undocumented immigrants to the O'Hare International Airport. Their arms were chained and linked together with pipes. The organization wrote, "Three buses which total 1,100 immigrants are deported every day." Organizers note that many deportees are low-priority cases; many deportees do not have criminal records. Given that Illinois is President Obama's home state, organizers hoped to draw attention to the immigration practices in the state of unfairly deporting men, women, and children. (See http://www.iyjl.org/stopdeportations for more details about their work.)

The SDDT, STAND, CIYJA, and the NIYA are some of the organizations that represent the wide variety of events and campaigns undocumented youth and allies are organizing. Using both offline and online tools, activists are pushing the boundaries to demand justice and equality for all immigrants. In the next section, I provide more information about the additional successes of activists despite the challenges they have faced.

Successes and Challenges

Undocumented youth continue to organize all over the United States. They have been speaking out against injustice regardless of the legal limitations on their status. Anyone undocumented is a target of deportation because of his or her immigration status. To be a public activist can lead to higher visibility with ICE. As a result, because undocumented activists increasingly have become tired of remaining in the shadows, even though they are aware that going public has its risks, they have become active in stopping deportations. In 2009, activists organized around one of the first public DREAMer deportation cases. Walter Lara, a DREAMer living in Florida, was facing deportation in July 2009. In reaction to his deportation case, activists created an online petition shared via e-mail, Facebook, Twitter, and Myspace. Activists also made phone calls to ICE urging it not to deport him.

As a result of the advocacy and support of Senator Bill Nelson, community and student organizations, and online organizing efforts, the Department of Homeland Security listened and stopped Lara's deportation (Hing 2009). Another example is the case of Rigo Padilla, an undocumented college graduate living in Chicago. He was placed in deportation proceedings after local police stopped him, charged him with driving under the influence (DUI), and found out he was undocumented. This second deportation proved a bit more challenging because of the circumstances under which

Padilla was caught. However, the fight to halt his deportation succeeded partly by highlighting his accomplishments (Olivo 2009). Undocumented activists often find that offline and online publicity can lead to more security because if ICE attempts to deport them, they can count on a large support network to organize around their cases.

The movement also involves political causes such as passing state-level DREAM Acts. Undocumented students are unable to receive federal financial aid, and each state has its own in-state tuition and financial aid policies. In California, undocumented students can be exempted from nonresident tuition at California's public colleges and universities if they (1) have attended a California high school for three or more years, (2) have graduated from a California high school or received the equivalent of a high school diploma, and (3) have filed or will file an affidavit stating that they will apply for legal residency as soon as possible (New Partnership Foundation 2010).

Now, California AB 540 students are also able to receive state financial aid under the California DREAM Act (AB 130 and AB 131). Under AB 130, AB 540 students were eligible to receive private scholarships after January 1, 2012, if attending a University of California (UC), California State University (CSU), or community college (California Student Aid Commission n.d.). With passage of AB 131, AB 540 students attending a UC, CSU, or community college were able to receive three types of state financial aid after January 1, 2013. The three types include: (1) Board of Governors (BOG) fee waiver, (2) institutional student aid (e.g., a CSU Grant or UC Grant), and (3) Cal Grant (California Student Aid Commission n.d). California is one of thirteen states that offer in-state tuition for undocumented students who meet similar requirements. Among the thirteen states, California, New Mexico, and Texas are the only three that offer state financial aid for undocumented students (National Conference of State Legislatures 2014).

Activism has been key in getting state policies passed that offer in-state tuition for eligible undocumented students. To advocate for state DREAM Acts, activists have created online petitions to share via e-mail, Twitter, Facebook, Myspace, and blog sites. They have also created graphics to share and raise awareness about the need for educational equality for undocumented students. When Oregon DreamACTivist was organizing regarding HB 2787, a bill that would allow eligible undocumented students there to pay in-state tuition fees, the group reached out to other groups to help share the message. One of the groups they reached out to was UndocuPickUpLines. Four undocumented women living in San Diego created UndocuPickUpLines—a Facebook page to share pick-up lines with a twist. Their goal is to bring awareness about issues affecting undocumented immigrants with humor and love. Lines ranging from the experiences of undocumented youth while dating to driving without a license have reached online users and are contributing to the movement by advocating for social, cultural, and political change. An example of a line featured on this page is, "Hey, you know what the immigrants rights movement and I have in common? We both really need you." After Oregon DreamACTivist reached out to UndocuPickUpLines for support, the page administrators created the line, "I need you like Oregon needs in-state tuition for undocumented students." Soon after, in March 2013, Oregon activists learned that their advocacy efforts helped lead to the passage of HB 2787.

Other advocacy groups use humor as well to humanize and illuminate the experiences of undocumented immigrants. For example, Dreamers Adrift is a group that created "Undocumented and Awkward" videos depicting socially awkward situations for undocumented youth and young people. Not having a state identification card, high school reunions, and inappropriate revelations of immigration status by school staff are just some of the themes of their videos. The YouTube channel features contributions from non-Latino/a groups, including the organization Asian Students Promoting Immigrant Rights Through Education. These videos portray the complex experiences of being undocumented while conveying a strong political message.

Activists in various states have had several successes to celebrate; however, undocumented youth living in states such as Georgia have faced the challenges of not qualifying for in-state tuition fees and being banned from the state's top five public universities (Brown 2010). Thus, educational attainment for undocumented students differs because policies affecting this population of students vary by state and institution. Many undocumented activists are focused on political gains that would address the challenges in pursuing higher education for undocumented youth. In Georgia, undocumented students formed Freedom University in 2011, after the ban, to provide access to higher education regardless of immigration status. Freedom University is a volunteer-run organization that offers free courses to undocumented youth and organizes to end the ban.

Next Steps for Undocumented-Youth-Led Organizing

Organizers have taken great steps in the movement to accomplish several changes in local, state, and national immigration policies. In 2001, when the DREAM Act was first introduced, the ideas of coming out of the shadows as undocumented and unafraid and stopping deportations were not yet introduced. The successes of undocumented-youth-led organizing have taken courage, persistence, inspiration, empowerment, and creativity. Activists know that the fight is not over. Although undocumented youth have been able to benefit from DACA, they are aware DACA is not enough. DACA temporarily benefits those that meet the requirements. Thus, DACA does not address the experiences of those already wrongfully deported. DACA also does not give undocumented youth and the 11 million undocumented immigrants certainty that they may live without fear in the United States.

An increasing number of campaigns are contributing to social and political changes beyond DACA. For example, the "UndocuBus" is an effort of undocumented youth and parents. Together they traveled the United States on a bus raising awareness about issues affecting *all* undocumented immigrants. The journey included visiting key southern cities such as Phoenix, Arizona (this is where the tour began on July 29, 2012). The beginning of the tour included a week of action calling on the federal government to stop allowing Sheriff Joe Arpaio, under SB 1070, to unjustly harass immigrants living in Arizona. The tour continued on to the following states: New Mexico, Colorado, Texas, Louisiana, Alabama, Georgia, and Tennessee. The tour's last stop was North Carolina, where UndocuBus activists staged an action outside of the Democratic National Convention (www.nopapersnofear.org).

Videos posted on YouTube have also been rallying cries for community members, students, and educators to take action. For example, a video a young woman made of her mother's arrest, detention, and impending deportation went "viral" and inspired activists and regular community members to protest her mother's deportation. David Guggenheim (maker of *Waiting for Superman* and *An Inconvenient Truth*) made a free-to-view thirty-minute documentary about her painful story. Ten-year-old Stephanie Pucheta created a video on YouTube in which she talked about her dad and how his deportation affected her. She did this every day for two weeks after the judge ordered her father's deportation. Several news outlets (Foley 2013b) and immigrant rights groups (e.g., Cúentame and Latino Rebels) have shown her video.

Because DACA is not enough, organizers, networks, and campaigns continue to fight regarding issues affecting undocumented communities across the United States. Undocumented youth have largely shaped the immigrant rights movement, aiding key successes and overcoming a series of challenges. It is up to many more of us to join in their fight to ensure justice for *all* immigrants.

10

Being a "DREAM Keeper": Lessons Learned

Every year, at my school, dozens of children new to the United States begin their educational journey. The student body is 95 percent Spanish speaking, Latino/a, and low income. In recent years, deportations of children, parents, and/or siblings have become frequent occurrences. Given the stress levels and aspirations of new immigrant families, I pride myself on being a "dream keeper," a term Gloria Ladson-Billings (1994) created to describe a teacher who is culturally relevant and who successfully teaches African American children. Educating and supporting undocumented students and their families is my everyday honor and privilege.

The past few years, I have been teaching kindergarten. As a bilingual teacher for more than twenty-two years in the San Diego region, I have taught at every elementary grade level. My greatest joy is when a student—eight years later or even fifteen years later—finds me to share how she or he has done in life. This is when I know, for the year that I had that child in my classroom, I did my job and did it well. Drawing on these experiences, I share my recommendations, best practices, and lessons learned for teaching new immigrants, especially undocumented Latino/a children.

Alma Ruiz-Pohlert wrote this chapter.

Five Recommendations

To begin, I offer five suggestions that could radically improve the learning of young, new immigrants. They are strategies an educator could implement immediately or plan to incorporate for the new academic year.

First, acknowledge students every day. Create rituals and interactions during the day that bring you eye to eye, hand to hand with your students on an individual basis. For me, this means I smile, hug, or give "high fives" to students as they do their work or go in and out of the classroom. I make sure I have contact with them every day as individuals. I may not be able to give them one-on-one feedback and work with them every day, but I do validate them as people and as individuals. The students in my classroom know that each one is valued as a learner in my classroom.

Second, adopt a *familia* (family) metaphor for how your classroom operates. I explain to my students that I am responsible for them to have a safe classroom, a place to learn, and a space to make friends. Some students come from chaotic households, and a calm, nurturing classroom may be one of their only safe spaces. Other students have solid, supportive families, and the *familia* metaphor works wonderfully as a bridge for their home-school learning. When the classroom is a safe, nurturing space, learning will follow.

Third, connect with parents or caregivers every day. Give parents a confirmation or information about how their children are doing and how they are learning. Communicate that a child had a wonderful day whenever possible and true. Always add something that she, he, and the class are learning. The parents I work with want to know, "*Sé porto bien*?" (Did my child behave?) Address them honestly, positively, and add on what the children learned that day, such as times tables or writing accomplishments. Reiterate the behavior and each time you can, make it a point to have contact with parents. Doing this makes it smoother when you have to deal with a negative situation. Even in this case, start from a positive place: "He is smart, but this time, he made a bad decision about. . . . " By having daily or weekly positive contact with parents, when there is a problem it will not be the first time you encounter the parents.

Fourth, use the students' and parents' language. Successful teachers of new Latino/a immigrants must learn some minimal Spanish. This will help with important parent communication. Even more important, you must learn Spanish to help get your lesson across to students. It goes against any research or practice that an English-only policy is established in a school where more than half the population speaks Spanish as its first language (Zentella 2005). Short of incorporating a fully realized, dual-immersion program, teachers of new Latino/a immigrants need to speak minimal Spanish. Just learning the basic word for apple (*manzana*) can help bridge the knowledge gap with children who have just arrived to the United States and increase their learning and confidence. It is a basic lesson of Vygotsky's (1978) "zone of proximal development" that you begin where the learner is in order to scaffold the learning until she or he is further along. In my twenty-plus years of being an official bilingual teacher, and especially as a Spanish-speaking teacher in an English-only school, I know that students "get it" when you use Spanish to help them understand English.

Recently, I happened to tell my students, "Make it snappy" and then followed up with telling them this means "*Hazlo rápido.*" ("Do it quickly.") This is something they hear on a regular basis at home and could instantly understand the English meaning. I then introduced "snapping" and explained that "make it snappy" is coming from "snapping" which indicates "hurry" or "fast." Then we repeated it. They loved snapping their fingers and repeating the words—in both Spanish and English. They know the meaning, and they know the words in two languages. I believe using Spanish bridges their prior knowledge and builds upon their strengths. From this strength-based approach, as opposed to seeing the language difference from a deficit lens, students become more confident learners.

My final (and fifth) recommendation is to use small groups. In my public school classroom, six students working in each group is the norm. For math and other subjects, I always rely on one student who is the most vocal in Spanish and English to lead and model language for the group. I also use mixed-ability groups; that is, I integrate abilities and rely on the stronger students to model and help the students who struggle. It is essential for students to learn from their peers, not just the teacher.

In a typical lesson using this approach, I model in front of the entire class how to solve a math problem: If we have three cats and three dogs, how many are there altogether? Then, I will ask the student in each group who is more readily able to speak to reiterate the math problem so that the students hear it in their own peers' voices. The bilingual vocal student is not always the one with the best academic knowledge in the lesson, so I have the ones with the best math abilities begin to do the math problem aloud with the other students. The students who are struggling watch and observe. Then, they do it with the group. With students who are struggling, bring in a student who is more advanced. Independent work only comes after several practices in a group setting. I rely on the strengths of students to build community and to achieve better learning.

Kindergarten: First Step in the Journey

For many undocumented, young immigrants, attending kindergarten is the first step in their educational journey in the United States. I have been a part of the prescreening process and also a kindergarten teacher. From this stage, I have witnessed students flourish and stayed in contact with the families as my former students advance, take breaks, and many times ultimately graduate from middle and high school. Yet, many of my Latino/a students begin kindergarten already "behind" in terms of the school standards (Collins et al. 2011; Gillanders and Jiménez 2004; Lee and Kao 2009). Gándara (2010) explains that Latino/as have the lowest rates of preschool experiences because "young Latino children are more than twice as likely to be poor as white children and are even more likely to be among the poorest of the poor" (27).

Kindergarten Prescreening Assessment

Our school does kindergarten registration in the middle of March. After our students have been registered, we invite each student to come for an individual thirty-minute assessment. We ask basic language questions as well as math questions. We also want to know how much oral language they have mastered. We ask them questions such as: What are the eight basic colors? Can they write their names? Do they know letters in the alphabet? Do they know their shapes? Can they count up to eight and identify numbers? We also determine whether they know basic addition (if you have four lollipops, how many will you have if you add one more?). For their oral language, we show them a picture of a cat with five kittens. We ask them questions using the words *under*, *on top of*, and *beside*. Every question is worth one or two points. At the end of the assessment each student is given a score depending on how she or he answered each question.

At the end of the assessment, we have a conference with the parents and review positive outcomes of the assessment along with what the children might be lacking. We give the parents a bag full of items so they can work with their child at home. The bag contains shapes and worksheets for them to trace their names, numbers, and all the color names. We also emphasize that they should talk to their children when they are walking to the store. We have them practice using complete sentences.

This assessment helps us distribute evenly students of varying abilities into the six kindergarten classrooms. Eventually all of the teachers will have some low-level academic students, some medium-level academic students, and some high-level academic students. Bilingual teachers also give this assessment. Many of the students come from Spanish-speaking homes. We accept their answers in Spanish or English. A note is added to the assessment if the test was conducted only in Spanish.

Each teacher receives all of this information after the students are assigned to her or his classroom so as to look at this information and get a small snapshot of each student.

Roberto Ramirez. One year, as I was getting my classroom ready for the first day of school, I walked into the office and found a mother with three little children. The secretary told me that one of the children was assigned to my classroom. I introduced myself to Mrs. Ramirez and to the small kindergarten student, Roberto. The mother asked me if I would be so kind as to help her fill out the reduced lunch application. She mentioned that she spoke Nahualt (an indigenous language spoken in Mexico and parts of Central America), spoke little Spanish, and did not know how to read it. Mrs. Ramirez mentioned that they had just arrived from Mexico a few weeks ago. As I was filling out her application, I tried to ask her information about Roberto. Did he attend preschool before? No, was the answer. Does he speak Spanish? Yes, he knew some Spanish, but mainly spoke Nahualt. Instead of panicking, I saw this as an opportunity to help this student gain a new language: English. It dawned on me that this five-year-old would be a trilingual student!

For his first days in the classroom, Roberto was like a little boy at Disneyland. He was curious and touched everything in the classroom. He was fascinated with all the new items. I had to be very specific with him. For instance, one thing we emphasize in kindergarten is for a student to sit with his or her feet crisscross and listen to the teacher. He had never been in a classroom, and the word *crisscross* did not register in his mind, so I had to speak to him in Spanish and show him how to sit on the carpet. Another thing we ask of students is to sit quietly for a period of five minutes (while the teacher is explaining the next activity). For many of them, this is a new situation they may not have experienced at home. It took Roberto several days just practicing until he finally got it. I could see the way he was processing this internally: "Oh, I need to sit quietly and listen to the teacher. Oh, by the way, I do not know what in the world she is saying, but I see her and the other children are sitting down." I was able to explain to him in Spanish every activity we were doing, and he nodded and did what was asked of him. Roberto was not able to communicate much with me, but he was able to see the other students working, and he applied himself to mimic their behavior.

I also needed to give his mother, Mrs. Ramirez, a lot of acknowledgment. I would tell her how he behaved each day. She worked with him at home. Finally, we were able to have Roberto follow directions and learn his letters along with their sounds. He was able to read simple, repetitive books by the end of the school year. I was so proud of all of his efforts and how much he had grown academically.

Leticia Guillen. Leticia was a very tiny girl who loved to come to school. Despite her small size, she let you know how she was feeling and if she had any questions. Several months into the school year, Mrs. Guillen, Leticia's mom, told me she took the Sprinter (our commuter train) to come and pick up Leticia.

It so happened that after she had told me this, the train suffered a brake malfunction, and it would take four months to fix it. The first week this happened, Mrs. Guillen was a half hour late. I had left Leticia at the front office so she could wait for her mom. I came back to my classroom and started setting up the papers and pencils needed for the next morning. Mrs. Guillen came into the classroom and apologized for being late. She told me she knew it was going to take some time for the bus to pick up the train riders but had not realized it was going to be half an hour late. She explained that she arrived early to catch the bus. Mrs. Guillen was panicking, thinking about Leticia getting stressed out, wondering where her mother was, and waiting in the front office.

Mrs. Guillen asked me if it would be possible for Leticia to come back to the classroom to help me clean up the room or read quietly on the days that she was late picking her up. I told her that would be great. Leticia was so proud that her mom had asked me if she could stay after school and help me. Thus, whenever her mom was late, Leticia was happy to come back and help me clean up the classroom.

Because Leticia had an older sister who was let out an hour later, Mrs. Guillen asked if she could *also* stay and help me set up the classroom. I was more than glad for the help. I would put on a Spanish station, and she would tell me about each artist who was playing. Mrs. Guillen talked to me about what she was going to cook for dinner. She told me stories of how she came to the same elementary school as a child. She explained that she cleaned a building and that one of the stores left items outside the trash can that were still useful. Some items were crayons, pencils, stickers, and notebooks. She would gather the items and take them home for her girls. However, then, Mrs. Guillen asked me if she could bring some of those items for the students in my classroom. She said there was nothing wrong with them except the package was torn and could not be sold. I told her I would gladly receive those items, and I could use them as incentives in my treasure box. It was a win-win situation for the three of us. I got to see more of Leticia, and she felt proud of helping in the classroom. Mrs. Guillen got to help in the classroom and was grateful I could keep Leticia in the classroom in case the bus was running late.

The Talavera Family. One amazing family I had the honor of knowing while we still offered bilingual classes at my elementary school was the Talavera family. Gustavo was in second grade in my classroom, and Silvia was in first grade. Gustavo was a very intelligent boy who loved to read. He loved science books and wanted to know how things worked. I saw the spark he had to acquire more knowledge, so I had him check out books from my library to take home and read. I also started to ask him basic information about what he had learned in that specific book. Sometimes he would write up a few sentences about the book. Then, I started writing inference questions and opened-ended questions. He would go home, read the book, and answer all the questions. I also challenged him to do more when he was learning a new skill in math.

One day, Gustavo got in trouble during recess. After school during dismissal, I talked to Mrs. Talavera about his behavior. She spoke only Spanish. She promised me he would not repeat the same offense. Sure enough, he never got in trouble again. However, Mrs. Talavera would check in with me every day to see how he was doing in the classroom and on the playground. Soon, she would ask me if she could come and help me in the classroom. I told her she was welcome to come anytime to help in the classroom. She took it seriously and made it a point to come for one hour every day. I had her sharpen pencils, clean the tables, and staple small workbooks. No job was too little or big for her.

Mrs. Talavera took pride in coming in every morning. Eventually, she asked if she could sit and take notes on the lesson I was giving. It turned out that she had never enrolled in school. Her parents lived in a small village in Mexico, and the children helped work the land. I told her that it was never too late to learn. She laughed and said that she was going to be the oldest student in second grade. Thus, alongside her son, she became a "nontraditional" second grader.

The following year, Gustavo moved up to third grade. However, Mrs. Talavera decided she wanted to continue her second-grade learning in my classroom. She still helped me do small jobs in the classroom, which freed me to do other things. Every day I could count on her being there. She would sit down at the end of the classroom and take notes on the lesson. One day, the principal happened to walk in while I was giving a spelling lesson. All students were on task, and I was using the overhead projector. She walked up and whispered in my ear: "Tell the parent that I love that she is also learning with all the students." I was happy that she felt that way.

Mrs. Talavera was not only there to help me in the classroom but also she taught me many valuable lessons. Mainly, she consistently reminded me about the perseverance of my students' families. They were creative and never gave up. Once, her husband, who worked in construction, was not working because of the rain. She came in with a bag full of beautiful embroidered tablecloths and placemats. She said that this was what she did when she stayed at home at the early age of seven with her mom. Everything was done by hand, and the colors and patterns she followed were amazing. She designed every one of them. Mrs. Talavera said she needed money to buy milk and cereal for her children, and this was the only way she could earn money. I told her that I could buy some placemats, and I would take some samples and place them in the teacher's lounge so they could see them and buy them. She was proud of her work, and she was thankful I was going to help her in this situation. She said that when she was nine years old she was selling her placemats in the little town near her village. That is how she helped her family have a hot meal. My heart went out to her because she always made sure her children were fed, their hair was combed, and their clothes were clean. She was determined that her children were going to have the schooling she only imagined and never had.

Teachers and Undocumented Latino/a Children

Most of my colleagues genuinely care about their students. However, many of them are not quite sure how to "handle" newly arriving immigrant students and, in particular, how to incorporate their parents as partners. I have already stated that learning Spanish—even a basic understanding—is key to educating young, undocumented, Latino/a students. In their national longitudinal study on kindergarteners, Lee and Kao (2009) found that "teachers rate non-White children of immigrants lower on reading test scores even after controlling for their socioeconomic status and their test score" (201). If teachers are not hyper-aware of their practices, they could seriously and negatively affect the future educational trajectory of their immigrant, Latino/a students. I will write more about the dynamics of language, teachers, and families in this section.

Writing this chapter at the end of the school year, I can recall a meeting I just had with the other kindergarten teachers. We were planning a picnic lunch to say good-bye to our students. I mentioned that I was planning to invite the parents of the children to the ritual of saying good-bye. Several of my colleagues balked at the idea of having parents attend. One teacher in particular was visibly stressed and uncomfortable with parents in her classroom on the last day. She explained that she would not know what to say to them and did not want them there. I wanted to be understanding of her opinion, but it also made me realize how the parents of her students might have been feeling all year—alienated and not welcome in the classroom space. This is the opposite of how I structure my classroom and build relationships with my students. I respectfully explained that for the parents to witness her saying good-bye to their children, and that her saying a simple "thank you" to them, would be so meaningful. I added that the parents might not speak English, but many understand it. This teacher would not budge. Sadly, my colleagues did not agree that parents could be included in the good-bye portion of the day. This issue was still not resolved as we entered into the last week of the year.

Lost in Translation

The teachers' discomfort about Spanish-speaking parents becomes a practical challenge in the daily routine of teaching. Communicating with parents about a student is something that happens on a daily basis—or should, in my opinion. Yet, most teachers wait until there is an "issue" with a student, such as a child not completing homework or misbehaving in class. Notes that must be sent home about field trips or special events for the class must be translated.

As a native Spanish speaker, I am frequently asked by my colleagues to translate written or verbal English into Spanish. For the sake of the student, I am usually happy to oblige, but the translations usually turn into longer, more important conversations in which I then must participate. These interactions take away from my own prep time and the time I want to spend with my students' parents. I now make it clear that I will help with two-minute translations for other teachers; beyond this time frame, they need to ask the school administration for a translator. However, arranging for a translator or waiting for someone to help may take longer than both teacher and parent prefer. In these cases, teachers tend to rely on siblings who may speak both English and Spanish to help communicate with parents. This is fine for low-level or mundane issues, but in my experience, older siblings can only translate up to a certain point and may not convey the message correctly to the parents, or they might use other words that transform the teacher's message. In addition, this places an undue burden on the siblings, who might already have to do this emotional and language labor outside the school setting on behalf of their parents.

What happens when a teacher can successfully communicate with Spanish-speaking parents? Everyone benefits. Take, for example, a child who was new in a colleague's classroom. He was not paying attention, and the teacher thought he was misbehaving. Because he could not speak English yet, she had him sitting at his desk for six hours a day with nothing to do. She felt helpless, and he felt restless. This teacher brought me in to speak to the student and later to his parents. I discovered that he had never been in school before, and he did not know any English. They had arrived in the United States mere days before he came to the school, and he arrived one month after the start of kindergarten. He knew a few of his colors and numbers but did not know them in English. I had to explain the setting of the classroom, how we sit, raise our hands, work together in the center of the classroom, and then do our worksheet. This was totally foreign to the little boy. It took about a week for him to really comprehend the routine of what to do and what to expect. Then, he started to get into the groove. This took quite a bit of talking to the parent and talking to the little boy. I used a warm, encouraging tone—"Okay, m'ijo" ("Okay, son")—and explained all the processes and lessons in his own language, using words he could understand so he could adapt to the classroom setting. As you can see, this was before I established my two-minute translation rule! Yet, with 95 percent of the students in similar situations in my very large elementary school, why are there only a handful of us who can speak Spanish?

When English-speaking teachers try to do their own translations, this can actually hurt relationships with parents rather than enhance them. First, there are nuances in Spanish that should be understood. A common one is the difference between "*atención*" and "*poner atención*." Teachers will use *atención* to mean "paying attention" when it is really a more urgent "be on alert" or a command to "watch out." Second, teachers may translate one sentence or phrase but leave the rest of what they need to convey in English (or leave it out altogether). I have seen this occur when teachers manage to communicate to a parent only that a child is coming late to class too often; however, the teacher is not able to communicate what happens in the morning, what the child is missing, and so forth. Google translator is a frequent tool for well-meaning teachers, but the process of translating is not just about getting the words right but also communicating meaning, nuance, and tone through word choices and structure of sentences.

Learning Spanish for your primarily Spanish-speaking students is just one piece of the competency puzzle to be a successful teacher of undocumented Latino/a children. Understanding the students' cultures, finding strengths in what they bring to school from home, and connecting with students and their families are key to establishing the best context for learning.

A Note About Parents of Undocumented Latino/a Children

I consider the parents of my students my most powerful allies in their education. Many teachers and administrators underestimate the motivation and innovation of Latino/a parents, especially if they are low income or do not speak English. The research tells us that Latino/a parents, in particular new immigrants, consider education a top priority but often are not sure how to go about achieving this. The school setting and some teachers can be extremely uninviting to parents, so this further reduces the potential for partnerships (Ardón Bejarano 2007).

In my school, we have witnessed the parent-teacher organization (PTO) rise to amazing heights through the leadership of a Latina who is a paraprofessional in my classroom. She has managed to include many parents and tap into their strengths to produce successful events and fund-raisers. Through supreme organization, she identifies who does what well and then lets them do it. She respectfully manages the parents and reminds everyone of the bigger picture. The yearly jog-a-thon at our school went from being a so-so event with very little fund-raising to being a large communitywide event with T-shirts sold at a reasonable price (instead of pledging laps). For teacher appreciation days, we were given lunch for every day that week. The parents had come together to cook and deliver the hot meals to each teacher in the school.

Although our PTO is led by Latino/a, Spanish-speaking parents, the State of California has mandated that K–12 public schools with twenty-one or more English learners must form an English-learner advisory committee (ELAC). The committee is comprised of parents, staff, and community members specifically designated to advise school officials on English-learner program services. The ELAC is responsible for advising the principal, staff, and the School Site Council on programs and services for English learners. The ELAC also assists the school in the development of needs assessment, annual language census, and ways to make parents aware of the importance of regular school attendance. The law mandates the school district must provide for all ELAC members

- appropriate training and materials to assist each member carry out his or her legally required advisory responsibilities,
- training planned in full consultation with ELAC members,
- and Economic Impact Aid-Limited English Proficient and/or district funds to cover costs of training and attendance of ELAC members. This may include costs for child care, translation services, meals, transportation, training cost, and other reasonable expenses.

How the ELAC operates depends on the school and district support. The ELAC at my own school is fairly small but has existed for some time. The nearby school in a medium-income neighborhood only recently formed an ELAC. My teaching colleagues have heard that in a higher-income neighborhood in this city, the administrators discuss their ELAC committee in disdainful tones. In a research study on Latino/a parent participation, Ardón Bejarano (2007) found that ELACs are often marginalized in the larger school and district settings. The standards set by the state—for example, providing child care so that parents can be on the committee—are not supported on the local level. The ELAC has the potential to be a powerful force for schools that have at least twenty-one Spanish-speaking students.

Tackling the Summer Slide

New immigrant children with whom I work have come with little knowledge of formal schooling, and their parents often have very little formal education. They are extremely motivated to learn but have to catch up in terms of basic concepts and understanding English. Teachers can do much to help bridge their home knowledge with school knowledge—then, summer happens! For most children, the "summer slide" is a real thing, especially for minority or low-income students. *Educational Leadership* recently reported that "low-income children . . . made as much progress in reading during the academic year as middle-income children did, [but] the poorer children's reading skills slipped away during the summer months" (Smith 2012). Some parents who possess the time and resources can provide summer camp or travel experiences for their children that will keep alive some of the academic learning and even advance it in preparation for the following school year.

I think the students at my school, especially those who are new and/or undocumented immigrants, would benefit from a six-week summer program that would enrich their understanding of what they needed to have learned in previous years and prepare them for subsequent years. In this sense, the program can be for any elementary school level. This program would involve classroom learning Monday through Thursday, 9 a.m. to noon, with Fridays being all-day field trips. Parents would be invited to participate or help. The first week would be community and team building—gaining trust and deepening the connection with the students. Then, each week, a new theme would be approached through writing, reading, art, math/science, and social studies, such as animals, sports, the world (geography), and space exploration. The final week would involve putting together all the students' knowledge, having students present their favorite portions of the session to each other, and creating portfolios for them to take home.

For the week on animals, students could learn about species, biodiversity, and body parts. Students could write stories and summaries about what they learned. The week's culminating activity could be going to the local zoo or animal safari park. For the sports week, teachers could incorporate math features such as statistics in baseball and soccer and scoring in gymnastics. Racial segregation in sports and Title IX issues of gender inequality could be social studies themes. Going to a local sport event such as a track and field meet or soccer, basketball, or baseball game could culminate the week's learning. In the week on the world, the geography and maps of the local region and home countries could be the focus. This could include a trip to city hall where students could look at old maps of our town and learn about urban planning for the future. Students could use Google Earth to better understand parts of the world with which they are familiar, where they have family, or where they wish to travel. In the case of undocumented young students, they could virtually visit their birth town or region. Creating dioramas and maps could involve math, science, and art. For the space exploration week, gravity, planets, and stars could be the focus. Students could create their own art projects showing constellations. The week's writing, reading, and science learning would culminate in a trip to the local planetarium. Inviting the local astronomy club to teach students about telescopes could also be a feature.

A program to prevent the summer slide would serve to strengthen the students' knowledge and achievement and provide innovative and enjoyable ways of learning. This could be a welcome relief to the teachers who participate in the program as well—the stress of standardized testing would melt away as teachers would actually teach across the curriculum. In addition students could put their learning to use every day.

The Welcome Center

A feature that used to exist in my school but was dismantled several years ago was the Welcome Center. Here, newly arrived immigrants would begin their classes with a bilingual, culturally competent teacher; the goal was to transition the students to mainstream classrooms as soon as possible. This was different from ability grouping, tracking, or de facto segregation. The focus for the Welcome Center was enrichment and acclimation for the new student. Sometimes, a student would arrive a few weeks into the school year and had never been to a school previously in his or her home country. The message of the Welcome Center was to nurture and prepare students to be successful both academically and socially. The curriculum was taught in Spanish, with English as the secondary language. This "gentle" boot camp successfully created more confident and informed students.

A Dream Keeper for Undocumented Latino/a Children

My passion and understanding of undocumented students comes from my personal background. I see the strength of all my students because previous teachers identified my strengths and encouraged me.

I was born in Tijuana, Mexico. My family immigrated to the United States when I was nine years old. I had attended school up to the third grade in Mexico. Because I did not speak English, I was assigned to third grade again. Within a year, I was able to understand what teachers and other students were saying. I was shy, and it took me another year to speak the English language. Because I was retained one school year, I had to make up the "lost" year in high school. Like the siblings in Chapter 5 in this book, I was able to take summer classes and night classes so I could graduate on time.

After my high school graduation, I attended Grossmont Community College in San Diego, California. I was able to secure a job at the college and attend classes. I was involved in Movimiento Estudiantil Chicano/a de Aztlán (MEChA) and student government. My boss at the time, Jesus Nieto, encouraged me to graduate and transfer to a four-year college. He even took me and four other students to visit Southern California universities. Eventually, after three years, I graduated and transferred over to San Diego State University (SDSU). There, I was able to complete my undergraduate program and continue on to finish my fifth year of student teaching as a bilingual teacher.

After graduation, I attended graduate school in the Community-Based Block (CBB) at SDSU. It was an intense program with a multicultural counseling emphasis. The "community-based" part of the program involved classes held off campus in the community—low-income, multicultural neighborhoods of urban San Diego. We also conducted counselor clinics for the members of these communities. The "block" portion of the program meant each cohort took our intensive classes with the same group of students for every class. With my teaching and counseling experience, I was ready to go into the classroom setting. I have been hired by three different school districts because of my bilingual skills and my cultural competency counselor background.

Ladson-Billings (1994) and Delpit (1995) wrote about what it takes to be excellent teachers for African American children and children of color. Ladson-Billings spent years in classrooms observing student teachers and more senior teachers. Delpit was a schoolteacher for many years before becoming an academic.

Ladson-Billing famously called culturally competent teachers "dream keepers" and found that they possessed high self-esteem, saw themselves as part of the community, viewed teaching as an art form, believed that all their students could succeed, and built on the students' strengths. These teachers know their students and their life outside of school. Dream keepers connect with parents as allies and as partners.

Delpit also found that teachers must have a strong bond and interpersonal relationship with students of color and their families. Teachers who were exceptional with students of color engaged in the community surrounding the school. She argued that teachers must realize the differences of learning styles and ways of listening. Delpit also explained the ways in which teachers of students of color can become burned out or pushed out during graduate school or by colleagues and administrators who do not value their contributions.

This chapter and my recommendations are written in the spirit of creating more "dream keepers" for undocumented Latino/a children. My fundamental contribution to continuing the work of Ladson-Billings and Delpit is to include the issue of language—in the case of my career and focus, Spanish. The teachers who support young DREAMers and want to see them flourish in the educational pipeline must speak Spanish, understand the cultural context of their students, be engaged *en la comunidad*, partner with parents in meaningful ways, and urge their own school sites to adopt Spanish-language curricula.

11 Rethinking the American Dream

In the midst of all the sociopolitical debates about immigration law and policy, the everyday lives of undocumented immigrants continue. It is clear educational experiences play a pivotal and central role in their daily lives. The accessibility of educational institutions, although limited, is still greater than the accessibility of many other US institutions. Thus, for both undocumented youth and adults, attending school is often one of the most consistent activities they have in their lives. This book offers a compelling examination of the educational pipeline for undocumented students. The participants who shared their experiences in our study explained how they navigated multiple social worlds. They not only traversed these social worlds but transformed them as well. As a result, we have a better understanding of the diversity of experiences of undocumented young people.

Reconsideration of the American Dream

The promise of the American dream—the relatively better opportunities and conditions the United States has to offer than their families' home countries—loomed over the participants in this study. Many told us of how their parents uprooted their families in order to earn more here and give their children a better chance. Now that the youth are here, they want to fulfill their parents' dreams. Most of the students sharing their stories with us felt a sense of betrayal in terms of what the United States actually promises immigrants. At the same time, they persisted and believed their efforts could and someday would make a difference. They hope to make an impact on the social worlds they inhabit and traverse.

The United States has a strong philosophical basis for extending educational rights. Horace Mann famously wrote, "Education is the great equalizer." He began the Common School Movement in 1837 when he advocated for the rights of all children under the law to receive public or free education. He believed education promoted social harmony and political stability. He picked up the work of Thomas Jefferson before him, who wrote to James Madison in 1787: "Above all things I hope the education of the common people will be attended to; convinced that on their good sense we may rely with the most security for the preservation of a due degree of liberty."[1] For the founders, whose families immigrated to the United States themselves, education was key to maintaining liberty.

These very notions underlie the Supreme Court *Plyler v. Doe* (1982) decision, which allows undocumented children to attend school. The American dream is a political struggle at the federal, state, and local levels. Yet, it is also a cultural struggle. Who is considered "American" and who has rights to higher education becomes a moral issue. The educational pipeline, therefore, is a metaphor for the American dream.

However, countless studies have found that schools replicate the socioeconomic hierarchy. Sociologists have long written about the ways in which school is structured to privilege certain students—in ways of learning and ways of interacting. In fact, the social reproduction of inequality is a leading theory in understanding inequality in schools. The participants interviewed for this book shared their experiences and, particularly some of the high school students, the ways in which their schools—from teachers and tracking to classmates—negatively affected their educational aspirations and outcomes.

Rather than focusing on the American dream, we are better served by relying on the discourse about universal human rights. The American dream has to be "achieved" or "earned," whereas human rights are assumed under a moral imperative for a just society and basic dignity. Too many immigration policies in the United States hinge on educational achievement and therefore exclude many people. The odds of a successful journey in the educational pipeline are not in favor of undocumented immigrants. Immigration reform, as it stands within the "dream" (or "equal opportunity" as opposed to "equal rights") discourse, unfairly privileges a few and does not consider the social location of most undocumented immigrants. I believe in education without borders, that is, education without socially constructed barriers to keep some in and others out.

The United Nations states that "education is a fundamental human right and essential for the exercise of all other human rights. It promotes individual freedom and empowerment and yields important development benefits" (UN Educational, Scientific, and Cultural Organization n.d.). As such, its members have created several binding treaties and agreements. In the UN general Declaration of Human Rights, Article 26 describes the right to education and focuses on developing human potential. Article 28 in the Convention on the Rights of the Child states, "Young people should be encouraged to reach the highest level of education of which they are capable."

In the United States, undocumented immigrants are promised access to public education from kindergarten to high school. However, given the current economy, we know how important it is to earn a college degree, which is not promised as a right to undocumented students by the federal government. This is why we see such variation of laws preventing access to higher education across states, as outlined in Chapter 2. Human rights provide a clear moral compass and a social justice framework on which to improve laws and practices for undocumented immigrants. Currently, Somalia and the United States are the only countries that have not ratified the entire Convention on the Rights of the Child.[2]

Some believe human rights documents lack the punitive enforcement power to make a difference, but the discourse is effective for making real change. Child labor, children living in the streets, child soldiers, and child marriage have been partially ameliorated in communities where advocates and the children themselves drew on the human rights discourse to stop the oppressive conditions.

The right legal, social, and economic conditions must exist in order for undocumented people to truly access and thrive throughout the entire educational pipeline. For undocumented students in the United States and elsewhere, economic conditions and uneven legal access are significant barriers to achieving this fundamental human right. Legally allowing undocumented students to attend public schooling from kindergarten to high school is just a minimal beginning; support for college tuition and smoother transitions through the educational pipeline must also be in place. Access is not enough. Creating reasonable and time-sensitive paths to citizenship along with granting immediate work permits would allow undocumented immigrants to use their skills, education, and talents to enhance not only their lives but also their communities. This would encourage even more participation in the educational system; one of the unforeseen functions of Deferred Action for Child Arrivals (DACA) could be that more undocumented youth enroll in college or stay in school in order to qualify for this legislation (Batalova, Hooker, and Capps 2013). Positive incentives benefit everyone, including our state and national economies.

Lessons from the Pipeline

We began our study knowing undocumented students experience a leaking educational pipeline, but we did not fully understand the nuances of students' experiences at each stage, especially those of young undocumented immigrants.

The children who participated in this research expressed joy and excitement for learning in elementary school. In middle school, several challenges arose for undocumented students, but intervention programs and outreach helped many remain in school. By high school, our undocumented students were still committed to school, and even going to college, but were not given much of the important information to help them continue on their pathways to college. In community college and at the university, we witnessed students feeling very stressed and fearful of all they could lose, yet also feeling hopeful about the future. After graduation, the outlook was bittersweet: these participants persisted through and some even thrived in college, yet many would not be able to apply their academic knowledge in a profession. Although participants granted DACA status could temporarily work "legally" in the United States and were happy about the outcomes of their applications, they also felt concerned about their situations and fearful because their parents continued to be unprotected from deportation.

Both the larger environment and their own efforts shaped the students' educational experiences throughout the pipeline. Our examination revealed that space and place mattered a great deal in access to education. The North County region of San Diego County and Southwest Riverside County were areas in which enforcement of laws against undocumented immigration permeated communities (Gonzales 2013). There was a resolutely chilling effect when Immigration and Customs Enforcement (ICE) patrolled near neighborhoods and schools during the beginning and end of the school day in these regions. The conservative politicians and active anti-immigrant hate groups in the area also encouraged such egregious practices by supporting legislation to allow sheriffs and police officers to work in tandem with ICE agents and to sponsor anti-immigration local ordinances.

Although these practices were viewed as negative ones by the students in this study, we learned that most of them were not politically active. Still, they shaped their local social worlds by making connections with educators and continuing their educational journeys. Others formed student clubs to conduct outreach and advocacy in support of younger undocumented students in the educational pipeline and on their local campuses (e.g., Alas con Futuro, STAND, and MEChA). Only one participant decided to return to his home country, and all others were firmly grounded in the notion of staying in the United States, hoping for a pathway to legally live and work.

Implications and Impacts

In the course of their educational experiences, students traversed multiple social worlds and shared information about those worlds with us as they considered their educational paths. Although our study was specifically focused upon participants' experiences of schools, other important themes emerged in the research process that helped us better understand the impacts of undocumented status on individuals and families.

Generations. We learned from participants of all ages, children to postgraduate adults, about the importance of family. The issue of not being able to visit grandparents was particularly salient to most of our participants. Sadness and grief overtook many when they recalled deciding not to return to see an ill or dying relative because they would not be able to return to the United States legally afterward. This study supports previous research that has documented the importance of grandparents and meaningful connections to extended families for young people (Yorgason, Padilla-Walker, and Jackson 2011). The absence of grandparents and other important kin added another layer of anxiety for undocumented students.

Undocumented Childhoods. Although some participants revealed that they were unaware of their immigration status until high school, most of the children in our sample (i.e., those in elementary school and middle school) were aware of being undocumented. In our regional context, the data do not support the notion that children were spending "their childhood in suspended illegality, in a buffer stage wherein they were legally integrated and immigration rarely limited activities" (Gonzales 2011:608). The level of deportation enforcement activity in their communities made it hard for them to ignore what it meant to be undocumented. Parents actively socialized their children on managing this information. It appears that similar to what research has revealed about how African American parents prepare children to deal with racism (Lesane-Brown 2006), undocumented parents may be socializing their undocumented children to better understand the consequences of their legal status and prepare them to deal with social backlash, possible violence, and detention. The importance of elementary school and middle school students' experiences informs existing analytical frameworks, such as Gonzales (2011), which is based on teenagers and young adults; for example, we encountered undocumented elementary school students engaging in discovery, learning to be "illegal," and coping simultaneously.

Educator Allies. Participants typically named one or more educators in the educational pipeline (e.g., staff person, teacher, or counselor) who reached out to them. These allies did not necessarily know their status but anchored the students to the pipeline. Numerous participants named educator-allies who worked for Gaining Early Awareness and Readiness for Undergraduate Programs (GEAR UP), Advancement Via Individual Determination (AVID), the Educational Opportunity Program (EOP), and Migrant Education, which points to the importance of such programs.

Libraries. Some participants mentioned school and public libraries as spaces where they could take control over their own learning. Many students mentioned the library in their interviews, usually as a place to study but in some cases, a place to "escape" from classes (or teachers) they disliked. Two of the high school students mentioned the library (and library books) as an indicator that they could read and think at a more sophisticated level than that at which they were placed. Librarians could become important allies in connecting undocumented youth to learning and books related to their lives and dreams (Houston and Spencer 2007; Morris 2012; Myhill et al. 2012; Plocharczyk 2008; Vaagan and Enger 2004). Libraries are typically free to the public and could offer some of the programs suggested by educator Alma Ruiz-Pohler in Chapter 10 that were cut from public schools.

Deportation. Almost all participants discussed the fear and stress of deportation for themselves and family members. Deportation causes emotional and financial devastation. The fear of being deported weighed heavily on students during their classroom time and outside of school. This fear prevented many from taking advantage of programs and other events that could have positively affected their educational experiences and outcomes.

The Sociological Imagination (Mills 1959) is helpful to understanding that personal devastation for undocumented immigrants is also directly related to a variety of large-scale factors upon which the Detention Watch Network and other social movement groups have elaborated: the existence of quotas for immigration detention (e.g., 34,000 beds must be occupied each day), the exploitation of detainee labor, the privatization of detention centers, the conditions of detention centers, the lack of adequate health care in detention facilities, and the citizen children living for months in immigration detention centers. There are also human rights violations related to a lack of legal representation: only 30 percent of deportations are administered through immigration court, so a majority of migrants is deported without due process (Werlin 2014). In addition, the American Immigration Council discovered that "DHS has bypassed the immigration courts entirely and instead employed summary removal processes that allow DHS officers to act as both the prosecutor and judge" (Werlin 2014). President Obama has aggressively expanded the reach of ICE: in 2009 there were 77 jurisdictions and in 2012 there were 3,074 (Gonzales 2013). Insightful research about the lived experiences of deportation in communities (Golash-Boza

2012), on children (Dreby 2014), by gender (Golash-Boza and Hondagneu-Sotelo 2013), and on the effects on youth during and after detention (Heidbrink 2014) is enlightening.

Role Conflict. The undocumented immigration status of the individuals in this study conflicted with many other roles with expectations attached to them. The participants in this project were more than just undocumented immigrants—they were romantic partners, friends, children, parents, students, men, women, and so on. Managing roles is something we all do with greater or lesser success; undocumented immigrants carried additional expectations often constrained by their circumstances. Children who wanted to go on field trips or attend after-school programs often could not do so because they needed to hurry home. High school students in our study reported having very limited social lives. The community college and university students mourned how little they could socially enjoy being eighteen- or twenty-one-year-olds. The postgraduate students had the most in-depth examples of the ways in which their immigration status held them back. For example, a male college graduate felt that he could not fulfill his role as a "man" because he did not have a car in which to pick up his date or money to pay for the date. Participants felt proud of their status of "college graduate," but the experience was greatly tainted by the fact that they could not then fulfill that role (i.e., working in a profession).

Navigating with Cultural Funds of Knowledge

We found evidence that throughout the educational pipeline, our participants drew on funds of knowledge (Moll et al. 1992) and cultural wealth (Yosso 2005) that helped them better navigate school, community, law enforcement, and other social worlds. Their immigration experiences and home life provided nontraditional forms of capital.

Aspirational Capital. Undocumented Latinos maintained hope despite many barriers and fears. Their immigration journey—from their own memories of being lifted onto their parents' shoulders to cross the border or their parents' recollections—helped create and grow this aspirational capital.

Navigational Capital. Many participants shared that they were forced to be resourceful and use their social networks to find out about and avoid immigration checkpoints. They transcended adversity, which helped them become stronger individuals.

Linguistic Capital. Speaking Spanish at school with friends and at home allowed students to achieve meaningful connections in the midst of hostile settings of school and city spaces. When students spoke in Spanish to their migrant education teachers or professors, this also helped forge relationships crucial to their educational success.

Familial Capital. Many participants carried family traditions, hopes, and culture with them. Most parents also hoped their children would pursue an education because they could not.

Resistance Capital. Many participants communicated that they knew what others thought of undocumented immigrants. They strived to become educated to combat these stereotypes. In this way, their forms of resistance were empowering rather than self-defeating; they did not leave the mainstream educational system as a means of signaling their opposition. As seen in the GEAR UP program, when interventions were positive and culturally appropriate, undocumented students as young as middle school age could turn around a negative trajectory of involvement in gangs or doing poorly in school.

Reflective Capital. Additionally, we found that many of the participants expressed a thoughtful and pragmatic reflection of what they endured here and what they had left behind, which could be termed *historically based, reflective capital.* Many newer immigrants possess a "dual reference." Gibson (1988) found it was what motivated the Sikh farmworker children in Central California to do well in school despite obligations to work in the fields, racism, and language barriers. The undocumented Latino/as in this study (and their families) know what life is like here and what it is like in their countries of origin. Most decide to stay here, although sometimes with regret and many times with hardships.

Future Research Directions

As in most studies, we came across many ideas and findings that deserve their own research project or exploration. We share with you here the ones related to research, and in Appendix A, we offer projects to develop related to the community.

Explore Supportive Educators

There must be more research on the "DREAM keepers" for undocumented students, such as the educators featured in this book who encouraged and empowered undocumented students to pursue their educational goals. Much of the research about undocumented students is from the perspective of the students (and their families). Yet, teachers (and other educators such as counselors and even school nurses) can be some of the most important allies for undocumented students. The theme of the 2013 UN Global Action Week on Education was "Every Child Needs a Teacher."[3] We would add that every child needs a "dream keeper." What are the main characteristics of educators who help keep the dreams of undocumented students alive?

We see from the stories shared by participants and the authors in this book that some educators are not equipped to support undocumented immigrants. To this end, some professional associations, such as the American Counseling Association, the Iowa School Counselors Association, and the American Psychology Association have begun to offer professional development and resolutions regarding undocumented youth (Storlie and Jach 2012). More on-the-ground training, outreach, and awareness must be pursued.

Widen the Conceptual Lens of the Pipeline

First, we believe it is important to study those students who "fall out" of the educational pipeline and do not return to school. We will likely learn a great deal about educational processes of undocumented students by studying who leaves school and why.

For example, one approach to accomplishing such a study is to capture middle school leavers by finding undocumented students in their last year of elementary school and closely following them into middle school. Another approach is to interview (and support) undocumented students in alternative or transitional high schools, similar to interviewing "early exiters" of high school, a strategy Gonzales (2011) successfully employed.

Second, the community college serves as an important starting point for many undocumented immigrants of all ages and countries of origin. Focusing on general education development (GED) and English as a second language (ESL) courses, along with certificate programs in vocational fields, may help us better understand how undocumented Latino/a adults experience the educational system.

Third, capturing students' experiences in middle school seemed to be the biggest challenge for this project. Very little research is done on undocumented middle school students in general. Most states are not required to keep track of middle school attainment data. More research on undocumented middle schoolers is crucial to understanding the entirety of the pipeline experiences.

Fourth, very few studies have been able to do what Covarrubias and Lara (2013) did with US Census Bureau data: access a representative sample and conduct "intersectional data mining" critical methodology to paint a comparative picture of the educational pipelines for groups with different immigration statuses. I believe these researchers have begun groundbreaking work toward detecting and following large national trends for undocumented immigrants' educational attainment.

Examine Mixed-Status Families

We came across many mixed-immigration-status families; exploring the interpersonal dynamics and educational aspirations of all members of the family would be important to understanding education in context in the larger undocumented immigrant community. An urgent social issue that became evident as we conducted our research for this book is the aftermath of parental deportation on citizen children. One of my graduate students, Diana Garcia, is examining children's experiences (both undocumented and citizens) in mixed-status families. We encourage others to engage in similar research in order to fill the large gap in knowledge that exists on this subject.

Explore Long-Term Effects on Undocumented (and Transnational) Families

For some time, David Thronson (2008) argued that there has been a *crisis of destabilization of immigrant families.* ICE and local authorities search homes extremely early in the morning, before migrants are awake. They enter people's homes without search warrants and disrupt all from their sleep to question them. In many cases, the children are forced to witness the interrogations and subsequent arrest of family members. Thronson (2008) shows that raids contribute to a climate of fear in the community.

A pathbreaking study by the Applied Research Center, *Shattered Families*, revealed the civil rights infractions and conditions experienced by citizen children in detention and in the foster-care system (Wessler 2011). The Applied Research Center conservatively estimates the number of children of detained or deported parents amounted to least 5,100 children, and projected that the number would increase to 15,000 by 2016. Many undocumented families already live at higher levels of poverty and economic hardship (Baum, Jones, and Barry 2010). For the families who lose one or both parents to deportations, their children are forced into more poverty, along with psychological and emotional distress.

In 2014, the United States experienced historically high rates of unaccompanied children, who mainly came from Central America, trying to cross the border into South Texas. These youth may or may not have family in the United States but are being detained in fairly dire conditions. Approximately 60,000 minors arrived at the US-Mexican border in fiscal year 2014. President Obama declared the situation a "humanitarian" issue and deployed resources to help with legal representation, social services, and deportation proceedings. However, according to Syracuse University's Transactional Access Records Clearinghouse, 43,000 cases have not been resolved and most detainees do not have legal representation. From October 1, 2014, to June 1, 2015, the Department of Homeland Security reported a dramatic reduction in the number of unaccompanied minors: 22,000 were detained at the southwest border in that fiscal year. Save the Children reports, however, that from October 2014 to February 2015, "more than 100,000 children risked their lives to *reach* the US border." Increased detention by the Mexican government is contributing to the decrease in arrivals to the United States (Llorente and Llenas 2015).

The UN High Commissioner for Refugees (2014) report, *Children on the Run*, explains that most of the minors are fleeing their hometowns because of violence in the community and in families. To be sure, this is currently one of the most pressing (and heart-wrenching) immigration issues. Some of our students in this book crossed over by themselves and made it. The trauma of *el cruce* (border crossing) along with the difficult life in the United States makes all too clear the type of situation in their home countries that motivated children to take such risks.

Comprehensive Reform: Sweeping, Definitive, and Positive Social Change

As discussed throughout this book, a multilevel approach to understanding undocumented immigration is paramount to discover the forms of inequality, oppression, and injustice experienced by the participants. It is also a useful approach to strategize about where structural, institutional, and microinteractional forms of social change must take place. Most of the educational pipeline chapters contained specific recommendations on educational institution reform; here, we suggest additional action for media and the economy. These final recommendations bring together the structural (macro) changes that must occur and include the importance of one-on-one interactions (micro). Although massive educational reform must take place at all levels of the educational pipeline for all students, we focus on those related to the diversity of undocumented immigrants' experiences. We hope to honor how our participants described their lives, challenges, and dreams.

Structural Level

Comprehensive and humane immigration reform is immediately needed at the federal level. Some states, counties, and cities have created humane conditions and opportunities for undocumented immigrants; cities creating sanctuaries can offer important relief for undocumented immigrants and families because this new type of status allows access to more public services on the local level. However, these services have been hard won by activists and are easily reversible. More often, anti-immigrant blocs operate at local and state levels against the interests of immigrant communities (Gonzales 2013). Legislation at the federal level must give clear parameters for states to maximize social justice–oriented opportunities.

Undocumented immigrants need a clear, accessible, and time-sensitive process to begin their journey to documentation. As many of us know, there is no "line to join" for many undocumented immigrants to apply for citizenship. The rare opportunity is wrought with complex paperwork, high costs, and an absurdly long timeline.

The participants in our study and their families would be positively affected by an *extended family* reunification process. Students spoke about separation of parents, aunts, uncles, and grandparents. As previously discussed, sociologists have detailed the socioemotional pain and loss of social capital when families are fractured.

Family reunification plans must include provisions to help those deported to return to the United States. The extremely high rate of deportation as a result of programs such as Secure Communities, the ICE enforcement policy, is disproportionately based on traffic violations and other such minor offenses. In *The Deportation Regime*, De Genova and Peutz (2010) argue that the deportation experience is most commonly characterized by the threat or fear of being potentially detained, and then the detainment itself, and ultimately deportation. The significant stigma, stress, and shame upon being deported take a toll not only on the deported migrants but also on their kin network (Schuster and Majidi 2014).

Changes must also be made to help immigrants who are detained. The American Civil Liberties Union (n.d.) found that in a central California detention facility, "the average length of detention for individuals who applied for relief from deportation was 421 days. . . . Out of 595 individuals detained for 180 days or longer, 176 of them—30%—had already won their immigration cases during the study period, and 207 or 35% were projected to win their cases." Basic human rights are being violated, especially for the children detained with their parents. As activists try to hold police officers accountable for shooting unarmed black men and women, we must also hold border enforcement officials responsible for using overly aggressive and even deadly force on unarmed, undocumented immigrants.

There are several *unacceptable* aspects of immigration reform that we gleaned from our study. Piecemeal reform and liberal-minded "bandages" (e.g., executive actions) are unhelpful and exclusionary, usually addressing the issues of only portions of the undocumented immigrant community. Be leery of reforms that provide only residency instead of citizenship with voting rights. Reject any inclusion of intensive border security and more immigration enforcement; advocate for open borders. Given the leaks in the educational pipeline, we are critical of reform efforts that grant undocumented immigrants opportunities based on educational achievement. We believe that immigrants in same-sex unions or who are transgendered must also be given equal rights for pathways to citizenship. Similarly, we would not support overly strict "morality" clauses in immigration legislation, which unfairly target lower-income immigrants and those subject to police and ICE profiling.

The biggest question looms: How do we ultimately achieve humane, comprehensive immigration reform? The optimist in me believes we must "dream big" in order to work for large-scale change. However, history has indicated that two "liberal" presidents have ushered in the most draconian policies affecting communities of color: President Clinton with welfare "reform" and President Obama with record-high levels of deportation. Therefore, the grassroots efforts of the social movements supporting immigrant social justice are paramount (Gonzales 2013). Activists draw on notions of insurgent citizenship that go beyond conventional claims of immigration rights (Leitner and Strunk 2014). Additionally, Eisema and colleagues (2014) found that for undocumented youth in Los Angeles, activism serves several purposes: skill building, social capital, and social mobility for the activists themselves; community building and empowerment; and creating effective social change at local, state, and national levels.

Effecting social change at the federal level can have an enormous impact as seen in President Obama's health-care program, based on the Affordable Care Act (ACA), in which the federal government required US citizens to have health insurance and leveraged funds and other incentives to facilitate state participation. As with the testimony of formerly uninsured people who helped pass the ACA, the experiences shared in this book help us to have a clear understanding of the need for comprehensive immigration reform, especially in regard to education. Thus far, immigration reform has been used as a political strategy to gain votes and win elections during periods of anti-immigrant sentiment in the country. To many of us, this seems like a vicious cycle that will always repeat during economic troubles. Studies have consistently shown the economic benefits of humane, comprehensive immigration reform. The type of reform the authors of this book support could result in a surplus in the economy; better wages for all citizens; more jobs; higher rates of Latino/as in higher learning institutions; fewer mental illnesses among immigrants; more Latino/as in politics; positive changes in media coverage; and an even greater surge in community organizations, advocacy groups, and civic engagement in general.

Social Institutions: Education, Media, and the Economy

We need to provide more access to higher education. I believe that we must revisit the *Plyler v. Doe* Supreme Court decision. It granted opportunities for undocumented youth to attend only K–12 public education in each state. The court left decisions about higher education to the states (e.g., access and forms of financial support). This leeway has allowed states to deny educational rights to undocumented students. Comprehensive immigration reform should have an extensive reach that shapes states' educational practices (e.g., milestones, outreach) for undocumented immigrants and their families.

Many participants in this book worked in agriculture or were from migrant farmworker families. Migrant labor laws related to children must be addressed and revised. Currently, for migrant children working on the same farm as their parents, there is no minimum age for working in agriculture and no limits to hours worked outside the school day. Human Rights Watch (2010) found that "children typically start working adult hours during the summers, weekends, or after school at age 11 or 12," and many of these children are as young as seven (5). In its study on US tobacco farms, Human Rights Watch (2014) found that children suffered from nicotine poisoning in addition to common ailments because of injuries, pesticides, and so forth. The study reported that "despite long days working outside in the heat, employers did not provide [children] with drinking water, and most said that they had limited or no access to toilets, hand washing facilities, and shade" (12). Both children and parents deserve protection from oppressive work conditions.

Unwillingness to address this particular issue is one of the reasons the United States has not ratified the UN Convention on the Rights of the Child. Specifically, Article 32 protects migrant children workers "from economic exploitation and from performing any work that is likely to be hazardous or to interfere with the child's education, or to be harmful to the child's health or physical, mental, spiritual, moral or social development." Whether we revise US labor law to include migrant children on its own or as a rider on a comprehensive immigration reform bill, addressing migrant child labor is most urgent.

Finally, many students shared that they "knew" how others thought of undocumented immigrants. For some, it provided motivation to prove the anti-immigrant hate groups wrong, whereas others felt saddened and angry about these negative stereotypes. Racist and nativist stereotypes communicated by individuals and perpetuated through media served as persistent attacks on their identities, their parents' integrity, and their aspirations. Chavez (2014) has written extensively about negative media portrayals of immigrants and Latino/as and deconstructed the narratives about 1.5-generation undocumented immigrants along with others dominating media and popular culture. Some news outlets followed the Associated Press in eliminating the use of *illegal immigrant* or *illegal alien*, but many others need to change this derogatory usage of the English language. In popular culture, portrayals of Latino/as (documented or not) are still in dire need of diversifying their experiences and professions. The socialization process through media and the power of news to inform our political decisions must also be addressed in reform efforts.

Micro Level

On an everyday (micro-interactional) level, when participants shared information about their statuses with trusted allies and friends, they enriched the immediate social landscape and educated others about their journeys. I have witnessed this in the safe-zone training for undocumented speakers and other outreach events at my university and in local communities. The sharing of one's self in a more intimate, interpersonal way is a precious thing and does make a difference. Although it is not the responsibility of undocumented students to teach others, Brown (2012) has found that being vulnerable actually enhances individuals' sense of efficacy and other positive outcomes. However, vulnerability about revealing immigration status comes at a risk. My message is that *when and if* a person shares immigration status, it matters. Institutions need to actively find ways to protect undocumented immigrants in terms of this vulnerability.

Now, we end this book with a request for you, the reader. You matter. You have become informed of the issues, complexities, and opportunities facing undocumented Latino/a immigrants. We hope you work to bring positive social change to your community, organization, region, and beyond. We also ask you to take a moment to ask a simple question to those with whom you come into contact around your town or city: "*¿Estás estudiando?*" The simple inquiry of "Are you studying?" or "Are you a student?" posed to a young person or adult can be powerful entry point to understanding where in the educational pipeline the person is and serves to encourage him or her to take the *avenida* (pathway) toward fulfilling educational goals.

Conclusion

At the beginning of this book, we introduced Omar, who also wrote a chapter in this book. From a very young age, Omar knew about his immigration status; he and his peers coped with the stress and fear of deportation through the games they played. Omar went on to attend college and graduate school. He is an activist and community resource for the Oaxacan migrant community. Alfredo, a participant in this study, experienced the real-life stress of living on his own and multiple "real" encounters with border patrol. Yet, he never missed school, was set to graduate, and begin at Palomar College.

It is important to note that many of the participants and authors in this book, by steadily staying in the educational pipeline (and even thriving) are shaping their schools and other social worlds. Author Yeraldín served as president of STAND, a student college club that advocates for undocumented immigrant students, and is pursuing her dream to become a teacher. After earning her master's degree in sociology, author Carolina has been a part of the San Diego DREAM Team and helped organize a large conference on undocumented college students who want to go to graduate school. She is in doctoral study at Harvard.

The journey through the educational pipeline for undocumented Latino/a students is not easy. Few make it through to the end. When they do graduate from college, an uncertain future awaits. Piecemeal, temporary, and partial immigration reform legislation does little to alleviate the hopelessness they feel for their family members, communities, and themselves. Although many felt relief and glimmers of hope with DACA, 49 percent of those eligible to apply could not because they were not already enrolled in school (Batalova, Hooker, and Capps 2013). Immigration status was a barrier for continuing their education. After a comprehensive analysis of current immigration policies, Schmid (2014) argues that a universal approach to immigration and the associated human rights is the right path. Comprehensive, humane immigration reform is needed, and nothing less will do.

Notes

1. Jefferson to Madison, http://www.monticello.org/site/jefferson/quotations-education.

2. The United States has signaled support of the general ideas but will not ratify the convention because it cannot support possible lessening of parental control, school corporal punishment, and the death penalty for minors.

3. "Global Action Week: 'We Will Not Meet Our Education Goals Without Teachers,'" UN Educational, Scientific, and Cultural Organization, http://www.unesco.org/new/en/education/themes/leading-the-international-agenda/right-to-education/single-view/news/global_action_week_we_will_not_meet_our_education_goals_without_teachers/.

Appendix A: Sociology *con y en la Comunidad*

This book emerged from community and scholarly projects undertaken with and for community members. Ultimately, we wanted to convey the complexity that results in a leaking educational pipeline for undocumented Latino/as. Each collaborator in this project worked on social justice causes related to education and immigration. We came together through shared interests and an appreciation for research. In this appendix I share the origins of the study and process of training the pipeline student researchers. I also discuss the other influences leading to this project and detail related community events.

The project evolved in three stages. It began when two students came to me with an idea for research. The second occurred when the project expanded. The third happened when the authors of these chapters had insightful questions about the postgraduate experience of undocumented Latino/a students and after the occurrence of recent legislative changes. I conclude with some reflections about my own immigrant and professional context.

Origin Story

I did not know it at the time, but the story of this book began when Gricelda and Fredi, two former students, walked into my university office and asked if I could teach them how to publish research. I was flattered but noted the unidirectional nature of their request (professor teaches student). Instead, I offered to coach them on the research process but told them they would be taking an active role. I pledged to be there to learn and grow with them. I was newly tenured and had completed several projects, so I was thrilled to start this new journey with Gricelda and Fredi.

The first step was finding a meaningful topic. We all agreed that undocumented immigration and, specifically, Latino/a college students who were undocumented would be the ideal research study. At the time, Fredi was a graduate student in my sociology master's program and was writing a thesis on immigration, "The Experiences of IRCA Immigrants in North San Diego County," which he completed in December 2010. Gricelda was an undergraduate majoring in human development and a founding member of the student group on campus that supported and advocated for undocumented students. Both were active mentors to their peers and in the community.

This project contributed to community outreach and advocacy. In the first year, Fredi organized an immigration speaker series on campus. He coordinated "A Day of Dialogue on AB 540 Students," which brought important speakers on immigration policy and researchers on undocumented immigration such as Alejandra Rincón (2008) and Carmen Martínez-Calderón (2009). Gricelda, as the cofounder and president of the club now known as Standing Together As oNe Dream (STAND), worked to organize rallies and teach-ins on the DREAM Acts and legislation at the state *and* federal levels that provided much-needed resources (state) and a path to citizenship (federal). Fredi and Gricelda demonstrated to me that this project *always* needed to respond to community needs.

We began going through each step of the research, about a two-year process, first reading the literature, which at the time (2008) was nascent. Then we searched for theories and found reports on undocumented immigration. We discussed methods and put together our university Institutional Review Board (IRB) application. It was approved, but not without struggle and negotiation with the IRB. For example, the psychologists on the board felt that we could not ask any questions about mental health. Through weekly meetings and many e-mails, we slowly and carefully began the interview stage of the project by sending out recruitment notices around campus. Gricelda and Fredi began interviewing a couple of participants per week. Then, they set about transcribing the responses.

At this stage, our constant contact and revisions diminished. Fredi and Gricelda immersed themselves in the interview process and occasionally contacted me to check in about logistics. When we did meet, they shared the transcripts, and we had talks about the emotionality of interviewing, especially on a topic with which they were so intimate.

Recall, their goal was to publish their findings. Fredi and Gricelda took the first steps of presenting a paper, "Experiences of Undocumented Latino College Students: Struggles, Strategies, and Successes," at the Pacific Sociological Association Meetings in 2009. This prompted us as a group to solidify some concrete analytical themes. We resumed our weekly meetings to discuss the themes emerging from the data. This time, we met in restaurants and coffee shops, a relaxing atmosphere compared with campus. (Reflecting upon these meetings, I realized that our eating, talking, and thinking together set the tone for the subsequent stages of this project.) I noted that while we examined themes, we also discussed the ways in which capturing college students' experiences was not enough to relay the undocumented experience as a whole. We agreed that if we were to go forward with the project, we would broaden our scope to the entire educational pipeline.

Around this time, we became aware of a call for papers for an edited volume on minorities in education. We collaborated on the e-mail inquiry to the editors, and we received an enthusiastic response from them to move forward with an extended abstract. Over the next several months, we met and exchanged e-mails (once again!) to write the chapter. With just a few rounds of revisions, it was accepted and published in 2011. We included some of this work in Chapter 7 of this book, about university students who are Latino/a and undocumented. Given the five years that had passed, we were happy to be able to revise our argument in significant ways.

These former students and now coauthors urged me to continue with the project, even if they could not. Gricelda confided that although she felt learning about the entire research process was rewarding, she realized that she was drawn to the helping professions. She applied to graduate school in counseling with an emphasis in art therapy.

Fredi left the United States on a voluntary departure (avoiding formal deportation) mere months before he should have walked across the graduation stage for his master's degree. A colleague, Alicia Gonzales, conducted a symbolic hooding with Fredi in Tijuana. Fredi is now living in Tijuana teaching sociology and political science at a local university. He is applying to doctoral programs as an international student. Fredi participated in this book project from afar by writing a chapter on immigration policy. Fredi and Gricelda drew the blueprint for what became a five-year project: passion for social justice, collaboration with researchers and community members, and outreach to undocumented immigrant youth and their families.

Research Project 2.0: The Pipeline Project

I continued our work and called together another group of interested student researchers. Toward the end of the spring 2010 semester, I e-mailed a notice to recruit potential student interviewers. I conveyed that I was seeking research assistants with these characteristics: ability to speak Spanish, connections to or within the immigrant community, already working in an educational setting with Latino/a or immigrant students, and an academic interest in undocumented immigrants.

Then, I set up two information sessions to inform students of the project and discuss compensation. Both sessions were very well attended, with mostly Latino/a students and a few white students interested in education and immigration issues.

The information sessions served one main purpose—to recruit student researchers who had connections and close ties to the undocumented community. I explained that the nature of this research required *trust and in-group* relationships. All but two of the white students realized they were not qualified to work on this project. Some Latino/a students declined because of the time commitment involved. Those who committed to the project would be compensated through independent study units; I negotiated with my Department of Sociology that these units could count as course substitutions for qualitative methods or a senior seminar called Sociology of Education. We recruited fifteen student researchers who committed to meet in the summer for training and to begin data collection as soon as the IRB process was complete (early fall semester).

Our group of researchers ranged from mostly sociology majors to history and teaching-credential students. All approached the project with dedication and passion. During the summer, I was late into my second pregnancy, and we were all grateful for the spacious, air-conditioned meeting room on campus. The launching of this project coincided with the birth of my daughter, Cecilia Catalina. (I had a son as well, Pablo Vicente, whose birth coincided with the first stage of the project. He was eighteen months old when we began this stage.) I suppose they were junior researchers on this project.

Several student researcher-authors, in addition to Fredi and Gricelda, were part of the pipeline research stage of the project. *Rhonda Avery-Merker* had a working understanding of Spanish and was determined to tell the stories of the young undocumented students. She was a white woman working in various local schools as a paraprofessional at the time. Since then, she graduated and finished her special-education teaching credential. *Yeraldín Montie*l conducted most of her interviews with high school students and had close relationships with many staff members at high schools across the region. She finished her undergraduate degree at California State University, San Marcos (CSUSM) and is beginning a teacher credential program. *Bettina Serna,* from the desert region, had learned about the undocumented student club at her community college and conducted her interviews with them; she wrote Chapter 6 drawing on her and others' interviews. She is currently in the CSUSM graduate program of sociological practice finishing a thesis on the experiences of female card dealers. *Omar*

Canseco, who began this project as an undergraduate with interests in Oaxacan immigration, conducted his interviews with high school students. He also analyzed the postgraduate data we collected in 2013 as a graduate student in sociology. Omar is finishing his master's degree in sociological practice with a thesis on border crossings. His childhood reflections were shared in Chapter 1 of this book. *Carolina Valdivia Ordorica* conducted her interviews with high school and community college students; note the richness of her interviews, especially with "Alfredo," which reflected her ability to connect with participants she had not previously known. She graduated from a master of arts program in sociology at San Diego State University and is in doctoral study at Harvard. She wrote Chapter 9, on DREAMer activism.

There were a handful of super researchers who not only completed amazing interviews but always communicated deep, meaningful levels of analysis and demonstrated their enthusiastic commitment to this project: Maria Baca, Monica Anguiano, Juanita Huerta, Perla Gracia, and Mayela Caro. They have all graduated and gone on to become successful professionals in the community. I am extremely grateful for their dedication to this project.

Other pipeline researchers participated in the summer training but had less success with their interviews. However, they each served an important role in providing an amazing foundation for the general pipeline project. Some excellent summer training contributors were Ester Alva, Gina Diaz, Moises Esteban, Elsa Gaytan, Maria Hose, Leo Cruz, and Jose Escobedo.

The Training

After our group was solidified, we met on six Monday evenings, from 5:30 p.m. to 7:30 p.m., in the summer of 2010. Participation was mandatory for completing the second part of the project, which was doing the actual interviews during fall semester 2010. I explain here how I structured the learning experiences and describe some of the processes and discussions. Because I have enjoyed teaching the undergraduate and graduate levels of qualitative methods, Latino/a communities, and sociology of education, it was truly rewarding to put together the curriculum for a singular, active project.

Session 1: Introduction to the Literature on Undocumented Students. This session began online with me posting numerous research articles on the topic of undocumented students and Latino/as in education. I had attended the preconference workshop for the American Association of Hispanics in Higher Education earlier in the year, where speakers discussed the Latino/a educational pipeline and gave each participant a compact disc with the latest research on the subject.[1] I also added my own selection of readings. The result was a comprehensive tutorial on how Latino/as are faring in the school system, from kindergarten onward.

Student researchers were asked to read a large selection of studies, write summaries, and pose critical questions through an online discussion format. I also asked students to reflect on how the research they read would inform our future study of undocumented Latino/a students in the educational pipeline.

When we met in person, the researchers had completed this important academic overview and analytical work, and we were ready to discuss the issues that had emerged during a face-to-face meeting. I pulled up their discussions on a large screen in our meeting room to prompt conversations. The student researchers left this first session with a solid understanding of the previous scholarship on our topic.

Session 2: Interviewing Skills. The second session was more hands-on. Student researchers were assigned readings on qualitative interviews and related issues such as being an "insider" in the field of study. They came prepared to discuss the main points of the readings. Then, I introduced several activities that helped them hone their listening skills and gave them role-playing scenarios in order to experience common occurrences in interview settings (e.g., participants not understanding a question, interruptions, silences). Shy student researchers felt unsure if they could succeed in the interview setting, but the role playing helped them see that they were acute listeners. Gregarious members of our group realized that their talkative nature was sometimes a distraction to realizing when a prompt was needed with their interviewee. I passed along stories my former professors had told me of working with Erving Goffman, renowned sociologist and qualitative researcher, who was also rather shy. I believe this was the most enjoyable day for us.

Session 3: Ethics in Research. I assigned readings on the background to why ethics in research is an important consideration. Surprisingly, although some had taken qualitative methods, few student researchers knew about the devastating history of medical and social science studies of marginalized groups.

I had been IRB chair for my university and an IRB member for six years. I felt very prepared to put my expertise into play and engage with the student researchers in a way to make them excited about ethics and research. I asked them to bring with them copies of our university's IRB forms for expedited and full reviews and encouraged them to review the campus website for IRB resources.

We met in a computer lab to complete the Collaborative Institutional Training Initiatives (CITI), which offers IRB training for faculty and student researchers. Everyone logged in separately, but we approached each module together, discussing the issues and then individually taking the assessments. The session lasted almost four hours, but the students were determined to finish the training. Their results were sent to the university IRB office, which produced a certificate of completion for each student researcher. The students would be certified to begin the research in the fall.

We believe that we worked through many of the ethical and sensitive issues involved to do sound and respectful research with undocumented Latino/a young people and adults. In their book *Humanizing Research: Decolonizing Qualitative Inquiry with Youth and Communities*, editors Django Paris and Maisha T. Winn (2014) created an impressive volume with on-the-ground researchers who wrote about the mind, body, soul, and justice of researching "marginalized" communities and populations. Their first chapter is about a collective of four scholars in the Chicago area who expressed the pain and wonder of researching undocumented immigration (Diaz-Strong et al. 2014). Although their book was published after we completed data collection, I believe the spirit of this important new research-methods book is at the heart of our work.

Session 4: Interview Questions Workshop. This session was our most intense because we created the interview schedule everyone would use for interviews. We worked in English but knew many student researchers would be doing their interviews in Spanish. We produced questions for elementary school, middle school, high school, and community college.

For me, this was the most satisfying session because the student researchers really challenged each other about why they were presenting the questions they thought necessary. To pose and respond to the challenges, they drew upon the ethical training and previous studies' approaches. Some student researchers also "schooled" each other on topics from previous sessions they had not grasped completely.

I could also see why the student researchers were crucial to this project. They thought of asking questions that would not have occurred to me, such as how friends at school and romantic relationships are affected by immigration status. I also did not think we should ask the high school students about deportation fears, but the student researchers believed this was an extremely important part of their reality and should not be overlooked. The student researchers also were the closest to the educational pipeline. Their experiences of arriving in this country, applying to schools, and dealing with counselors were fresh in their minds.

Our most involved discussion was about what to ask the elementary and middle school students. To what extent the younger participants knew about their status created a tricky situation. I tentatively introduced a methodology I had used with much success: photo-elicitation interviews.[2] In my previous research, students took photos of what was important to them, and the researcher used those photographs as prompts in the interview. This immediately caught the attention of the student researchers because it would solve the problem of asking them about their status when we would not know the extent of their knowledge or the consequences of revealing their status to others.

The research group decided the younger students would need to know they were undocumented before being interviewed by the researcher, but that status would not be the focus of their photo interviews. Our young participants would be asked to document aspects of their lives important to them. Then, we as researchers would analyze the data as the work of undocumented children. If immigration status came up, we would "roll with it" and let the child speak about her or his experience naturally within the flow of the photographs. Our in-depth and thoughtful discussion prepared me to respond to questions from the IRB committee and defend our rationale.

As discussed previously, we elected to not share the images of the children due to considerable risk to them (and that of their friends and family) should their status or location be detected. As a visual sociologist, I loved working with their images and learning about their lives with Rhonda Avery-Merker. However, these circumstances were clear: ethics and commitment to our social justice ideals were prioritized over presenting compelling visual data. Having members of our research team ask good, hard questions about consequences for deportation and sharing their own stories shaped each step of our project.

Session 5: Practice Interviews and Recruitment Plan. The student researchers came to this session prepared to think through who they could interview and to practice the finalized interview questions we created.

Practicing all of our interview questions on each other was extremely beneficial because we could "hear" the rhythm and sequencing of the question. We also caught repetitions. The student researchers practiced the questions in a conversational way, as opposed to a neutral-toned survey approach. In addition, student researchers experienced the "meandering river" style of qualitative interviews, as opposed to the "ping-pong match" approach of survey interviews. We made extensive revisions to our questions based on this session, and I believe our research project was strengthened.

The student researchers completed a "commitment contract" in which they outlined their strategies for recruitment and the possible participants they had in mind, their relationship to them, and so forth. I went through and reviewed each contract with them; sometimes we made changes or clarifications in terms of ethical approaches to recruitment and realistic goals. Although some students did not ultimately meet their goals or fulfill their commitments, they each began with a solid plan.

Even though some of the student researchers worked in middle schools or had family members at middle schools, *none* of the planned middle school interviews came to fruition. (It was intriguing to me at the time. Since then, I have worked even more collaboratively with Cecilia Rocha, author of the middle school chapter, to better understand the dynamics of middle school. I have implemented a service-learning project in under-resourced middle schools in our region.)

Online Sessions: Finalizing IRBs and Resources. In between the in-person meetings, I sent out drafts via e-mail collaborating with student researchers on creating three IRB applications for our project. We submitted our applications in August and September of 2011. The first two were relatively easy—high school and community college student studies were expedited and required little revision from the IRB committee. The children's photo-elicitation interview research project underwent full review and took much longer. In fact, we did not receive IRB approval until late October, days before I gave birth to my daughter.

We also collaborated to create a comprehensive resource document for legal, medical, mental health, and scholarship information. This guide was to be given to all participants and also to anyone who we spoke to about the study. In this way, we strived to conduct outreach and education in our communities.

Final Sessions: Individual Meetings. As each IRB application was approved, I met with individuals or small groups of student researchers for lunch or coffee to give them their printed stacks of interview questions, resource packets, and consent forms. We finalized their plans of action and went over the main goals of our project again. This is where they truly earned their independent study credits because they began the data collection stage and kept track of their interviews, transcribed them, and followed up with participants. A handful of student researchers experienced significant obstacles and never collected data. However, those who did yielded rich and often heart-wrenching data. Among those who collected data with children (elementary school), some experienced challenges to gain permission from parents. As mentioned, middle school interviews never solidified despite trusted relationships with these possible participants.

I commend the student researchers for their dedication and hard work. They participated in nearly every stage of the research process. As data were sent to me, I discerned general themes, sent them out via e-mail, and asked for feedback. Several students consistently replied with their reflections. They were the students I invited to cowrite chapters with me for this book.

Pipeline Project 3.0: Responding to New Developments

Toward the end of this project, several undocumented coauthors asked me if we were going to include the experiences of postgraduate undocumented students. They were at this stage of their academic careers, and I agreed that there was very little research on the topic. I contacted additional postgraduate DREAMers and worked with a core group of postgraduate undocumented students. Together, we created an extensive open-ended survey about how they felt about graduation, what they were doing now, and what they hoped to do in the future. Deferred Action for Childhood Arrivals (DACA) had just passed, and we were also able to capture some of the compelling mixed emotions participants experienced as they were deciding to apply for benefits or waiting for notification.

Participatory Research

We considered two types of participation for this project. First, I focused on the participation of the student researchers. Throughout this project, it was my intention to make sure that the student researchers were collaborators and even leaders in the research process. My goal for the student researchers, as young people and often first-generation college students, was to mentor them (and connect them with colleagues) about research, graduate school, and critical analysis.

The story of the leaking pipeline is also the story of my collaborative authors in this book. All of the authors but myself are first-generation college students. Each author made it to college but knows countless others—family, friends, partners—who have fallen or are falling through the educational pipeline at various levels. This book is their story, too. I encouraged them to write themselves into the chapter as much as *they* felt comfortable.

The ethics of authors' revealing immigration status, in a permanent public format, were discussed frequently. Up until the last week before submitting the manuscript for publication, we were returning to this issue. Our conversations reflected larger ones occurring elsewhere: some people felt "undocumented and unafraid," and others felt extremely protective of information about their immigration status even if it had changed to "resident" or "citizen."

Most had a keen awareness of *how, when,* and *with whom* they shared their immigration status. A part of this consideration was that "outing" yourself as undocumented could mean repercussions for family members. I took these issues very seriously. Yet, preventing any of the authors who wanted to share their immigration status would be paternalistic on my part and deny them agency. Open, honest, and authentic conversations were the foundation of all of our communications in general and were especially required for ethical, tricky, and sensitive issues such as immigration status.

Fredi wrote, "I think disclosing immigration status gives justice to all the voices expressed in the book. It is also liberating for one's self from the oppressive immigration system. Disclosing immigration status gives greater connection to the immigrant community, undocumented immigrants in particular, to the point of saying 'thank you' for giving voice to my experience. Throughout my educational path, I wished I had encountered a book like this, a book that I could relate to. Our experiences speak for themselves. We are the experts on this topic and we can incite social change."

Similarly, Yeraldín shared, "It took me a long time to be able to come out of the shadows. The reason I decided to share my status or my story in the book is because I want our readers to see that being undocumented is a struggle and it continues to be. You don't *learn* to be undocumented; it is our reality. There are no guidelines for us to follow or script to read. I also want other students to read our story and be motivated to continue a higher education and to keep fighting for the changes they want to see in our community."

However, other contributors felt that off-campus work experiences made it clear that sharing their immigration status, even if it had changed from undocumented to resident, left them vulnerable to hostility from coworkers and supervisors. Thus, they felt more protective about sharing their status in a public way.

As a professor, I needed to truly hear what my collaborators were explaining. Contributors were not pressured either way to disclose or not disclose their status. I know these thoughtful conversations will continue long after this book is published.

We aimed to include the perspectives, voices, and direction of our research participants. The interviews with the high school, community college, and college students were the least participatory in terms of engaging the "subjects" of the research to collaborate on the project. The photo-elicitation interviews with the children were semiparticipatory in the sense that they guided the pacing and content of the interviews.

Sherry Arnstein (1969), in her original concept for empowered political processes, and Roger Hart (1992), regarding researching children, rate research participation approaches from the lowest level of engagement to highest:

1. Youth are manipulated.
2. Youth are used as decoration.
3. Youth are used for tokenism.
4. Youth are informed.
5. Youth are consulted and informed.
6. Adults initiate and share decisions with youth.
7. Youth initiate and are directed by adults.
8. Youth initiate and share decisions with adults.

The student researchers in our project, many of whom were undocumented, certainly experienced high levels of participation in the research process. However, our adult and young adult research "subjects" mostly experienced the fourth and fifth levels; children in the photo-elicitation study were at the sixth level of participation.

Taking the Project to the Community

This six-year research project had many forms of community collaborations. In 2009, we created "Day of Dialogue" and invited the emerging scholars and policy experts on the burgeoning area of undocumented immigration to CSUSM. Carolina, Gricelda, and Yeraldín—all three authors in this book—were presidents of campus club STAND. Throughout the years, I worked with them to hold rallies, teach-ins, and workshops that brought awareness to the campus and larger region about undocumented immigrants.

Those connected to this project and others have joined in efforts to improve the campus climate and student services for undocumented students. For example, with STAND and colleague Xuan Santos, we organized the first "safe-space" training for the undocumented student population on our campus. We followed the efforts of other ally trainings held at the University of California, Berkeley; University of Arizona; and California State University, Long Beach (CSULB). The CSULB (2009) *AB 540 Ally Handbook* was particularly helpful.

For years, I have been an active member of the AB 540 Task Force on my campus, which brings together representatives of many departments and administrative units on campus to discuss issues of undocumented students and to respond to students' needs. We recently overhauled our AB 540 campus webpage (www.csusm.edu/ab540) to provide even more comprehensive bilingual information and support for AB 540 students. The research we have shared from this book has had a direct and positive effect on our institution.

We are working to make an even greater impact in the region. To imagine what is possible with collaboration and *ganas* (determination), I share an event to demonstrate how the Pipeline Research Collective and allies strived to make a difference. Frequently, sociologists conduct research read by only a small group of scholars and students. From the beginning, this project has been firmly rooted *en la comunidad*—research and activism by and for members of undocumented communities. We hope that by describing the details of an event such as the one we organized, it could serve as a blueprint for others to organize events in their communities.

Cecilia Rocha and I stood before 200 registered guests who were members of and allies to the undocumented immigrant community. We were gathered in a lecture hall at Palomar College for "Avenidas [Pathways] to Success for AB 540 Students," an event that combined social networking, dinner, scholarship, and legal information for undocumented students and their families. Numerous educators attended to learn and also brought their students. These important allies were counselors, teachers, Advancement Via Individual Determination (AVID) staff, and Migrant Education coordinators; they came from all over the San Diego and Southwest Riverside region.

The summer before, I called on trusted colleges Cecilia Rocha (a coauthor in this book and GEAR UP coordinator at Palomar College) and Adrean Askerneese (a general counselor at MiraCosta College) to brainstorm about creating a workshop to help undocumented students navigate the legal and scholarship terrain that could increase their chances of doing well in school or college. We had not known of any other event like this in our region and knew it was needed. With additional colleagues from each of our campuses, we met on a regular basis to write a grant to partially fund the event; to ask our campus administrations for institutional, monetary, and symbolic support; and, of course, to plan the actual event.

Over that fall semester, we sent e-mails to schools, immigrant listservs, and immigration rights groups. We also physically distributed flyers in the community. More than 300 people expressed interest in registering and wanted more information about Avenidas, and about 200 attended the actual event.

Starting at 4 p.m. on Thursday, February 3, 2012, students, parents, educators, and community members registered at the Palomar College Student Union and picked up their packets of materials. GEAR UP staff warmly welcomed the participants in Spanish and English.

We began with a social and networking hour—student clubs from the three colleges staffed tables and chatted with the participants. STAND from CSUSM and Movimiento Estudiantil Chicano/a de Aztlán (MEChA) from Palomar College, MiraCosta College, and CSUSM brought materials and chatted with participants across five tables.

We—the organizers and volunteers—personally served lasagna and salad for all participants. (An educational alliance foundation for the region funded us for 100 dinners; GEAR UP at Palomar College and the president of MiraCosta College personally contributed the remaining amounts.) The registrar of Palomar College, Herman Lee, and I welcomed the participants and thanked them for being there.

We moved from the dining area to the large lecture hall, where financial aid directors Vonda Garcia and Mary San Agustin of CSUSM and Palomar College, respectively, gave a joint presentation on the financial aid process and resources for AB 540 students. Leo Melena, a representative from the BECA Foundation (a regional scholarship organization), gave an overview on applying for private scholarships and offered tips for personal essays to accompany the application. He offered valuable insider information to the students and families on what a selection committee looks for in successful applications.

Then, Miko Tokuhama-Olsen, an attorney from San Diego Legal Aid, gave a one-hour overview of the AB 540 status in terms of the law. In simple language and an engaging style, she let the audience know the "do's and don't's" of immigration law. Many students and parents told us they had not known some of these important contours of the law. She also had all her material in Spanish.

Finally, four more immigration attorneys—three of whom spoke Spanish—were assigned their own classrooms to do breakout sessions in a more intimate atmosphere for questions and answers. The legal aid speaker brought her intern, and both did one-on-one private sessions with participants; they stayed in the lecture hall.

Evaluations were collected at the end of the evening. According to the 127 evaluations returned to us, the event was a success. Yet, we learned there was much more to be done for the next event. First, we should have had more Spanish translators. Second, although we had decided to make Avenidas one evening, participants wanted more time and more information (100 percent of those who completed the evaluation wanted to see another event like this). Third, the venue really mattered. Unfortunately, the college presented some obstacles that made it challenging to host our event, such as problematic issues with catering, parking, and reserving rooms. Overall, we felt proud we had created this event and realized that it was just one of the community-related activities that made this public sociology project meaningful.

At the time of Avenidas, the DREAM Act in California had passed but would not be in effect until the following year. DACA did not exist. We believe that the space and networks provided by Avenidas may have supported the future workshops and community events in the following years that would once again bring a number of people together to become more informed and empowered about immigration. (Some of these events, such as the DACA workshops at MiraCosta College, have been mentioned by interviewees and in chapter discussions.)

I continue to maintain a listserv (which has grown to more than 400 members) to communicate news, pass along information about local workshops, and alert members to events related to the undocumented community of the San Diego region. In this way, I work as a public sociologist in my region.

Being a Latina Professor: My Immigrant and Academic Journey

This final section discusses my social location and how it is related to this project. I tried to be conscious of my relative privilege and my position as an academic throughout this study and even as I cowrote the book with the students.

I am Latina. Spanish is my first language. I came to the United States as a young child. To some extent, I share some superficial aspects of immigration experiences with undocumented youth. However, my journey was one of relative privilege.

I was born in Lima, Peru, to a Peruvian mother (Mercedes Ibáñez Rosazza) and Irish American father (Bill Clark) who came to Peru initially as a Peace Corps volunteer. My parents met in the 1960s, married, and became parents to my younger sister and me. My mother was an accomplished poet and playwright and my father a Peace Corps volunteer trainer. We left Peru so my father could attend graduate school in public policy at the University of California, Berkeley. We had a long journey to the United States, driving most of the way in a green Volkswagen "square-back" station wagon. The US government paid for our furniture to be shipped to the United States. (Ironically, we moved into an apartment in graduate student housing with little space for the enormous hand-carved wooden furniture.)

My parents are college-educated intellectuals, professionals, and artists. They exposed us to issues of social justice, international folk art, and high art. We lived in a "good" neighborhood (in a predominantly white college town) and attended excellent public schools.

Growing up, my experiences being identified as a Latina were mainly through my mother—speaking up for her because of how she was treated as a result of her accent—and our annual summer vacations living with our family in Lima and Trujillo, Peru. My skin is "Irish white," and my English-language accent is decidedly West Coast American.

In the United States, I strived to fit into the white, middle-class norm of my school peers. For a while, dropping "Ibáñez" and just using Clark helped, but then there was my first name, Marisol. Friends teased that it rhymed with "aerosol." I begged my parents to change my name, like those of my Peruvian American cousins who immigrated to Texas: José became Bucky and Javier changed to Andy. My sister and I even proposed our new names as Linda and Judy. Alas, and thankfully, our parents never once let us think this was possible, always pronounced our names correctly, and insisted we use our legal last names.

Flash forward to attending Third College (now Thurgood Marshall College) at the University of California, San Diego, where I *fully* realized my cultural identity and its relative privilege among other groups. Chicano studies, global economic systems, white privilege, and "third world" literature were the types of classes that fundamentally changed the way I viewed my origins and upbringing. The year I spent studying Mexican literature at the national university in Mexico City, Mexico, was also formative. I traveled by bus through many states within Mexico (and also to various Central American nations). In the capital, I conducted research in the national archives to better understand changes to post–Mexican Revolution agrarian land reform, such as the *ejido* system or communal farmland. From this point onward, my research interests and activities were situated in radical praxis.

As an undergraduate, I was mentored by Professors Rae Lesser Blumberg and Ivan Evans. I did my first independent research projects on economic development (an interview study with Quechua-speaking microentrepreneurial women in Ayacucho, Peru). After I was in a doctoral program in sociology at the University of California, Davis, my research projects were on migrant education, paroled teenage fathers, and interracial dating. My dissertation was based on a yearlong ethnography in South Central Los Angeles, comparing the classroom dynamics in charter and noncharter fourth-grade elementary schools. My analysis focused on how classroom microinteractions produced mechanisms of inequality across gender, race, (perceived) ability, and language (Clark-Ibáñez 2003).

Postdissertation, I conducted photo-elicitation interviews (PEI) with the almost sixty children I met during my dissertation work and thus extended my connection to Los Angeles for two more years. This project, I believe, solidified my scholarly identity. I have given numerous workshops in the United States and Europe on the PEI methodology. I have been contacted by scholars around the world with encouragement and questions about PEI. Apparently, one of my articles has been cited more than 400 times. I believe my commitment to social justice with a focus on children's rights has served as a good research moral compass. I have learned a great deal from each participant in this book whether they published here with me, conducted interviews, or were an interviewee or survey taker. I believe we accomplished our goal.

Langston Hughes wrote "I Dream a World" when African Americans were at the beginning of a long fight for educational equality and inclusion. He dreamt about "a world where all will know sweet freedom's way" and "no other man will scorn." It aptly describes the way many of us in and associated with this project feel about social justice and undocumented immigration.

This book illuminates the journeys and experiences of Latino/a undocumented youth throughout the educational pipeline and from a number of different perspectives. Real and meaningful community collaboration characterized this project and continues today. My collaborators and I hope the rich nature of these stories—across grade levels and beyond—yields a compelling narrative and social snapshot of current education and immigration policies in practice.

Notes

1. For more information on the American Association of Hispanics in Higher Education, see http://www.aahhe.org/.

2. See the following for more information: Clark-Ibáñez (2005) for an overview of PEI as it compares to ethnography, Clark-Ibáñez (2007) for a focus on PEI and theories of childhood, and Clark-Ibáñez (2009) on how PEI was used to better understand the experiences of alleged "bad" girls and "bad" boys in an inner-city context.

Appendix B: Brief Overview of the Field

A rich, interdisciplinary field of research on Latino/as and education and a growing subfield of work on undocumented Latino/as contributed to our understanding of the strengths and challenges of these populations as they navigate the educational pipeline. As a collective research group, we read and discussed studies of undocumented immigration and education that featured Latino/as in the United States. In this section, I provide an overview of the studies that informed our research project.

Overall, Latino/as are attending college in increasing numbers but continue to experience many challenges to educational achievement. To survive and thrive in the educational pipeline, many Latino/as from low-income families must overcome structural and institutional inequalities (Chávez, Soriano, and Olivarez 2007). For example, underfunded schools, poor-quality teachers, high teacher turnover, lack of advanced placement (AP) courses, and formal and informal tracking systems are just some of the obstacles poor Latino/a students face when navigating the pipeline (Covarrubias and Lara 2013; Gonzales 2010). Rotherham (2011) reports that only 17 percent of Hispanic fourth graders score proficient or better on the National Assessment of Educational Progress (a test given to samples of students each year) whereas 42 percent of non-Hispanic white students do. Because of the demographics of low-income Latino/a communities, undocumented Latino/a students are likely also affected by these dynamics.

Aspirations

Research shows that although Latino/as have aspirations to attend college, they sometimes lack the social and cultural capital to achieve their goals. Research also shows that school counselors often act as agents of inequality by actively dampening the aspirations of Latino/a students. Often, college is not presented as an option (McKillip, Rawls, and Barry 2012). Martinez and Cervera (2012) found that, compared with black, white, and Asian students, Latino/as have the least access to college support resources. In addition, although most Latino/as aspire to attend four-year universities, they are the group least likely to apply to these schools in their senior year.

As a result, many Latino/a students take the community college route to a four-year university (Ortiz, Valerio, and López 2012). This may result in stalled aspirations or a "cooling out" period (Bahr 2008; Ellis 2013). In California, "after 7 years only 17 percent of Latino and 19 percent of African American students who had intended to transfer to a 4-year college had actually successfully done so" (Gándara et al. 2012).

One optimistic and refreshing finding emerges from the literature on undocumented students: they are highly motivated (Gonzales 2007). Many undocumented students express the desire to participate in the "American dream" (Chavez 2008). Morales and colleagues (2011) found that in the Midwest, undocumented students are highly motivated to succeed despite cultural isolation from larger Latino/a communities.

We need to be cautious, however, because much of this research is conducted at higher levels of education such as high school, community college, and four-year universities. Cohort peer students may have already fallen from the pipeline. As mentioned previously, Súarez-Orozco and her colleagues (2010) conducted a pathbreaking immigration study of younger children and found that the undocumented children were among the least academically successful group. Covarrubias and Lara (2013) also warned of the "brown model minority" image of undocumented students; they found this group is, in general, not performing at the same level as its "documented" counterparts (24). Thus, when we examine undocumented college-bound or college students, we must note that they are a uniquely resilient and successful group. Many of their cohort peers may have fallen from the pipeline long before reaching a college or even "college-bound" educational environment.

Academic Preparation

Although the number of Latinos attending college is increasing, scholars have found that the lack of academic preparation is a significant factor for not attending college (Burciaga, Pérez Huber, and Solórzano 2010; Súarez-Orozco and Paez 2008). Structural issues and institutional inequalities exist and present significant challenges for Latino/a students. For example, poorly funded schools (Gándara et al. 2012), less availability of qualified teachers (Castro-Salazar and Bagley 2010), lack of college-level required courses (e.g., college-prep requirements of the California universities), absence of AP courses (Gándara et al. 2012), and lack of culturally relevant curricula (Milner 2011; Ortiz, Valerio, and López 2012; Ramirez 2012) are some of the obstacles these students face. Tracking in high schools funnels Latino/a and other marginalized students into non-college-track courses (Mulkey et al. 2009; Oakes 1985).

These structural factors shape students' identities. Directly related to whether students see themselves as capable and prepared to attend college are the direct and indirect socialization experienced by students as children (Pérez Huber 2010; Wilkinson 2010). There is evidence of a hidden curriculum embedded in daily schoolwork (Anyon 1997; Apple 1995; Clark-Ibáñez 2005).[1] Despite these formidable obstacles, many scholars study the effects of self-efficacy and schooling for Latino/a students (Boden 2011; Bordes-Edgar et al. 2011; Niehaus, Rudasill, and Adelson 2012). For example, Cavazos, Johnson, and Sparrow (2010) found positive self-talk and positive reframing led to higher grades for the Latino/a students in their study.

In his study of undocumented students in Los Angeles, Gonzales (2010) presented compelling data on Latino/a high school students. Those in lower tracks experienced bullying, labels, and low expectations; those in higher academic tracks were supported by institutional gatekeepers. In addition, in a comprehensive study across multiple schools in the United States, researchers found that undocumented students of all ages and countries of origin experienced *low levels* of educational achievement, grade-point averages (GPAs), and classroom participation (Súarez-Orozco et al. 2011).

Family and Community Strengths

Families and community create sources of strength for Latino/a students. Latino/a parents are *very supportive* of their children's college aspirations, but frequently are unsure of the processes for applying for college and financial aid (Boden 2011; Castro-Salazar and Bagley 2010; Pérez and McDonough 2008).

Súarez-Orozco and colleagues (2010) report that undocumented parents with children (who have citizenship) often hold oppressive, low-paying jobs and do not have access to subsidized day care. These factors affect future educational outcomes for students of undocumented parents. Reyes

(2010) reports that often, undocumented mothers cannot fully participate in their children's education and are often unable to attend teacher meetings or go to the library. Level of parental participation in a child's education is yet another predictor of educational success or failure for a child.

Latino/a students, undocumented or citizens, often cite *familia* as their main motivator for attending and succeeding in college (Clark-Ibáñez, García-Alverdín, and Alva 2011; Easley, Bianco, and Leech 2012). Parents provide students the cultural connection often lacking on a college campus (Torres 2004). Scholars argue that instead of viewing Latino/a parents as lacking cultural capital, we should perceive Latino/a parents as providing the "cultural wealth" needed for students to succeed (Yosso 2005).

Financial Concerns

Latino/a families who are lower middle class, working class, or working poor may believe college is out of financial reach for their children. The median household income for Latino/a families is $34,300; for white families it is $50,000 (US Census Bureau 2012, data cited in Diaz-Strong et al. 2014). The poverty rate for Latino/as is 22.2 percent, whereas for whites it is 7.4 percent; the average poverty rate in the United States is 12.4 percent (US Census Bureau 2012 data, cited in Diaz-Strong et al. 2014). There is not a national average for undocumented immigrant family income; however, many of our participants had parents who worked in the agricultural fields, and the average family income for farmworkers is $15,000 to $17,499 (Mejía and McCarthy 2010). Parents, for a variety of reasons previously noted, may not have the ability to complete the financial aid forms that would provide aid to their children.

In particular, financial struggles negatively affect undocumented students' success (Clark-Ibáñez, García-Alverdín, and Alva 2011; Contreras 2009; Olivérez 2006; Pérez Huber 2010; Solórzano et al. 2013). Formal financial aid and employment are outside the reach of many because of their undocumented status. As of June 2014, only thirteen states allow undocumented students to pay in-state tuition. Numerous studies cite financial concerns as a top issue for undocumented students (Chávez et al. 2007; Pérez Huber 2010). Lack of access to financial aid helps to explain the higher enrollment of undocumented students in community colleges, where the tuition is considerably lower. Covarrubias and Lara (2013) found that undocumented Mexican immigrants end their educational careers with an associate's degree (community college) more frequently than do other groups. (See Jauregui, Slate, and Brown 2008 for examination of undocumented immigrant enrollment trends in Texas community colleges.)

Peer and Social Capital

Peer support can be a powerful factor influencing Latino/a students' college success. For example, Valenzuela (1999) found that when Latino/a immigrants connect for scholarly support, they acquire social capital in the form of information or tangible resources, such as the use of a friend's computer. This results in positive effects on school attainment and success. Subsequent studies show that when social capital is acquired by marginalized youth, it produces powerful effects on educational goals and self-efficacy (Valdez and Lugg 2010).

Despite the gains made through peer contact, undocumented Latino/a students also experience unique challenges related to their immigration status. For example, as discussed previously, social support is extremely important to academic success (as confirmed by studies about college students in general), but negative or unsupportive networks may be even *more* detrimental to undocumented students than to their citizen counterparts (Castellanos and Orozco 2005) because undocumented students are more vulnerable. However, the research confirms they are resilient when they reach the college level. Clearly, for undocumented students, there are complex interactions resulting from both positive and negative sources of social support.

Stress and Fear

One of the most important findings from research on undocumented college-bound or college students is the enormous amount of stress they experience. The uncertainty of their status and the threat of deportation, whether their own or a family member's, is a continual source of stress (Abrego 2011; Clark-Ibáñez, García-Alverdín, and Alva 2011; Dozier 1993; Herdoiza 2012; Hernandez 2008; Muñoz 2008). Clark-Ibáñez, García-Alverdín, and Alva (2011) report that even coming and going to college is a source of stress because of the excessive monitoring of drivers and the presence of Immigration and Customs Enforcement (ICE) on public transportation.

In addition, the university setting itself (attending class, campus climate, campus activities) brings its own form of stress through the perpetuation of stereotypes and stigmas in the curriculum (Castellanos and Orozco 2005). In addition, compared with the average college student, undocumented students experience more depression (Hovey 2000; Mejía and McCarthy 2010). There is a high degree of stress related to issues of legality. Undocumented students also face role strain and thus more stress with acculturation compared with the average college student and Latino/a students who are documented (Hovey and King 1996; Neff and Hoppe 1993). As will be discussed, many students engage in political activism and civic engagement to alleviate the sense of isolation and despondency associated with their immigration status.

Legal Liminality and Civic Engagement

Undocumented students exist in "legal liminality" (Menjívar 2006, 2008; Menjívar and Abrego 2012; Nakano Glenn 2011), a state of being "neither from here nor there" (Castro-Salazar and Bagley 2012:30). This inbetweenness has led researchers to study how undocumented students perceive their "Americaness" (Perez 2009), levels of civic engagement (DeJaeghere and McCleary 2010; Perez et al. 2010), activism (Nakano Glenn 2011; Seif 2004), and knowledge of the legal system (Abrego 2006; King and Punti 2012; Rincón 2008). Perez and colleagues (2010) conducted an in-depth study of undocumented Mexican students and compared them with others in high school. They found that 90 percent of the undocumented students were "civically engaged in activities such as providing social services, activism, and tutoring" (260).

The University of California, Los Angeles (UCLA) Center for Labor Research and Education has produced two books authored by undocumented college students that describe ways in which they engaged in the political process on the route to finishing their college degrees (Wong 2009; Wong et al. 2011). Of those awarded DACA benefits, "41% of respondents participated in a political rally or demonstration compared to just 6% of voters surveyed in the 2012 American National Election Study (ANES)" (Wong and Valdivia 2014:4).

Status, Role, and Life Course

We believe Erving Goffman's sociological concept of *status* is central to how the undocumented students experienced their personal and academic lives. Students operated in multiple and sometimes conflicting statuses, and often, this results in *role conflict*. In the case of our participants, they simultaneously occupied the status of "child" (or youth) and "undocumented immigrant"—both subordinate positions in our society. These identity statuses come attached with specific social expectations (roles). Tensions arise when these expectations require divergent behavior. The role attached to a young person in the United States is to be carefree, to play, and to explore independence, whereas the role of an undocumented immigrant is to be cautious and to "live in the shadows." We explored how students navigated these identity contradictions in roles and expectations.

In a related way, life course theory, traditionally used to understand the process of aging, can be used as an analytical lens in exciting and new ways with our data. Macmillan (2005) explained, "Life course theory emphasizes in various and often disparate ways life stages, role trajectories and transitions, and the timing and ordering of events in the life course. All these coalesce to produce a 'normative' life course that corresponds to social timetables of given times and given places" (3). Gonzales (2011) theorized about this phenomenon for undocumented young people and explained that as students transitioned from the ascribed statuses of children to teenagers to young adults, they encountered (and collided) with notions of their "illegality."

Our participants revealed that status and role *related to their age* significantly affected the experiences of undocumented young people. To understand the experiences of undocumented students is to know where they are in terms of life events predicated on rites of passages or developmental age, such as obtaining a driver's license. In California, undocumented immigrants were not allowed to drive because they were ineligible for driver's licenses. Our teenaged and college-aged participants mentioned their realization of being unable to drive was a fundamental moment in their self-discovery and identities as undocumented immigrants.

From giving us a baseline understanding of the state of education for Latino/as to shaping our interview questions, previous research studies were essential to our project. We believe we add to this field of study by delivering an intimate look at growing up as undocumented Latino/a immigrants and analyzing the social and legal dynamics that shape everyday life in and out of school.

Note

1. The hidden curriculum refers to the pedagogy (and content) taught to different types of students, which replicates or intensifies existing inequalities inside and outside of the school context. A classic example comes from Anyon's (1997) work on social class: working-class students were given worksheets, middle-class students were taught to focus on the "right" answers, and upper-class students were taught free and critical thinking. The way in which students were taught often mirrored the types of jobs their parents held and they were expected to hold in the future.

Appendix C: Summary Tables of the Participants

Table C.1 High School Participants

Name	Age at Arrival (years)	Grade at Arrival	Age When Interviewed
Diana	3	Prekindergarten	17
Yadira	7	Fifth grade	18
Ana María	11	Seventh grade	17
Patricia	13	Eighth grade	14
Carmen	14	Ninth grade	17
Daniela	16	Ninth grade	18
Alfredo	15	Ninth grade	17
Joel	16	Ninth grade	17

Table C.2 Community College Participants

Name	Time Spent in College	Age at Arrival	Age When Interviewed
Esperanza	3 semesters	7	20
Ariana	3 semesters	10	19
Selena	1 semester	3	19
Deysi	1 semester	14	18
Lupita	3 years	10	20
Sofia	2.5 years	9	20
Martin	2 years	1.5	21
Julio	3 years	12	24
Elizabeth	3 years	1.5	23
Paulina[a]	1 semester	Less than a year	18
Maria[a]	2 years	Less than a month	18
Leticia	2 years	12	21
Alejandro[a]	4 semesters	15	29
Christina[a]	1 year	17	21
Teresa	1 semester	4	20

Note: a. Indicates they did not qualify for AB 540 status.

Table C.3 Demographics Given by Postgraduate Survey Respondents

	Birth Country	Age at Arrival	Undergraduate Major and School	Graduate School Affiliation and Program
Flor (female)	Mexico	20	BA in communications, California State University, San Marcos (CSUSM)	MA in CSUSM
Noemi (female)	Mexico	12	BA in sociology, second major in criminology and justice studies	MA program in sociology, San Diego State University (SDSU) applying to PhD programs
Blanca (female)	Mexico	13	BS in business administration, CSUSM	MA in educational leadership; apply to PhD programs
Esperanza (female)	Mexico	4	BA in psychology, CSUSM	MA in psychology, SDSU
Luna (female)	Costa Rica	11	BA in religious studies, second major in women's studies, SDSU	Hopes to go to graduate school
Julio (male)	Mexico	n/a	BA in political science, CSUSM	Plans to complete a master's degree in criminology and justice administration, SDSU; apply to law school
Olga (female)	Mexico	4	BA/BS in health education	n/a
Antonio (male)	Mexico	15	BS in electrical engineering, California State University, Los Angeles (CSULA)	MA in mechatronic intelligent systems, Universidad De Las Americas Puebla (UDLAP), Mexico
Gerardo (male)	Mexico	10	BA in visual and performing arts and music, CSUSM	n/a
Santiago (male)	Mexico	5	BA in criminal justice, Sam Houston State University (Texas)	n/a
Rosa (female)	Mexico	15	BS in business administration, second major in medicine, California State University Sacramento	n/a
Rigoberta (female)	Guatemala	15	BS in computer science, City University of New York (CUNY), Lehman College	n/a
Pedro (male)	Peru	15	BBA, Wisconsin	MBA in professional accountancy
Catarino (male)	Mexico	10	BA/BS in sociology, Whitman College, Washington State	MSW, University of Chicago, Illinois
Female	Mexico	9	Texas	n/a

Manuel (male)	Mexico	13	BA/BS in civil engineering, California State University, Long Beach	n/a
Perla(female)	Mexico	3	AA in Chicano studies, San Bernardino City College (California)	n/a
Laura (female)	Mexico	6	BA in sociology, minor in political science, SDSU	n/a
Lucia (female)	Mexico	9	BA/BS in biochemistry, California State University Bakersfield	MS in chemistry, CSULA; applied for PhD program
Female	Ghana	11	BA/BS in public health, Southern Connecticut State University	n/a
Carla (female)	Mexico	2	BA in criminology and justice studies, minor in psychology, CSUSM	n/a
Male	Mexico	14	BA in sociology, 2nd major in political science, CSUSM	MA, CSUSM
Male	Mexico	4	BA/BS	n/a
Male	Guatemala	2	BS in social work, second major in early childhood education, CUNY, Borough of Manhattan College	n/a
Female	Mexico	3	BA/BS, CSUSM	n/a
Female	Mexico	4	BS in Texas	n/a
Gloria (female)	N/A	10	BS in computer science, CUNY	n/a
Male	Mexico	12	BA in Latino/a studies, University of California, Los Angeles (UCLA)	n/a
Female	Philippines	4	BS in nursing, California State University Fullerton (CSUF)	n/a
Lupe (female)	Trinidad	12	BA in corporate communications, second major in black studies, Baruch College (New York)	n/a
Male	Mexico	7	BA in political science	MA in SDSU
Female	Mexico	10	BA in sociology, 2nd major in psychology and urban planning, at California State University Northridge	n/a
Male	Mexico	14	BA/BS in psychology, 2nd major in education, University of California Santa Barbara (UCSB)	n/a
Female	Mexico	5	n/a	n/a

Notes: Pseudonyms given for those discussed in the text. Respondents are listed in order of submission to the online survey. Some participants left portions of their demographic information blank (e.g., major, university).

References

Abrego, Leisy J. 2006. "'I Can't Go to College Because I Don't Have Papers': Incorporation Patterns of Latino Undocumented Youth." *Latino Studies* 4:212–231.

———. 2008. "Legitimacy, Social Identity, and the Mobilization of Law: The Effects of Assembly Bill 540 on Undocumented Students in California." *Law and Social Inquiry* 33(3):709–734.

———. 2011. "Legal Consciousness of Undocumented Latinos: Fear and Stigma as Barriers to Claims-Making for First- and 1.5-Generation Immigrants." *Law and Society Review* 45(2):337–369.

Abrego, Leisy J., and Roberto G. Gonzales. 2010. "Blocked Paths, Uncertain Futures: The Postsecondary Education and Labor Market Prospects of Undocumented Latino Youth." *Journal of Education for Students Placed at Risk* 15(1–2):144–157.

Adger, W. Neil. 2003. "Social Capital, Collective Action, and Adaptation to Climate Change." *Economic Geography* 79:387–404.

Aguilera, Elizabeth. 2013. "Cal Grants for 'Dream' Student Roll Out." *Union Tribune*, April 8. Retrieved April 13, 2013 (http://www.utsandiego.com/news/2013/apr/08/calgrants-illegal-immigration-college-university/).

Akers-Chacón, Justin, and Mike Davis. 2006. *No One Is Illegal: Fighting Racism and State Violence on the U.S.-Mexico Border.* Chicago: Haymarket Books.

Alba, Richard, and Victor Nee. 2005. *Remaking the American Mainstream: Assimilation and Contemporary Immigration.* Cambridge, MA: Harvard University Press.

Alex-Assensoh, Yvette M., and Lawrence Hanks. 2000. *Black and Multiracial Politics in America.* New York: New York University Press.

Altstadt, Dave, Gretchen Schmidt, and Lara K. Couturier. 2014. *Driving the Direction of Transfer Pathways Reform: Helping More Students Achieve Their Baccalaureate Goals by Creating Structured Transfer Pathways with the End in Mind* (April 2014 report by Jobs for the Future and Completion by Design). Retrieved April 2, 2015 (http://www.jff.org/sites/default/files/publications/materials/Driving-the-Direction-Pathways-Reform-042414.pdf).

American Civil Liberties Union. n.d. *Prolonged Detention Fact Sheet.* Retrieved January 8, 2015 (https://www.aclu.org/sites/default/files/assets/prolonged _detention _fact_sheet.pdf).

———. 2014. "Supreme Court Refuses to Allow Arizona to Deny Drivers' Licenses to Immigrant Youth." Retrieved December 18, 2014 (https://www.aclu.org /immigrants-rights/supreme-court-refuses-allow-arizona-deny-drivers-licenses -immigrant-youth).

Amnesty International. 2009. *Jailed Without Justice* (Amnesty International Report). New York: Amnesty International. Retrieved October 2, 2013 (http:// www.amnestyusa.org/research/reports/usa-jailed-without-justice?page=show).

Anyon, Jean. 1981. "Social Class and School Knowledge." *Curriculum Inquiry* 11(1):3–42.

———. 1997. *Ghetto Schooling: A Political Economy of Urban Educational Reform.* New York: Teachers College Press.

Apple, Michael W. 1995. *Education and Power.* 2nd ed. New York: Routledge.

Aranda, Elizabeth, and Elizabeth Vaquera. 2015. "Racism, the Immigration Enforcement Regime, and the Implications for Racial Inequality in the Lives of Undocumented Young Adults." *Sociology of Race and Ethnicity* 1(1):88–104.

Araújo Dawson, Beverly. 2009. "Discrimination, Stress, and Acculturation Among Dominican Women." *Hispanic Journal of Behavioral Sciences* 31(1):96–111.

Ardón Bejarano, Ana Maríe. 2007. "Democratic Parent Involvement: A Qualitative Study of School-Community Relations." Thesis, Department of Sociology, California State University, San Marcos.

Arnstein, Sherry R. 1969. "A Ladder of Citizen Participation." *JAIP* 35(4):216–224.

Arya, Neelum, Francisco Villarruel, Cassandra Villanueva, and Ian Augarten. 2009. *America's Invisible Children: Latino Youth and the Failure of Justice* (Race and Ethnicity Series Policy Brief, vol. 3). Washington, DC: Campaign for Youth Justice. Retrieved August 3, 2013 (www.ramseyjdai.org/pdf/readings /latino-invisible-children.pdf).

Bahr, Peter Riley. 2008. "'Cooling Out' in the Community College: What Is the Effect of Academic Advising on Students' Chances of Success?" *Research in Higher Education* 49(8):704–732.

Balfanz, Robert. 2011. "Back on Track to Graduate." *Educational Leadership* 68(7):54–58.

Batalova, Jeanne, Sarah Hooker, and Randy Capps. 2013. *Deferred Action for Childhood Arrivals at the One-Year Mark: A Profile of Currently Eligible Youth and Applicants* (MPI Issue Brief No. 8). Washington, DC: Migration Policy Institute. Retrieved September 6, 2013 (http://www.migrationpolicy.org /research/deferred-action-childhood-arrivals-one-year-mark-profile-currently -eligible-youth-and).

Baum, Jonathan, Rosha Jones, and Catherine Barry. 2010. *In the Child's Best Interest?: The Consequences of Losing a Lawful Immigrant Parent to Deportation* (IHRLC Report). Berkeley, CA: International Human Rights Law Clinic. Retrieved June 19, 2014 (http://www.law.berkeley.edu/files/IHRLC/In_the _Childs_Best_Interest.pdf).

Benmayor, Rina. 2002. "Narrating Cultural Citizenship: Oral Histories of Latina/o First Generation College Students." *Social Justice* 29(4):96–121.

Boden, Karen. 2011. "Perceived Academic Preparedness of First-Generation Latino College Students." *Journal of Hispanic Higher Education* 10(2):96–106.

Bolton, Alexander. 2014. "Dems Press Obama to Wait on Immigration." *The Hill*, November 18. Retrieved December 14, 2014 (http://thehill.com/homenews /senate/224473-dems-press-obama-to-wait-on-immigration).

Bonilla-Silva, Eduardo. 2003. *Racism Without Racists: Color Blind Racism and the Persistence of Racial Inequality in the United States*. Lanham, MD: Rowman and Littlefield.

Bonsteel, Alan. 2011. "California Acknowledges Middle-School Dropouts." *SFGate*, August 12. Retrieved January 30, 2013 (http://www.sfgate.com/opinion/openforum/article/California-acknowledges-middle-school-dropouts-2335195.php).

Bordes-Edgar, Veronica, Patricia Arredondo, Sharon Robinson Kurpius, and James Rund. 2011. "A Longitudinal Analysis of Latina/o Students' Academic Persistence." *Journal of Hispanic Higher Education* 10(4):358–368.

Borkowski, John W., and Lisa E. Soronen. 2009. *Legal Issues for School Districts Related to the Education of Undocumented Children* (NSBA Report). Alexandria, VA: National School Boards Association. Retrieved November 11, 2014 (http://www.ncpie.org/WhatsHappening/UndocumentedChildrenNov2009.pdf).

Boutte, Gloria Swindler, Julia Lopez-Robertson, and Elizabeth Powers-Costello. 2011. "Moving Beyond Colorblindness in Early Childhood Classrooms." *Early Childhood Education Journal* 39(5):335–342.

Brand, Jennie E., Fabian T. Pfeffer, and Sara Goldrick-Rab. 2014. "The Community College Effect Revisited: The Importance of Attending Heterogeneity and Complex Counterfactuals." *Sociological Science* (October 1):448–465.

Brint, Stephen, and Jerome Karabel. 1989. *The Diverted Dream: Community Colleges and the Promise of Educational Opportunity in America, 1900–1985*. New York: Oxford University Press.

Brown, Brené. 2012. *Daring Greatly: How the Courage to Be Vulnerable Transforms the Way We Live, Love, Parent, and Lead*. New York: Gotham.

Brown, Robbie. 2010. "Five Public Colleges in Georgia Ban Illegal-Immigrant Students." *New York Times*, October 13. Retrieved April 9, 2013 (http://www.nytimes.com/2010/10/14/us/14georgia.html?_r=0).

Burawoy, Michael. 2005. "2004 Presidential Address: For Public Sociology." *American Sociological Review* 70:4–28.

Burciaga, Rebeca, Lindsay Pérez Huber, and Daniel G. Solórzano. 2010. "Going Back to the Headwaters: Examining Latina/o Educational Attainment and Achievement Through a Framework of Hope." Pp. 422–437 in *Handbook of Latinos and Education: Theory, Research, and Practice*, edited by E. Murillo, S. Villenas, R. T. Galvan, J. S. Munoz, C. Martinez, and M. Machado-Casas. New York: Routledge.

California Community College Chancellor's Office. n.d. Retrieved January 12, 2015 (http://www.cccco.edu/).

California Department of Education. 2013. *Dropouts by Ethnic Designation by Grade in San Diego County, 7–12 Grade, 2011–2012* (CDE Report). Sacramento, CA: Data Reporting Office. Retrieved January 11, 2015 (http://www.cde.ca.gov/ds/sd/sd/filesdropouts.asp).

California DREAM Act. 2011a. Assembly Bill No. 130. Retrieved January 15, 2013 (http://www.csac.ca.gov/pubs/forms/grnt_frm/AB130.pdf).

California DREAM Act. 2011b. Assembly Bill No. 131. Retrieved April 9, 2013 (http://www.csac.ca.gov/pubs/forms/grnt_frm/AB131.pdf).

California State University Long Beach. 2009. *AB 540 Ally Handbook* (CSULB Handbook). Long Beach: California State University Long Beach. Retrieved January 15, 2013 (http://www.csulb.edu/president/government-community/ab540/handbook/ab_540_handbook.pdf).

California Student Aid Commission. 2011a. "Assembly Bill No. 130." Retrieved April 9, 2013 (http://www.csac.ca.gov/pubs/forms/grnt_frm/AB130.pdf).

———. 2011b. "Assembly Bill No. 131." Retrieved April 9, 2013 (http://www.csac.ca.gov/pubs/forms/grnt_frm/AB131.pdf).

———. n.d. "California Dream Act." Retrieved February 21, 2015 (http://www.csac.ca.gov/dream_act.asp).

Campanile, Carl. 2012. "Illegal Aliens OK: Poll." *New York Post*, December 11. Retrieved January 15, 2013 (http://www.nypost.com/p/news/national/illegal_aliens_ok_poll_RLa3W712b3tJqWCGdXYUtN).

Capps, Randy, Genevieve Kenney, and Michael Fix. 2003. *Health Insurance Coverage of Children in Mixed-Status Immigrant Families* (Urban Institute Report, No. 12). Washington, DC: Urban Institute. Retrieved March 21, 2014 (http://www.urban.org/UploadedPDF/310886_snapshots3_no12.pdf).

Capps, Randy, and Marc R. Rosenblum. 2014. "Executive Action for Unauthorized Immigrants: Estimates of the Populations That Could Receive Relief." *Migration Policy Institute* 10 (September):1–14. Retrieved January 12, 2015 (http://migrationpolicy.org/research/executive-action-unauthorized-immigrants-estimates-populations-could-receive-relief).

Castellanos, Gloria, and Veronica Orozco. 2005. "Perceived Educational Barriers, Cultural Congruity, Coping Responses, and Psychological Well-Being of Latina Undergraduates." *Hispanic Journal of Behavioral Sciences* 27(2):161–183.

Castillo, Mariano. 2012. "For Immigrants, 'Deferred Status' Still Means No Federal Health Insurance." *CNN*, September 20. Retrieved November 28, 2012 (http://www.cnn.com/2012/09/20/us/immigration-daca-health-care/index.html).

Castro-Salazar, Ricardo, and Carl Bagley. 2010. "Ni de Aquí Ni from There—Navigating Between Contexts: Counter-Narratives of Undocumented Mexican Students in the United States." *Race, Ethnicity, and Education* 13(1):23–40.

Catron, Peter. 2013. "Immigrant Unionization Through the Great Recession." *American Sociological Review* 78(2):315–332.

Cavazos, Javier, Michael B. Johnson, and Gregory Scott Sparrow. 2010. "Overcoming Personal and Academic Challenges: Perspectives from Latina/o College Students." *Journal of Hispanic Higher Education* 9(4):304–316.

Centers for Disease Control and Prevention. 2013a. *Teen Birth Rates Drop, but Disparities Persist* (CDC Report). Atlanta, GA: Centers for Disease Control and Prevention. Retrieved August 3, 2013 (http://www.cdc.gov/features/dsteenpregnancy/).

———. 2013b. *Preventing Repeat Teen Births* (CDC Report). Atlanta, GA: Centers for Disease Control and Prevention. Retrieved August 3, 2013 (http://www.cdc.gov/vitalsigns/TeenPregnancy/index.html).

Cerutti, Mario, and Miguel Gonzalez Quiroga. 1990. "Guerra y Comercio en Torno al Río Bravo (1855–1867): Línea Fronteriza, Espacio Económico Común." *Historia Mexicana* 40(2):217–297.

Chapman, Chris, Jennifer Laird, Nicole Ifill, and Angelina Kewal-Ramani. 2011. *Trends in High School Dropout and Completion Rates in the United States: 1972–2009 Compendium Report* (NCES Report). Washington, DC: US Department of Education. Retrieved August 19, 2013 (http://files.eric.ed.gov/fulltext/ED524955.pdf).

Chapman, Mimi V., and Krista M. Perreira. 2005. "The Well-Being of Immigrant Latino Youth: A Framework to Inform Practice." *Families in Society* 86(1):104–111.

Chavez, Hugo. 2008. *The Latino Threat: Constructing Immigrants, Citizens, and the Nation.* Palo Alto, CA: Stanford University Press.

Chavez, Leo R. 2014. "'Illegality' Across Generations: Public Discourse and the Children of Undocumented Immigrants." Pp. 84–110 in *Constructing Immigrant "Illegality": Critiques, Experiences and Responses*, edited by Cecilia Menjívar and Daniel Kanstroom. New York: Cambridge University Press.

Chávez, María Lucia, Mayra Soriano, and Paz Olivarez. 2007. "Undocumented Students' Access to College: The American Dream Denied." *Latino Studies* 5:254–263.

Clark-Ibáñez, Marisol. 2003. *Lessons in Inequality: A Comparative Study of Two Urban Schools*. Dissertation. Department of Sociology at University California, Davis. (http://search.proquest.com/docview/305345601).

———. 2004. "Framing the Social World with Photo-Elicitation Interviews." *American Behavioral Scientist* 47(12):1507–1527.

———. 2005. "Making Meaning of Ability Grouping in Two Urban Schools." *International Review of Modern Sociology* 31(1):57–79.

———. 2007. "Inner-City Children in Sharper Focus: Sociology of Childhood and Photo-Elicitation Interviews." Pp. 167–196 in *Visual Research Methods: Image, Society, and Representation*, edited by G. Stanczak. Thousand Oaks, CA: Sage.

———. 2008. "Gender and Being 'Bad': Inner-City Students' Photographs." Pp. 95–113 in *Doing Visual Research with Children and Young People: Stories from the Field,* edited by P. Thomas. New York: Routledge.

Clark-Ibáñez, Marisol, Fredi García-Alverdín, and Gricelda Alva. 2011. "A Passport to Education: Undocumented Latino University Students Navigating Their Invisible Status." Pp. 497–513 in *International Handbook of Migration, Minorities, and Education: Understanding Cultural and Social Differences in the Process of Learning*, edited by Z. Bekerman and T. Geisen. Dordrecht, Netherlands: Springer.

College Board. n.d. "Advising Undocumented Students." Retrieved January 22, 2015 (http://professionals.collegeboard.com/guidance/financial-aid/undocumented-students).

Collins, Brian A., Claudio O. Toppelberg, Carola Suárez-Orozco, Erin O'Connor, and Alfonso Nieto-Castañon. 2011. "Cross-Sectional Associations of Spanish and English Competence and Well-Being in Latino Children of Immigrants in Kindergarten." *International Journal of Sociology of Language* 208(1):5–23.

The Colorado Oral History and Migratory Labor Project. 2008. *The Bracero Program: 1942–1964*. Retrieved June 2, 2013 (http://www.unco.edu/cohmlp/pdfs/Bracero_Program_PowerPoint.pdf).

Conger, Dylan, and Colin C. Chellman. 2013. "Undocumented College Students in the United States: In-State Tuition Not Enough to Ensure Four-Year Degree Completion." *Education Finance and Policy* 8(3):364–377.

Congress.gov. 2014. All Actions: H.R. 15—113th Congress (2013–2014). Retrieved January 12, 2015 (https://www.congress.gov/bill/113th-congress/house-bill/15/all-actions).

Constantine, Madonna G., Eric C. Chen, and Paulette Ceesay. 1997. "Intake Concerns of Racial and Ethnic Minority Students at a University Counseling Center: Implications for Developmental Programming and Outreach." *Journal of Multicultural Counseling and Development* 25(3):210–218.

Contreras, Frances. 2009. "Sin Papeles y Rompiendo Barreras: Latino Students and the Challenges of Persisting in College." *Harvard Educational Review* 79(4): 610–634.

———. 2011. "Strengthening the Bridge to Higher Education for Academically Promising Underrepresented Students." *Journal of Advanced Academics* 22:500–526.

Cooper, Betsy and Kevin O'Neil. 2005. *Lessons from the Immigration Reform and Control Act of 1986* (MPI Policy Brief). Washington, DC: Migration Policy Institute. Retrieved January 10, 2015 (http://migrationpolicy.org/research/lessons-immigration-reform-and-control-act-1986).

Corsaro, William A. 2003. *We're Friends, Right? Inside Kid's Culture*. Washington, DC: Joseph Henry.

Covarrubias, Alejandro, and Argelia Lara. 2013. "The Undocumented (Im)Migrant Educational Pipeline: The Influence of Citizenship Status on Educational Attainment for People of Mexican Origin." *Urban Education* (advance online publication March 5, 2013:1–36). Retrieved October 2, 2013 (http://uex.sagepub.com/content/early/2013/01/31/0042085912470468.abstract).

Covered California. 2014. *Covered California Open Enrollment: Lessons Learned 2013–2014* (Covered California Report). Sacramento, CA: California Department of Health Care Services. Retrieved January 8, 2015 (https://www.coveredca.com/PDFs/10-14-2014-Lessons-Learned-final.pdf).

Craig, Richard B. 1971. *The Bracero Program: Interest Groups and Foreign Policy*. Austin: University of Texas Press.

Cruz, Jeanette, and John M. Littrell. 1998. "Brief Counseling with Hispanic American College Students." *Journal of Multicultural Counseling and Development* 26(4):227–240.

De Genova, Nicholas P. 2002. "Migrant 'Illegality' and Deportability in Everyday Life." *Annual Review of Anthropology* 31:419–447.

De Genova, Nicholas, and Nathalie Peutz. 2010. *The Deportation Regime: Sovereignty, Space, and the Freedom of Movement*. Durham, NC: Duke University Press.

DeJaeghere, Joan, and Kate S. McCleary. 2010. "The Making of Mexican Migrant Youth Civic Identities: Transnational Spaces and Imaginaries." *Anthropology and Education Quarterly* 41(3):228–244.

Delgado Bernal, Dolores. 2002. "Critical Race Theory, Latino Critical Theory, and Critical Raced-Gendered Epistemologies: Recognizing Students of Color as Holders and Creators of Knowledge." *Qualitative Inquiry* 8(1):105–126.

Delpit, Lisa. 1995. *Other People's Children: Cultural Conflict in the Classroom*. New York: New Press.

Dias, Elizabeth, Steven Gray, and Michael Scherrer. 2011. "Missing: Hispanic Schoolchildren." *Time* (October 17): 14.

Diaz-Strong, Deysi, Maria Luna-Duarte, Christina Gómez, and Erica R. Meiners. 2014. "Too Close to the Work/There Is Nothing Right Now." Pp. 3–20 in *Humanizing Research: Decolonizing Qualitative Inquiry with Youth and Communities*, edited by D. Paris and M. T. Winn. Thousand Oaks, CA: Sage.

Dika, Sandra L., and Kusum Singh. 2002. "Applications of Social Capital in Educational Literature: A Critical Synthesis." *Review of Educational Research* 72(1):31–60.

Doll, Jonathan Jacob, Zohreh Eslami, and Lynne Walters. 2013. "Understanding Why Students Drop Out of High School, According to Their Own Reports: Are They Pushed or Pulled, or Do They Fall Out? A Comparative Analysis of Seven Nationally Representative Studies." *SAGE Open* 3:1–15.

Dowd, Alicia C. 2007. "Community Colleges as Gateways and Gatekeepers: Moving Beyond the Access 'Saga' Toward Outcome Equity." *Harvard Educational Review* 77(4):407–419.

Doyle, Martha, Ciara O'Dywer, and Virpi Timonen. 2010. "'How Can You Just Cut Off a Whole Side of the Family and Say Move On?': The Reshaping of Paternal Grandparent-Grandchild Relationships Following Divorce or Separation in the Middle Generation." *Family Relations* 59(5):587–598.

Dozier, S. B. 1993. "Emotional Concerns of Undocumented and Out-of-Status Foreign Students." *Community Review* 13:33–38.

Dream ACTivist. 2015. "Dream ACTivist, Political Organization." Retrieved March 31, 2015 (https://www.facebook.com/dreamactivist.org).

Dreby, Joanna. 2014. "The Modern Deportation Regime and Mexican Families: The Indirect Consequences for Children in New Destination Communities." Pp. 181–186 in *Constructing Illegality in America: Critiques, Experiences, and Responses,* edited by C. Menjívar and D. Kanstroom. Cambridge, UK: Cambridge University Press.

Drive California. n.d. "Bill AB60." Retrieved December 30, 2014 (http://driveca.org/bill-ab60/).

Durand, Jorge. 2007. "El Programa Bracero (1942–1964): Un Balance Critico." *Migración y Desarrollo* 2(9):27–43.

Easley, Julia Ann. 2014. "Student Helps Establish Center for Fellow Undocumented Students." *UC Davis News Service.* Retrieved December 15, 2014 (http://news.ucdavis.edu/search/news_detail.lasso?id=11033).

Easley, Nate, Margarita Bianco, and Nancy Leech. 2012. "Ganas: A Qualitative Study Examining Mexican Heritage Students' Motivation to Succeed in Higher Education." *Journal of Hispanic Higher Education* 11(2):164–168.

Eisema, Dirk, Tara Fiorito, and Martha Montero-Sieburth. 2014. "Beating the Odds: The Undocumented Youth Movement of Latinos as a Vehicle for Upward Social Mobility." *New Diversities* 16(1):23–39. Retrieved December 12, 2014 (http://newdiversities.mmg.mpg.de/wp-content/uploads/2014/11/2014_16-01_03_Montero.pdf).

Eisen, George. 1990. *Children and Play in the Holocaust: Games Among the Shadows.* Amherst: University of Massachusetts Press.

Ellis, Martha M. 2013. "Successful Community College Transfer Students Speak Out." *Community College Journal of Research and Practice* 37(2):73–84.

Epstein, Reid J. 2014. "National Council of La Raza Leader Calls Barack Obama 'Deporter-in-Chief.'" *POLITICO*, March 4. Retrieved May 26, 2014 (http://www.politico.com/story/2014/03/national-council-of-la-raza-janet-murguia-barack-obama-deporter-in-chief-immigration-104217.html).

Fassinger, Polly A. 1995. "Understanding Classroom Interaction: Students' and Professors' Contributions to Students' Silence." *Journal of Higher Education* 66(1):82–96.

Feldmann, Linda. 2011. "Obama Bemoans Congress's Inaction on Immigration Reform, Too." *Christian Science Monitor*, July 25. Retrieved December 13, 2014 (http://www.csmonitor.com/USA/Politics/2011/0725/Obama-bemoans-Congress-s-inaction-on-immigration-reform-too).

Fernández, José M. 2012. *Reaching for the Stars: The Inspiring Story of a Migrant Farmworker Turned Astronaut.* New York: Center Street Hachette Book Group.

Fix, Michael, and Wendy Zimmermann. 1999. *All Under One Roof: Mixed-Status Families in an Era of Reform* (Urban Institute Report). Washington, DC: Urban Institute. Retrieved January 10, 2015 (http://www.urban.org/UploadedPDF/409100.pdf).

Flores, Stella M. 2010. "State DREAM Acts: The Effect of In-State Resident Tuition Policies and Undocumented Latino Students." *Review of Higher Education* 33(2):239–283.

Flow of History, The. 2013. "A Brief Timeline of U.S. Policy on Immigration and Naturalization." Retrieved January 12, 2013 (http://www.flowofhistory.org/themes/movement_settlement/uspolicytimeline.php).

Foley, Elise. 2013a. "Obama Deportation Toll Could Pass 2 Million at Current Rates." *Huffington Post*, January 31. Retrieved April 20, 2013 (http://www.huffingtonpost.com/2013/01/31/obama-deportation_n_2594012.html).

———. 2013b. "Stephanie Pucheta, 10-Year-Old, On Dad's Deportation: 'Why Do They Have to Be So Cruel?'" *Huffington Post*, May 20, 2013. Retrieved February 1, 2015 (http://www.huffingtonpost.com/2013/05/20/stephanie-pucheta-deportation_n_3303435.html).

Frost, Joe. 2005. "Lessons from Disasters: Play, Work, and the Creative Arts." *Childhood Education* 82(1):2–8.

Galarza, Ernesto. 1964. *Merchants of Labor: The Mexican Bracero Story*. Charlotte, CA: McNally and Loftin.

Gamboa, Eramso. 1990. *Mexican Labor and World War II: Bracero in the Pacific Northwest, 1942–1947*. Austin: University of Texas Press.

Gándara, Patricia. 2010. "The Latino Education Crisis." *Educational Leadership* 67(5):24–30.

Gándara, Patricia, Elizabeth Alvarado, Anne Driscoll, and Gary Orfield. 2012. *Building Pathways to Transfer: Community Colleges That Break the Chain of Failure for Students of Color* (Civil Rights Project/Projecto Derechos Civiles Report). Los Angeles: University of California Los Angeles. Retrieved January 10, 2015 (http://civilrightsproject.ucla.edu/research/college-access/diversity/building-pathways-to-transfer-community-colleges-that-break-the-chain-of-failure-for-students-of-color).

García-Alverdín, Fredi. 2010. "The Experiences of First-Generation Mexican Immigrants in North San Diego County." Thesis, Department of Sociology, California State University, San Marcos.

Gates, Sara. 2012. "California DUI Checkpoint Program Targets Undocumented Immigrants (video)." *Huffington Post,* March 12. Retrieved May 19, 2014. (http://www.huffingtonpost.com/2012/03/12/california-dui-immigration-checkpoint_n_1339772.html).

Gibson, Margaret A. 1988. *Accommodation Without Assimilation: Sikh Immigrants in an American High School*. Ithaca, NY: Cornell University Press.

Gildersleeve, Ryan Evely. 2010. "Access Between and Beyond Borders." *Journal of College Admission* 206(Winter):3–10.

Gillanders, Cristina, and Robert T. Jiménez. 2004. "Reaching for Success: A Close-Up of Mexican Immigrant Parents in the USA Who Foster Literacy Success for Their Kindergarten Children." *Journal of Early Childhood Literacy* 4(3):243–269.

Glick, Jennifer E., and Michael J. White. 2004. "Post-Secondary School Participation of Immigrant and Native Youth: The Role of Familial Resources and Educational Expectations." *Social Science Research* 33:272–299.

Goffman, Erving. 1959. *The Presentation of Self in Everyday Life*. Garden City, NY: Doubleday.

———. 1963. *Stigma: Notes on the Management of Spoiled Identity*. Englewood Cliffs, NJ: Prentice-Hall.

Golash-Boza, Tanya M. 2012. *Immigration Nation: Raids, Detentions, and Deportations in Post-9/11 America*. Boulder: Paradigm Publishers.

Golash-Boza, Tanya M., and Pierrette Hondagneu-Sotelo. 2013. "Latino Immigrant Men and the Deportation Crisis: A Gendered Racial Removal Program." *Latino Studies* 11(3):271–292.

Gonzales, Alfonso. 2013. *Reform Without Justice: Latino Migrant Politics and the Homeland Security State*. New York: Oxford University Press.

Gonzales, Roberto G. 2007. "Wasted Talent and Broken Dreams: The Lost Potential of Undocumented Students." *Immigration Policy: In Focus* 5:1–11.

———. 2010. "On the Wrong Side of the Tracks: Understanding the Effects of School Structure and Social Capital in the Educational Pursuits of Undocumented Immigrant Students." *Peabody Journal of Education* 85:469–485.

———. 2011. "Learning to Be Illegal: Undocumented Youth and Shifting Legal Contexts in the Transition to Adulthood." *American Sociological Review* 76(4):602–619.

Gonzales, Roberto G., Carola Suárez-Orozco, and Maria Cecilia Dedios-Sanguineti. 2013. "No Place to Belong: Contextualizing Concepts of Mental Health Among Undocumented Immigrant Youth in the United States." *American Behavioral Scientist* 57(8):1174–1199.

GovTrack. 2013. "S. 744: Border Security, Economic Opportunity, and Immigration Modernization Act. On Passage of the Bill in the Senate." Retrieved December 13, 2014 (https://www.govtrack.us/congress/votes/113-2013/s168).

Greenwood, Michael J., and Fred A. Ziel. 1997. "The Impact of the Immigration Act of 1990 on U.S. Immigration." Retrieved February 20, 2013 (http://migration.ucdavis.edu//mn/cir/greenwood/combined.htm).

Grossman, Jennifer M., and Linda Charmaraman. 2009. "Race, Context, and Privilege: White Adolescents' Explanations of Racial-Ethnic Centrality." *Journal of Youth and Adolescence* 38(2):139–152.

Guevara, Diana. 2013. "San Diego Immigrants Go Public with Undocumented Status." *NBC San Diego,* March 13. Retrieved April 9, 2013 (http://www.nbcsandiego.com/news/local/San-Diego-Immigrants-Go-Public-With-Undocumented-Status-197688241.html).

Guillory, Raphael M., and Mimi Wolverton. 2008. "It's About Family: Native American Student Persistence in Higher Education." *Journal of Higher Education* 79(1):58–87.

Hall, Roberta M., and Bernice R. Sandler. 1982. *The Classroom Climate: A Chilly One for Women?* Washington, DC: Association of American Colleges.

Hart, Roger A. 1992. *Children's Participation: From Tokenism to Citizenship* (Inocenti Essays, No. 4). Florence, Italy: UNICEF ICDC. Retrieved January 10, 2015 (http://www.unicef-irc.org/publications/pdf/childrens_participation.pdf).

Heckman, James, Seong Hyeok, Rodrigo Pinto, Peter A. Savelyev, and Adam Yavitz. 2009. "The Rate of Return to the High/Scope Perry Preschool Program" (NBER Working Paper Series, No. 15471). Cambridge, MA: National Bureau of Economic Research. Retrieved June 19, 2014 (http://www.nber.org/papers /w15471.pdf).

Heidbrink, Lauren. 2014. *Migrant Youth, Transnational Families, and the State: Care and Contested Interests*. Philadelphia: University of Pennsylvania Press.

Herdoiza, Patricia C. 2012. "Undocumented Status and Educational Outcomes Among Latino Students." Thesis, Department of Psychology, American University, Washington, DC.

Hernandez, David Manuel. 2008. "Pursuant to Deportation: Latinos and Immigrant Detention." *Latino Studies* 6:35–63.

Hernandez, Susana, Ignacio Hernandez, Rebecca Gadson, Deneece Huftalin, Anna M. Ortiz, Mistalene Calleroz White, and DeAnn Yocum-Gaffne. 2011. "Sharing Their Secrets: Undocumented Students' Personal Stories of Fear, Drive, and Survival." *New Directions for Student Services* 131:67–84.

Hing, Julianne. 2009. "DREAMer Walter Lara's Delayed Deportation a Pyrrhic Victory for Immigrant Rights." Colorlines.com. Retrieved March 1, 2015 (http://colorlines.com/archives/2009/07/dreamer_walter_laras_delayed_d.html).

Hinojosa-Ojeda, Raúl. 2010. *Raising the Floor for American Workers: The Economic Benefits of Comprehensive Immigration Reform* (Center for American Progress and Immigration Policy Center Report). Washington, DC: Center for American Progress. Retrieved December 18, 2014 (http://cdn.americanprogress.org/wp-content/uploads/2012/09/immigrationeconreport3.pdf).

———. 2012. "The Economic Benefits of Comprehensive Immigration Reform." *Cato Journal* 32(1):175–199. Retrieved October 4, 2013 (http://www.cato.org/sites/cato.org/files/serials/files/cato-journal/2012/1/cj32n1-12.pdf).

Hinojosa-Ojeda, Raúl, and Sherman Robinson. 2013. *Adding It Up: Accurately Gauging the Economic Impact of Immigration Reform* (Immigration Policy Center Report). Washington, DC: American Immigrant Council. Retrieved September 5, 2013 (http://www.immigrationpolicy.org/just-facts/adding-it-accurately-gauging-economic-impact-immigration-reform).

Hondagneu-Sotelo, Pierrette. 1994. *Gendered Transitions: Mexican Experiences of Immigration*. Berkeley: University of California Press.

Houston, Cynthia R., and Roxanne M. Spencer. 2007. "From Aula Biblioteca to Biblioteca Aula: Integrating a School Library Program into the English Language Program of a Spanish School." *Library Review* 56:34–44.

Hovey, Joseph D. 2000. "Acculturative Stress, Depression, and Suicidal Ideation Among Central American Immigrants." *Suicide and Life-Threatening Behavior* 30:125–139.

Hovey, Joseph D., and C. A. King. 1996. "Acculturative Stress, Depression, and Suicidal Ideation Among Immigrant and Second Generation Latino Adolescents." *Journal of the American Academy of Child and Adolescent Psychiatry* 35:1183–1192.

Human Rights Watch. 2010. *Fields of Peril: Child Labor in US Agriculture*. Published May 2010, Report 1-56432-628-4. Retrieved January 8, 2015 (http://www.hrw.org/sites/default/files/reports/crd0510webwcover_1.pdf)

———. 2014. *Tobacco's Hidden Children: Hazardous Child Labor in United States Tobacco Farming*. Published May 2014, Report 978-1-62313-1340. Retrieved January 8, 2015 (http://www.hrw.org/sites/default/files/reports/us0514_UploadNew.pdf).

Illinois General Assembly. 2011. "Full Text of SB 0957." Retrieved January 9, 2013 (http://www.ilga.gov/legislation/fulltext.asp?DocName=&SessionId=84&GA=97&DocTypeId=SB&DocNum=957&GAID=11&LegID=&SpecSess=&Session=).

———. 2012. "State of Illinois 97th General Assembly Senate Vote. Senate Bill No. 957, Third Reading." Retrieved January 9, 2013 (http://www.ilga.gov/legislation/votehistory/97/senate/09700SB0957_12042012_008000T.pdf).

———. 2013. "State of Illinois Ninety-Seventh General Assembly. House Roll Call Senate Bill 957. Transportation-Tech, Third Reading, Passed." Retrieved January 9, 2013 (http://www.ilga.gov/legislation/votehistory/97/house/09700SB0957_01082013_009000T.pdf).

Immigration Policy Center. 2011. "The DREAM Act." Retrieved April 15, 2014. (http://www.immigrationpolicy.org/just-facts/dream-act).

———. 2013. "An Immigration Stimulus: The Economic Benefits of a Legalization Program" Retrieved May 10, 2013 (http://www.immigrationpolicy.org/just-facts/immigration-stimulus-economic-benefits-legalization-program).

Ingold, John. 2012. "Immigration Activists Stage Sit-In at Denver Obama Office." *Denver Post,* June 5. Retrieved January 16, 2013 (http://www.denverpost.com/breakingnews/ci_20791243/immigration-activists-stage-sit-at-denver-obama-office).

Institute of Portland Metropolitan Studies. 2011. "Immigration and Naturalization Act of 1965: Origin of Modern American Society." Retrieved February 25, 2013 (http://www.upa.pdx.edu/IMS/currentprojects/TAHv3/Immigration_Act.html).

Irizarry, Jason G. 2011. *The Latinization of U.S. Schools: Successful Teaching and Learning in Shifting Cultural Contexts.* Boulder: Paradigm Publishers.

IYJL. 2015. "Immigrant Youth Justice League." Retrieved March 31, 2015. (http://www.iyjl.org/stopdeportations/).

Jauregui, John A., John R. Slate, and Michelle Stallone Brown. 2008. "Texas Community Colleges and Characteristics of a Growing Undocumented Student Population." *Journal of Hispanic Higher Education* 7(4):346–355.

Jauregui, John Andrew, and John R. Slate. 2009. "Texas Borderland Community Colleges and Views Regarding Undocumented Students: A Qualitative Study." *College Retention* 11(2):183–210.

Jefferies, Julián. 2014. "Fear of Deportation in High School: Implications for Breaking the Circle of Silence Surrounding Migration Status." *Journal of Latinos and Education* 13(4):278–295.

Jiménez, Tomás R. 2011. *Immigrants in the United States: How Well Are They Integrating into Society?* (MPI Report). Washington, DC: Migration Policy Institute. Retrieved February 26, 2013 (http://www.migrationpolicy.org/pubs/integration-jimenez.pdf).

Johnson, Allan G. 2008. *The Forest and the Trees: Sociology as Life, Practice, and Promise.* Philadelphia, PA: Temple University Press.

Junn, Jane, and Kerry L. Haynie, eds. 2008. *New Race Politics in America: Understanding Minority and Immigrant Politics.* New York: Cambridge University Press.

Kerwin, Donald M. 2010. *More Than IRCA: US Legalization Programs and the Current Policy Debate* (MPI Policy Brief). Washington, DC: Migration Policy Institute. Retrieved January 10, 2015 (http://migrationpolicy.org/research/us-legalization-programs-by-the-numbers).

Khokha, Sasha. 2006. "MySpace Roots of Student Protests." *NPR,* March 29. Retrieved April 9, 2013 (http://www.npr.org/2006/03/29/5309238/text-message-myspace-roots-of-student-protests).

King, Desmond S., and Roger M. Smith. 2012. *Race and Politics in Obama's America.* NJ: Princeton University Press.

King, Kendall, and Gemma Punti. 2012. "On the Margins: Undocumented Students' Narrated Experiences of (Il)legality." *Linguistics and Education* 23(3):235–249.

King, Ryan D., Michael Massoglia, and Christopher Uggen. 2012. "Employment and Exile: U.S. Criminal Deportations, 1908–2005." *American Journal of Sociology* 117:1786–1825.

Ladson-Billings, Gloria. 1994. *The Dreamkeepers: Successful Teachers of African American Children.* San Francisco, CA: Jossey-Bass.

Lal, Prerna. 2015. "Prerna Lal, Immigration Attorney and Human Rights Advocate." Retrieved March 31, 2015 (www.prernalal.com/).

Lambert, Lisa. 2012. "Obama Seeks Comprehensive Immigration Reform in Early 2013." Reuters, November 14. Retrieved March 20, 2013 (http://www.reuters.com/article/2012/11/14/usa-obama-immigration-idUSL1E8MEHCB20121114).

Lareau, Annette. 2003. *Unequal Childhoods: Class, Race, and Family Life*. Berkeley: University of California Press.

Lee, Elizabeth M., and Grace Kao. 2009. "Less Bang for the Buck?: Cultural Capital and Immigrant Status Effects on Kindergarten Academic Outcomes." *Poetics* 37:201–226.

Leitner, Helga, and Christopher Strunk. 2014. "Assembling Insurgent Citizenship: Immigrant Advocacy in the Washington DC Metropolitan Area." *Urban Geographer* 35(7):943–964.

LeMay, Michael C. 2007. *Illegal Immigration: A Reference Handbook*. Santa Barbara, CA: ABC-Clio.

León, Esmeralda. 2014. "Demandan Pago para ex Braceros en el PRI." *Enfoque Oaxaca*, April 7. Retrieved April 30, 2014 (http://enfoqueoaxaca.com/en-portada/demandan-pago-para-ex-braceros-en-el-pri/).

Lesane-Brown, Chase L. 2006. "A Review of Race Socialization Within Black Families." *Developmental Review* 26:400–426.

Linthicum, Kate. 2014. "Obama Ends Secure Communities Program as Part of Immigration Action." *Los Angeles Times*, November 21. Retrieved December 18, 2014 (http://www.latimes.com/local/california/la-me-1121-immigration-justice-20141121-story.html).

Llorente, Elizabeth, and Brian Llenas. 2015. "The Border Surge, a Year Later: Tens of Thousands of Immigrant Children Remain in Limbo." Fox Latino News, June 2. Retrieved June 14, 2015 (http://latino.foxnews.com/latino/politics /2015/06/02/border-surge-year-later-tens-thousands-immigrant-children-remain-in-limbo/).

Macias, Jorge Luis. 2014. "Gobierno: Braceros y Sus Familias Siguen Exigiendo Su Dinero." *La Prensa*, April 11. Retrieved April 30, 2014 (http://www.laprensaenlinea.com/noticias/noticias-historias/20140411-gobierno-braceros-y-sus-familias-siguen-exigiendo-su-dinero.ece).

Macmillan, Ross, ed. 2005. *The Structure of the Life Course: Standardized? Individualized? Differentiated?* Amsterdam: Jai.

Mandeel, Elizabeth W. 2014. "The Bracero Program, 1942–1964." *American International Journal of Contemporary Research* 4(1):171–184.

Martin, Philip, and Elizabeth Midgley. 2003. "Immigration: Shaping and Reshaping America." *Population Bulletin* 58(2):1–46.

Martinez, Lisa M. 2014. "Dreams Deferred: The Impact of Legal Reforms on Undocumented Youth." *American Behavioral Scientist* 58(4):1873–1890.

Martinez, Silvia, and Yesenia Lucia Cervera. 2012. "Fulfilling Educational Aspirations: Latino Students' College Information-Seeking Patterns." *Journal of Hispanic Higher Education* 11(4):388–402.

Martínez-Calderón, Carmen. 2009. *Out of the Shadows: Undocumented Latino College Students* (ISSC Working Paper Series, No. 34). Berkeley, CA: Institute for the Study of Societal Issues. Retrieved August 28, 2013 (http://escholarship.org/uc/item/9zj0694b).

Massey, Douglas S., Jorge Durand, and Nolan J. Malone. 2002. *Beyond Smoke and Mirrors: Mexican Immigration in an Age of Economic Integration*. New York: Russell Sage Foundation.

McKillip, Mary E. M., Anita Rawls, and Carol Barry. 2012. "Improving College Access: A Review of Research on the Role of High School Counselors." *Professional School Counseling* 16:49–58.

Meckler, Laura. 2014. "Obama Delays Executive Action on Immigration Until After Elections." *Wall Street Journal*, September 6. Retrieved December 12, 2014 (http://www.wsj.com/articles/obama-to-delay-executive-action-on-immigration-until-after-elections-1410015015).

Mejía, Olga, and Christopher J. McCarthy. 2010. "Acculturative Stress, Depression, and Anxiety in Migrant Farmwork College Students of Mexican Heritage." *International Journal of Stress Management* 17(1):1–20.

Melendez Salinas, Claudia. 2014. "Alejo to Host Town Hall Meeting on Driver's Licenses." *Monterey Herald*, September 2. Retrieved December 12, 2014 (http://www.montereyherald.com/20140902/alejo-to-host-town-hall-meeting-on-drivers-licenses).

Menjívar, Cecilia. 2006. "Liminal Legality: Salvadoran and Guatemalan Immigrants' Lives in the United States." *American Journal of Sociology* 111(4):999–1037.

———. 2008. "Educational Hopes, Documented Dreams: Guatemalan and Salvadoran Immigrants' Legality and Educational Prospects." *Annals of the American Academy of Political and Social Science* 620:177–191.

Menjívar, Cecilia, and Leisy Abrego. 2012. *Legal Violence in the Lives of Immigrants: How Immigration Enforcement Affects Families, Schools, and Workplaces*. Washington, DC: Center for American Progress.

Mexican American Legal Defense and Education Fund. 2009. "AB 540: Access to College for All." Retrieved December 20, 2012 (http://www.maldef.org/education/public_policy/ab540/index.html).

Mills, C. Wright. 1959. *The Sociological Imagination*. New York: Oxford University Press.

Milner, H. Richard. 2011. "Culturally Relevant Pedagogy in a Diverse Urban Classroom." *Urban Review* 43(1):66–89.

Mintz, Steven. 2014. "Childhood and Transatlantic Slavery." *Children and Youth in History*, Item 57. Retrieved June 17, 2014 (http://chnm.gmu.edu/cyh/case-studies/57).

Mize, Ronald L. 2006. "Mexican Contract Workers and the U.S. Capitalist Agricultural Labor Process: The Formative Era, 1942–1964." *Rural Sociology* 71(1):85–108.

Moll, Luis, Cathy Amanti, Deborah Neff, and Norma Gonzalez. 1992. "Funds of Knowledge for Teaching: Using a Qualitative Approach to Connect Homes and Classrooms." *Theory into Practice* 31(2):132–141.

Monning, Elizabeth. 2014. "Coping Strategies of Jewish Children Who Suffered the Holocaust." *Arizona Journal of Interdisciplinary Studies* 3:42–56.

Moorman, Sara M., and Jeffrey E. Stokes. 2013. "Does Solidarity in the Grandparent/Grandchild Relationship Protect Against Depressive Symptoms?" Paper presented at the annual meeting of the American Sociological Association, August 12, New York, NY.

Morales, Amanda, Socorro G. Herrera, and Kevin Murry. 2011. "Navigating the Tides of Social and Political Capriciousness: Inspiring Perspectives from DREAM-Eligible Students." *Journal of Hispanics in Higher Education* 10(3):266–283.

Morris, Rebecca J. 2012. "Find Where You Fit in the Common Core, or the Time I Forgot About Librarians and Reading." *Teacher Librarian* 39:8–12.

Mulkey, Lynn M., Sophia Catsambis, Lala Carr Steelman, and Melanie Hanes-Ramos. 2009. "Keeping Track of or Getting Offtrack: Issues in the Tracking of Students." *International Handbook of Research on Teachers and Teaching* 21:1081–1100.

Muñoz, Susana Maria. 2008. "Understanding Issues of College Persistence for Undocumented Mexican Immigrant Women from the New Latino Diaspora." PhD dissertation, Department of Education, Iowa State University, Ames, IA.

Myhill, William N., Renee Franklin Hill, Kristen Link, Ruth V. Small, and Kelly Bunch. 2012. "Developing the Capacity of Teacher-Librarians to Meet the Diverse Needs of All Schoolchildren: Project ENABLE." *Journal of Research in Special Educational Needs* 12:201–216.

Nakano Glenn, Evelyn. 2011. "Constructing Citizenship: Exclusion, Subordination, and Resistance." *American Sociological Review* 76(1):1–24.

National Conference of State Legislatures. 2012. "Ensuring Latino Success in College and the Workforce." Retrieved February 11, 2013 (http://www.ncsl.org/research/education/ensuring-latino-success-in-college-and-workforce.aspx).

———. 2014. "Allow In-State Tuition for Undocumented Students." Retrieved April 9, 2013 (http://www.ncsl.org/issues-research/educ/undocumented-student-tuition-state-action.aspx).

National Immigration Law Center. 2012. "DACA and Driver's Licenses: Will Individuals Granted Deferred Action Under the Deferred Action for Childhood Arrival (DACA) Policy Be Eligible for Driver's Licenses?" Retrieved January 4, 2013 (http://www.nilc.org/dacadriverslicenses.html).

Nault, Kyle. 2014. "Titan Dreamers Center Opens Its Doors." *Daily Titan*, April 23. Retrieved December 14, 2014 (http://www.dailytitan.com/2014/04/titan-dreamers-resource-center-opens-its-doors/).

Navarrete, Julio N. 2013. "The Implications of Using Creative Writing as a Way of Coping with the Socio-Emotional Challenges of Undocumented College Students and Graduates." Unpublished thesis, Department of Education, National Hispanic University, San Jose, CA. Retrieved January 11, 2015 (http://www.julionavarrete.com/uploads/8/6/9/6/8696856/julio_navarrete_-_undocumented_student_voices.pdf).

Neff, James Alan, and Sue Keir Hoppe. 1993. "Race/Ethnicity, Acculturation, and Psychological Distress: Fatalism and Religiosity as Cultural Resources." *Journal of Community Psychology* 21(1):3–20.

Negrón-Gonzales, Genevieve. 2013. "Navigating 'Illegality': Undocumented Youth and Oppositional Consciousness." *Children and Youth Services Review* 35: 1284–1290.

New Partnership Foundation. 2010. "What Is AB 540?" Retrieved April 9, 2013 (http://ab540.com/whatisab540.html).

Nguyen, David H. K., and Gabriel R. Serna. 2014. "Access or Barrier? Tuition and Fee Legislation for Undocumented Students Across the States." *Clearing House: A Journal of Educational Strategies, Issues, and Ideas* 87(3):124–129.

Nhan, Doris. 2012. "Electoral Maps: Results Indicate Deepening Racial Divide Among Voters." *National Journal*, November 8. Retrieved January 20, 2012 (http://www.nationaljournal.com/thenextamerica/politics/electoral-maps-results-indicate-deepening-racial-divide-among-voters-20121107).

Nicholls, Walter J., and Tara Fiorito. 2015. "Dreamers Unbound: Immigrant Youth Mobilizing." *New Labor Forum* 24(1):1–7. Retrieved April 1, 2015 (http://newlaborforum.cuny.edu/2015/01/17/winter-2015/).

Niehaus, Kate, Kathleen Mortiz Rudasill, and Jill L. Adelson. 2012. "Self-Efficacy, Intrinsic Motivation, and Academic Outcomes Among Latino Middle School Students Participating in an After-School Program." *Hispanic Journal of Behavioral Sciences* 34(1):118–136.

NIYA. 2015. "National Immigrant Youth Alliance." Retrieved March 31, 2015 (http://theniya.org/).

No Papers No Fear. 2015. "About the 'No Papers, No Fear' Ride for Justice." Retrieved March 31, 2015 (http://nopapersnofear.org/).

Nuñez-Alvárez, Arcela, and Ana Ardón. 2012. "Latinos in San Diego County: Understanding the Contributions and Challenges of Families in 2012 and Beyond." Report given at conference, April 4, 2012, California State University, San Marcos. Retrieved December 1, 2014 (http://www.csusm.edu/nlrc/2012_Latino_Conference.html).

Oakes, Jeannie. 1985. *Keeping Track: How America's Schools Structure Inequality*. New Haven, CT: Yale University Press.

Ochoa, Gilda L. 2013. *Academic Profiling: Latinos, Asian Americans, and the Achievement Gap*. Minneapolis: University of Minnesota Press.

Ojeda, Lizette, Brandy Piña-Watson, Linda G. Castillo, Rosalinda Castillo, Noshaba Khan, and Jennifer Leigh. 2012. "Acculturation, Enculturation, Ethnic Identity, and Conscientiousness as Predictors of Latino Boys' and Girls' Career Decision Self-Efficacy." *Journal of Career Development* 39(2):208–222.

Olivas, Michael A. 1995. "Storytelling out of School: Undocumented College Residency, Race, and Reaction." *Hastings Constitutional Law Quarterly* 22:1019–1086.

———. 2004. "IIRIRA, the DREAM Act, and Undocumented College Student Residency." *Journal of College and University Law* 30:435–464.

———. 2010. Plyler v. Doe: *Still Guaranteeing Unauthorized Immigrant Children's Right to Attend U.S. Public Schools* (Migration Information Source Feature). Washington, DC: Migration Policy Institute. Retrieved May 3, 2014 (http://www.migrationinformation.org/feature/display.cfm?ID=795).

Olivérez, Paz Maya. 2006. "Ready but Restricted: An Examination of the Challenges of College Access and Financial Aid for College-Ready Undocumented Immigrant Students in the United States." PhD dissertation, Rossier School of Education, University of Southern California, Los Angeles. Retrieved June 10, 2012 (http://digitallibrary.usc.edu/cdm/ref/collection/p15799coll127/id/168544).

Olivo, Antonio. 2009. "Student's Deportation Is Stayed." *Chicago Tribune*, December 11. Retrieved April 9, 2013 (http://articles.chicagotribune.com/2009-12-11/business/chi-121109-immigration-rigo-padilla_1_rigo-padilla-illegal-immigration-homeland-security).

Ortiz, Carlos J., Melissa A. Valerio, and Kristina López. 2012. "Trends in Hispanic Academic Achievement: Where Do We Go from Here?" *Journal of Hispanic Higher Education* 11(2):136–148.

Ortiz Uribe, Monica. 2013. "Guest Worker Programs Have a Long History in U.S." *Fronteras Desk*. Retrieved November 9, 2014 (http://www.fronterasdesk.org/news/2013/apr/17/guest-worker-programs-have-long-history-us/).

Oseguera, Leticia. 2012. *High School Coursework and Postsecondary Education Trajectories: Disparities Between Youth Who Grew Up in and out of Poverty* (PATHWAYS to Postsecondary Success Research Brief, No. 2). Los Angeles, CA: UC/ACCORD. Retrieved October 7, 2013 (http://pathways.gseis.ucla.edu/publications/201201_OsegueraRB_online.pdf).

Otiniano, Angie Denisse, Amy Carroll-Scott, Peggy Toy, and Steven P. Wallace. 2012. "Supporting Latino Communities' Natural Helpers: A Case Study of Promotoras in a Research Capacity Building Course." *Journal of Immigrant Minority Health* 14(4):657–663.

Paral, Rob, Madura Wijewardena, and Walter Ewing. 2009. *Economic Progress via Legalization: Lessons from the Last Legalization Program* (IPC Special Report). Washington, DC: Immigration Policy Center. Retrieved January 11, 2015 (http://immigrationpolicy.org/sites/default/files/docs/economic_progress_via_legalization_-_paral.pdf).

Paris, Django, and Maisha T. Winn, eds. 2014. *Humanizing Research: Decolonizing Qualitative Inquiry with Youth and Communities.* Thousand Oaks, CA: Sage.

Parker, Ashley, and Robert Pear. 2014. "Senate Passes $1.1 Trillion Spending Bill, Joining House." *New York Times*, December 13. Retrieved December 18, 2014 (http://www.nytimes.com/2014/12/14/us/senate-spending-package.html).

Parra-Cardona, Jos, Laurie A. Bulock, David R. Imig, Francisco A. Villaruel, and Steven J. Gold. 2006. "'Trabando Duro Todos los Días': Learning from the Life Experiences of Mexican-Origin Migrant Families." *Family Relations* 55(3):361–375.

Passel, Jeffrey S. 2005. *Estimates of the Size and Characteristics of the Undocumented Population* (Pew Research Hispanic Trends Project Report). Washington, DC: Pew Research Center. Retrieved June 30, 2013 (http://www.pewhispanic.org/2005/03/21/estimates-of-the-size-and-characteristics-of-the-undocumented-population/).

Passel, Jeffrey S., and D'Vera Cohn. 2011. *Unauthorized Immigrant Population: National and State Trends, 2010* (Pew Research Hispanic Trends Project Report). Washington, DC: Pew Research Center. Retrieved October 4, 2013 (http://www.pewhispanic.org/2011/02/01/unauthorized-immigrant-population-brnational-and-state-trends-2010/).

Passel, Jeffrey S., D'Vera Cohn, and Ana Gonzalez-Barrera. 2013. *Population Decline of Unauthorized Immigrants Stalls, May Have Reversed* (Pew Research Hispanic Trends Project Report). Washington, DC: Pew Research Center. Retrieved March 25, 2014 (http://www.pewhispanic.org/files/2013/09/Unauthorized-Sept-2013-FINAL.pdf).

Passel, Jeffrey S., and Paul Taylor. 2010. *Unauthorized Immigrants and Their U.S.-Born Children* (Pew Research Hispanic Trends Project Report). Washington, DC: Pew Research Center. Retrieved August 28, 2013 (http://www.pewhispanic.org/2010/08/11/iii-household-structure-mixed-families/).

Pérez, Patricia A., and Patricia M. McDonough. 2008. "Understanding Latina and Latino College Choice: A Social Capital and Chain Migration Analysis." *Journal of Hispanic Higher Education* 7:249–265.

Perez, William. 2009. *We Are Americans: Undocumented Immigrants Pursuing the American Dream.* Sterling, VA: Stylus.

Perez, William, Roberta Espinoza, Karina Ramos, Heidi Coronado, and Richard Cortes. 2009. "Academic Resilience Among Undocumented Latino Students." *Hispanic Journal of Behavioral Sciences* 31:149–181.

———. 2010. "Civic Engagement Patterns of Undocumented Mexican Students." *Journal of Hispanic Higher Education* 9(3):245–265.

Pérez Huber, Lindsay. 2010. "Using Latina/o Critical Race Theory (LatCrit) and Racist Nativism to Explore Intersectionality in the Educational Experiences of Undocumented Chicana College Students." *Educational Foundations* 24:77–96.

Planas, Roque. 2012. "Lawsuit Challenges Arizona Driver's License Ban for DACA Immigrants." *Huffington Post*, November 29. Retrieved March 27, 2013 (http://www.huffingtonpost.com/2012/11/29/arizona-immigrants-drivers-license_n_2212261.html).

Plocharczyk, Leah. 2008. "Meeting Multicultural Needs in School Libraries: An Examination of Mexican Migrant Families and Factors That Influence Academic Success." *Journal of Access Services* 3:45–50.

Portes, Alejandro. 2000. "The Two Meanings of Social Capital." *Sociological Forum* 15:1–12.

Portes, Alejandro, and Rubén G. Rumbaut. 2001. *Legacies: The Story of the Immigrant Second Generation.* Berkeley: University of California Press.

———. 2006. *Immigrant America: A Portrait.* Berkeley: University of California Press.

Prengaman, Peter. 2006. "Thousands Rally in California for Immigrants' Rights." *Lawrence Journal World* (March 26). Retrieved January 16, 2013 (http://www2.ljworld.com/news/2006/mar/26/thousands_rally_california_immigrants_rights/).

Preston, Julia. 2012. "Latino Groups Warn Congress to Fix Immigration, or Else." *New York Times: The Caucus,* December 12. Retrieved January 20, 2013 (http://thecaucus.blogs.nytimes.com/2012/12/12/latino-groups-warn-congress-to-fix-immigration-or-else/).

Ramirez, Axel Donizetti. 2012. "Latino Cultural Knowledge in the Classroom Setting." *Journal of Hispanic Higher Education* 11(1):213–226.

Raskoff, Sally. 2010. "Ritual Season." Retrieved August 28, 2013 (http://www.everydaysociologyblog.com/2010/06/ritual-season.html).

Reyes, Barbara. 2010. *Defensive Motherhood: The Negotiation of the Everyday Lives of Undocumented Mexican Mothers.* Thesis. Master of Arts in Sociological Practice at California State University, San Marcos. Retrieved January 20, 2012 (http://csusm-dspace.calstate.edu/handle/10211.3/122497).

Rickerd, Chris. 2012. "Whitewashing S-Comm's Immigration Enforcement Failures." Retrieved January 25, 2013 (http://www.aclu.org/blog/immigrants-rights-racial-justice/whitewashing-s-comms-immigration-enforcement-failures).

Rincón, Alejandra. 2008. *Undocumented Immigrants and Higher Education: Sí Se Puede!* New York: LFB Scholarly Publishing.

Rivera-Silber, Natasha. 2013. "'Coming Out' Undocumented in the Age of Perry." *NYU Review of Law and Social Change* 37(1):71–78.

Robertson, Charlotte. 2014. "Slacktivism: The Downfall of Millennials." *Huffington Post*, October 14. Retrieved March 15, 2015 (http://www.huffingtonpost.com/charlotte-robertson/slacktivism-the-downfall-_b_5984336.html).

Rosenblum, Marc R., and Kate Brick. 2011. *US Immigration Policy and Mexican/Central American Migration Flows: Then and Now* (MPI Report). Washington, DC: Migration Policy Institute. Retrieved January 11, 2015 (http://migrationpolicy.org/research/RMSG-us-immigration-policy-mexican-central-american-migration-flows).

Ross, Terris, Grace Kena, Amy Rathbun, Angelina Kewal-Ramani, Jijun Zhang, Paul Kristapovich, and Eileen Manning. 2012. *Higher Education: Gaps in Access and Persistence Study* (NCES Report, NCES 2012-046). Washington, DC: Government Printing Office. Retrieved August 16, 2013 (http://nces.ed.gov/pubs2012/2012046.pdf).

Rotherham, Andrew J. 2011. "The Education Crisis No One Is Talking About." *Time* (May 12). Retrieved January 24, 2013 (http://www.time.com/time/nation/article/0,8599,2070930,00.html#ixzz2IuetfhzW).

Rural Migration News. 2006. "Bracero: History, Compensation." Retrieved January 20, 2013 (https://migration.ucdavis.edu/rmn/more.php?id=1112).

Ryabov, Igor. 2009. "The Role of Peer Social Capital in Educational Assimilation of Immigrant Youths." *Sociological Inquiry* 79(4):453–480.

Sacchetti, Maria. 2013. "Program Deports Many with No Criminal Record." *Boston Globe*, February 17. Retrieved December 14, 2014 (http://www.bostonglobe.com/metro/2013/02/17/seccomm/5T1u8iv24z48Y19t4UHmTJ/story.html).

Saenz, Victor B., and Luis Ponjuan. 2009. "The Vanishing Latino Male in Higher Education." *Journal of Hispanic Higher Education* 8(1):54–89.

Salazar Parreñas, Rhacel. 2005. *Children of Global Migration: Transnational Families and Gendered Woes*. Palo Alto, CA: Stanford University Press.

San Diego Dream Team. 2015. "San Diego Dream Team, Immigrant Youth Led Community Organization Based in San Diego County." Retrieved March 31, 2015. (http://sandiegodreamteam.org/).

Save the Children. n.d. "U.S. Border Crisis." Retrieved June 14, 2015 (http://www.savethechildren.org/site/c.8rKLIXMGIpI4E/b.9152023/k.9C56/US_Border_Crisis.htm?msource=wexgpubx0614).

Schelzing, Erik. 2014. "Corker Hits Fellow Republicans over Immigration." *Tennessean*, November 6. Retrieved December 14, 2014 (http://www.tennessean.com/story/news/politics/2014/11/06/corker-hits-fellow-republicans-immigration/18622409/).

Schmid, Carol L. 2014. "Undocumented Childhood Immigrants, the DREAM Act, and Deferred Action for Childhood Arrivals (DACA) in the United States." *International Journal of Sociology and Social Policy* 33:693–707.

Schuster, Liza, and Nassim Majidi. 2014. "Deportation Stigma and Re-migration." *Journal of Ethnic and Migration Studies*, 1–18. Retrieved on January 8, 2015 (http://www.tandfonline.com/doi/abs/10.1080/1369183X.2014.957174#.VLOPl2TF_yN).

Seif, H. 2004. "Wise Up!: Undocumented Latino Youth, Mexican-American Legislators, and the Struggle for Higher Education Access." *Latino Studies* 2:210–230.

Shapiro, Doug, Afet Dundar, Jin Chen, Mary Ziskin, Eunkyoung Park, Vasti Torres, and Yi-Chen Chiang. 2012. *Completing College: A National View of Student Attainment Rates*. Signature Report 4, November 2012, National Student Clearinghouse Research Center. Retrieved December 3, 2014 (http://content.nwacc.edu/publicrelations/CostContainment/NSC_Signature_Report_4.pdf).

Shifman, Limor. 2013. "Memes in a Digital World: Reconciling with a Conceptual Troublemaker." *Journal of Computer-Mediated Communication* 18:362–377.

Smith, Lorna. 2012. "Slowing the Summer Slide." *Resourceful School* 69(4):60–63. Retrieved May 1, 2013 (http://www.ascd.org/publications/educational-leadership/dec11/vol69/num04/Slowing-the-Summer-Slide.aspx).

Solis, Carmen, Edwardo L. Portillos, and Rod K. Brunson. 2009. "Latino Youths' Experiences with and Perceptions of Involuntary Police Encounters." *Annals of the American Academy of Political and Social Science* 623:39–51.

Solórzano, Daniel G., Amanda Datnow, Vicki Park, and Tara Watford. 2013. *Student Success and the Value of Postsecondary Education: Maximizing Access for Youth in Poverty* (PATHWAYS to Postsecondary Success Report). Los Angeles, CA: UC/ACCORD. Retrieved October 7, 2013 (http://pathways.gseis.ucla.edu/newsroom/publications/PathwaysReport.pdf).

Solórzano, Daniel G., Octavio Villalpando, and Leticia Oseguera. 2005. "Educational Inequities and Latina/o Undergraduate Students in the United States: A

Critical Race Analysis of Their Educational Progress." *Journal of Hispanic Higher Education* 4:272–294.

Southern Poverty Law Center. 2012. "SPLC Asks Tenn. Supreme Court to Block Illegal 287(g) Immigration Agreement in Nashville." Retrieved October 4, 2013 (http://www.splcenter.org/get-informed/news/splc-asks-tenn-supreme-court-to-block-illegal-immigration-agreement-in-nashville).

Stanton-Salazar, Ricardo. 2001. *Manufacturing Hope and Despair: The School and Kin Support Networks of U.S.-Mexican Youth.* New York: Teachers College Press.

———. 2011. "A Social Capital Framework for the Study of Institutional Agents and Their Role in the Empowerment of Low-Status Students and Youth." *Youth and Society* 43:1066–1109.

Starkweather, Sarah. 2007. "U.S. Immigration Legislation Online." Retrieved January 12, 2013 (http://library.uwb.edu/guides/usimmigration/USimmigrationlegislation.html).

Stawski, Jennifer. 2008. "Annotated Bibliography: Criminalization of Immigrants." Retrieved on January 12, 2013 (http://library.uwb.edu/guides/usimmigration/USimmigrationlegislation_criminalization.html).

Steele, Claude M. 1997. "A Threat in the Air: How Stereotypes Shape Intellectual Identity and Performance." *American Psychologist* 52(6):613–629.

———. 2010. *Whistling Vivaldi: And Other Clues to How Stereotyping Affects Us.* New York: Norton.

Storlie, Cassandra A., and Elizabeth A. Jach. 2012. "Social Justice Collaboration in Schools: A Model for Working with Undocumented Students." *Journal for Social Action in Counseling and Psychology* 4(2):99–116.

Storz, Mark G. 2008. "Educational Inequity from the Perspectives of Those Who Live It: Urban Middle School Students' Perspectives on the Quality of Their Education." *Urban Review* 40:247–267.

Suárez-Orozco, Carola, María G. Hernández, and Saskias Casanova. 2015. "'It's Sort of My Calling': The Civic Engagements and Social Responsibility of Latino Immigrant-Origin Young Adults." *Research in Human Development* 12(1–2):84–99.

Suárez-Orozco, Carola, Marcelo M. Suárez-Orozco, and Irina Todorova. 2010. *Learning a New Land: Immigrant Students in American Society.* Cambridge, MA: Belknap Press of Harvard University Press.

Suárez-Orozco, Carola, Hirokazu Yoshikawa, Robert T. Teranishi, and Marcelo M. Suárez-Orozco. 2011. "Growing Up in the Shadows: The Developmental Implications of Unauthorized Status." *Harvard Educational Review* 81(3):438–472.

Suárez-Orozco, Marcelo, and Mariela Paez. 2008. *Latinos: Remaking America.* Berkeley: University of California Press.

Sutter, Molly Hazel. 2005. "Mixed-Status Families and Broken Homes: The Clash Between the U.S. Hardship Standard in Cancellation of Removal Proceedings and International Law." *Transnational Law and Contemporary Problems* 15:783–813.

Swedback, Arielle. 2014. "Napolitano Announces Legal-Support Program for Undocumented Students." *Daily Californian,* November 23. Retrieved December 14, 2014 (http://www.dailycal.org/2014/11/23/napolitano-announces-legal-support-program-undocumented-students/).

Taxin, Amy. 2013. "Calif. Gov. Jerry Brown Signs Allowing Undocumented Immigrants to Apply for Driver's Licenses (UPDATE)." *Huffington Post Los Ange-*

les, October 3. Retrieved December 5, 2014 (http://www.huffingtonpost.com/2013/10/03/drivers-licenses-for-undocumented-immigrants_n_4037387.html).

Terriquez, Veronica. 2014. "Dreams Delayed: Barriers to Degree Completion Among Undocumented Community College Students." *Journal of Ethnic and Migration Studies* (published online October 30). Retrieved January 2, 2015 (http://www.tandfonline.com/doi/abs/10.1080/1369183X.2014.968534#.VLRbNWTF_yN).

Texas Higher Education Coordinating Board. 2008. *Overview: Residency and In-State Tuition* (THECB Report). Austin: Texas Higher Education Coordinating Board. Retrieved November 15, 2012 (http://www.thecb.state.tx.us/reports/PDF/1528.PDF).

Thomson, Ginger, and Sarah Cohen. 2014. "More Deportations Follow Minor Crimes, Records Show." *New York Times*, April 6. Retrieved May 26, 2014 (http://www.nytimes.com/2014/04/07/us/more-deportations-follow-minor-crimes-data-shows.html?_r=0).

Thronson, David B. 2008. "Creating Crisis: Immigration Raids and the Destabilization of Immigrant Families." *Wake Forest Law Review* 43:391–418. Retrieved June 19, 2014 (http://digitalcommons.law.msu.edu/cgi/viewcontent.cgi?article=1328&context=facpubs).

Tilsley, Alexandra. 2012. "DREAM Act Passes in Maryland." *Inside Higher Ed*, November 7. Retrieved February 7, 2013 (http://www.insidehighered.com/news/2012/11/07/maryland-passes-dream-act).

Tinto, Vincent. 1993. *Leaving College: Rethinking the Causes and Cures of Student Attrition*. Chicago: University of Chicago Press.

Torres, Vasti. 2004. "Familial Influences on the Identity Development of Latino First-Year Students." *Journal of College Student Development* 24(4):457–469.

Torresa, Rebecca Maria, and Melissa Wicks-Asbunb. 2014. "Undocumented Students' Narratives of Liminal Citizenship: High Aspirations, Exclusion, and 'In-Between' Identities." *Professional Geographer* 66(2):195–204.

Transactional Access Records Clearinghouse. n.d. "Representation for Unaccompanied Children in Immigration Court." Retrieved June 14, 2015 (http://trac.syr.edu/immigration/reports/371/).

Turnbull, Lornet. 2006. "Stunning Turnout Credited to Word-of-Mouth Network." *Seattle Times*, April 12. Retrieved January 16, 2013 (http://community.seattletimes.nwsource.com/archive/?date=20060412&slug=aftermath12m).

Undocu Pick-Up Lines. 2015. "Undocu Pick-Up Lines." Retrieved March 31, 2015 (www.Facebook.com/UndocuPickUpLines).

UN Educational, Scientific, and Cultural Organization. n.d. "The Right to Education." Retrieved September 6, 2013 (http://www.unesco.org/new/en/education/themes/leading-the-international-agenda/right-to-education/).

UN High Commissioner for Refugees. 2014. *Children on the Run: Unaccompanied Children Leaving Central America and Mexico and the Need for International Protection* (UNHCR Report). Washington, DC: UN Refugee Agency. Retrieved June 19, 2014 (http://www.unhcrwashington.org/sites/default/files/1_UAC_Children%20on%20the%20Run_Full%20Report.pdf).

United We Dream. 2015. "About Us." Retrieved March 31, 2015 (http://unitedwedream.org/about/our-missions-goals/).

University of California, Berkeley. 2013. *Undergraduate Students: A–G Completion Rates* (Division of Equity and Inclusion Report). Berkeley: University of California, Berkeley. Retrieved August 19, 2013 (http://diversity.berkeley.edu/undergraduate-students-a%E2%80%93g-completion-rates).

University of California San Diego, Social Science and Humanities Library. 2010. "Timeline: *Brown v. Board of Education:* The Southern California Perspective." Retrieved March 25, 2013 (http://sshl.ucsd.edu/brown/timeline.html).

US Bureau of Labor Statistics. 2013. *Education Pays* (USBLS Report). Washington, DC: US Department of Labor. Retrieved September 5, 2013 (http://www.bls.gov/emp/ep_chart_001.htm).

US Census Bureau. 2012. *Hispanic Heritage Month 2012: Sept. 15–Oct. 15* (Profile America: Facts for Features Report, CB12-FF.19). Washington, DC: US Census Bureau. Retrieved March 15, 2013 (http://www.census.gov/newsroom/releases/pdf/cb12ff-19_hispanic.pdf).

US Citizenship and Immigration Services. n.d.a. "Immigration Reform and Control Act of 1986 (IRCA)." Retrieved January 4, 2013 (http://www.uscis.gov/portal/site/uscis/menuitem.5af9bb95919f35e66f614176543f6d1a/?vgnextchannel=b328194d3e88d010VgnVCM10000048f3d6a1RCRD&vgnextoid=04a295c4f635f010VgnVCM1000000ecd190aRCRD).

———. n.d.b. "Immigration Act of 1990." Retrieved January 4, 2013 (http://www.uscis.gov/portal/site/uscis/menuitem.5af9bb95919f35e66f614176543f6d1a/?vgnextoid=84ff95c4f635f010VgnVCM1000000ecd190aRCRD&vgnextchannel=b328194d3e88d010VgnVCM10000048f3d6a1RCRD).

———. n.d.c. "Consideration of Deferred Action for Childhood Arrivals Process." Retrieved January 4, 2013 (http://www.uscis.gov/portal/site/uscis/menuitem.eb1d4c2a3e5b9ac89243c6a7543f6d1a/?vgnextoid=f2ef2f19470f7310VgnVCM100000082ca60aRCRD&vgnextchannel=f2ef2f19470f7310VgnVCM100000082ca60aRCRD).

———. n.d.d. "Press Release: Secretary Napolitano Announces Final Rule to Support Family Unity During Waiver Process." Retrieved January 4, 2013 (http://www.uscis.gov/portal/site/uscis/menuitem.5af9bb95919f35e66f614176543f6d1a/?vgnextoid=dc9af51016bfb310VgnVCM100000082ca60aRCRD&vgnextchannel=68439c7755cb9010VgnVCM10000045f3d6a1RCRD).

———. 2013. *Deferred Action for Childhood Arrivals* (USCIS Report, August). Washington, DC: USCIS Office of Performance and Quality. Retrieved January 11, 2015 (http://www.uscis.gov/sites/default/files/USCIS/Resources/Reports%20and%20Studies/Immigration%20Forms%20Data/All%20Form%20Types/DACA/daca-13-8-15.pdf).

———. 2014. *Number of I-821D, Consideration of Deferred Action for Childhood Arrivals by Fiscal Year, Quarter, Intake, Biometrics, and Case Status: 2012–2014* (USCIS Report, May). Washington, DC: USCIS Office of Performance and Quality. Retrieved January 11, 2015 (http://www.uscis.gov/sites/default/files/USCIS/Resources/Reports%20and%20Studies/Immigration%20Forms%20Data/All%20Form%20Types/DACA/I821d_daca_fy2014qtr2.pdf).

US Department of Education. 2014. "The Condition of Education 2014 (NCES 2014-083): Status Dropout Rates." Retrieved April 2, 2015 (http://nces.ed.gov/programs/coe/indicator_coj.asp).

US Department of Homeland Security. n.d. "Southwest Border Unaccompanied Children." Retrieved June 14, 2015 (http://www.cbp.gov/newsroom/stats/southwest-border-unaccompanied-children).

US Government Printing Office. 2014. "S. 744." 113th Congress, 1st Session. Retrieved December 12, 2014 (http://www.gpo.gov/fdsys/pkg/BILLS-113s744es/pdf/BILLS-113s744es.pdf).

US Immigration and Customs Enforcement. 2012. "Secure Communities." Retrieved December 22, 2012 (http://www.ice.gov/secure_communities/).

US Senate. 2010a. "A Bill to Authorize the Cancellation of Removal and Adjustment of Status of Certain Alien Students Who Are Long-Term United States Residents and Who Entered the United States as Children and for Other Purposes." 111th Congress, 2d Session. S. 3992. Retrieved January 8, 2015 (https://www.congress.gov/bill/111th-congress/senate-bill/3992).

———. 2010b. "To Authorize the Cancellation of Removal and Adjustment of Status of Certain Alien Students Who Are Long-Term United States Residents and Who Entered the United States as Children and for Other Purposes, Public Law 103-159, S. 952." Statutes at Large 110 (2010).

———. 2013. "To Provide for Comprehensive Immigration Reform and for Other Purposes, Public Law 89-732, S. 744." Statutes at Large 54 (2013). Retrieved December 12, 2014 (http://www.gpo.gov/fdsys/pkg/BILLS-113s744es/pdf/BILLS-113s744es.pdf).

Vaagan, Robert, and Gry Enger. 2004. "Developing the Multicultural School Library: Vahl Primary School, Oslo." *New Library World* 105:337–344.

Valdez, Trina M., and Catherine Lugg. 2010. "Community Cultural Wealth and Chicano/Latino Students." *Journal of School Public Relations* 31(3):224–237.

Valdivia Ordorica, Carolina. 2013. "DREAM ACTivism: College Students' Offline and Online Activism for Undocumented Immigrant Youth Rights." Thesis, Department of Sociology, San Diego State University, San Diego, CA.

Valenzuela, Angela. 1999. *Subtractive Schooling: US-Mexican Youth and the Politics of Caring*. Albany: State University of New York Press.

Valle, Ramon. 2006. "Thousands of Students Walk Out of Schools in Southern California to Protest Anti-Immigration Legislation." Retrieved October 5, 2014 (http://www.wsws.org/en/articles/2006/03/stud-m30.html).

Vygotsky, Lev. 1978. *Mind in Society: The Development of Higher Mental Processes*. Cambridge, MA: Harvard University Press.

Walker, Lauren. 2014. "Promise Fulfilled? Activists Respond Differently to Obama's Executive Order." *Newsweek* (November 11). Retrieved December 5, 2014 (http://www.newsweek.com/promise-fulfilled-activists-respond-differently-obamas-executive-order-286214).

Weigel, David. 2014. "Republicans Want Comprehensive Immigration Reform. The Republican House? Less So." *Slate: Weigel*, May 19. Retrieved May 19, 2014 (http://www.slate.com/blogs/weigel/2014/05/19/republicans_want_comprehensive_immigration_reform_the_republican_house_less.html).

Wells, Amy Stuart. 1989. *Middle School Education: The Critical Link in Dropout Prevention* (ERIC/CUE Digest Report, No. 59). New York: ERIC Clearinghouse on Urban Education. Retrieved May 30, 2013 (http://files.eric.ed.gov/fulltext/ED311148.pdf).

Werlin, Beth. 2014. "Drop in Court-Ordered Deportation Means Little to Overhaul Deportation Numbers." Retrieved January 11, 2015 (http://immigrationimpact.com/2014/04/23/drop-in-court-ordered-deportations-means-little-to-overall-deportations-numbers).

Wessler, Seth Freed. 2011. *Shattered Families: The Perilous Intersection of Immigration Enforcement and the Child Welfare System* (ARC Report). New York: Applied Research Center. Retrieved September 5, 2013 (http://arc.org/shatteredfamilies).

White House. 2011. "Fact Sheet—The State of the Union: President Obama's Plan to Win the Future." Office of the Press Secretary. Retrieved May 28, 2014 (http://www.whitehouse.gov/the-press-office/2011/01/25/fact-sheet-state-union-president-obamas-plan-win-future).

Wiggins, David K. 1980. "The Play of Slave Children in the Plantation Communities of the Old South, 1820–1860." *Journal of Sport History* 7(2):21–39.

Wiles, John, ed. 2009. *Developing Successful K–8 Schools: A Principal's Guide*. Thousand Oaks, CA: Corwin.

Wilkey, Robin. 2011. "California DREAM Act Signed by Jerry Brown: Second Bill Passes." *Huffington Post*, October 8. Retrieved December 20, 2012 (http://www.huffingtonpost.com/2011/10/08/california-dream-act_n_1001828.html).

Wilkinson, Lindsey. 2010. "Inconsistent Latino Self-Identification in Adolescence and Academic Performance." *Spring Science and Business Media* 2:179–194.

Wong, Kent, ed. 2009. *Underground Undergrads: UCLA Undocumented Immigrant Students Speak Out*. Los Angeles: University of California, Los Angeles, Center for Labor Research and Education.

Wong, Kent, Janna Shadduck-Hernández, Fabiola Inzunza, Julie Monroe, Victor Narro, and Abel Valenzuela. 2011. *Undocumented and Unafraid: Tam Tran, Cinthya Felix, and the Immigrant Youth Movement*. Los Angeles: University of California, Los Angeles, Center for Labor Research and Education.

Wong, Tom K., and Carolina Valdivia. 2014. *In Their Own Words: A Nationwide Survey of Undocumented Millennials* (CCIS Working Paper, No. 191). La Jolla, CA: Center for Comparative Immigration Studies. Retrieved June 1, 2014 (http://ccis.ucsd.edu/in-their-own-words-a-nationwide-survey-of-undocumented-millennials-working-paper-191/).

Xu, Qingwen, and Kalina Brabeck. 2012. "Service Utilization for Latino Children in Mixed-Status Families." *Social Work Research* 36(3):209–221.

Yang, K. Wayne. 2007. "Organizing MySpace: Youth, Walkouts, Pleasure, Politics, and New Media." *Educational Foundations* 2(1–2):9–28.

Ye Hee Lee, Michelle. 2014. "Has House Republicans' Inaction on Immigration Cost $37 Million a Day?" *Washington Post*, December 2. Retrieved December 14, 2014 (http://www.washingtonpost.com/blogs/fact-checker/wp/2014/12/02/has-house-republicans-inaction-on-immigration-reform-cost-37-million-a-day/).

Yorgason, Jeremy B., Laura Padilla-Walker, Jami Jackson. 2011. "Non-Residential Grandparents' Financial and Emotional Involvement in Relation to Early Adolescent Grandchild Outcomes." *Journal of Research on Adolescence* 21(3):552–558.

Yosso, Tara J. 2005. "Whose Culture Has Capital? A Critical Race Theory Discussion of Community Cultural Wealth." *Race Ethnicity and Education* 8(1):69–91.

Zentella, Ana Celia. 2005. *Building on Strength: Language and Literacy in Latino Families and Communities*. New York: Teachers College Press.

Index

AB 540. *See* California Assembly Bill 540
Ability grouping, 191
Academic preparation, 228–229
Activism, 130–131, 159–160
Administrators, schools, 60–61, 138
Advancement Via Individual Determination (AVID), 64–65, 67, 82, 100, 102–103, 221; importance, 198, 200
Affordable Care Act (ACA), exclusion from, 36, 205
African American: dream keeper, 179; families, 56; parents, 197; percentage with college prerequisites, 97; teachers of, 192; transfer students, 228
Alabama, 4, 29, 32, 178
Alas con Futuro, 109, 111, 115, 119–120, 130, 196. *See also* Student clubs
Allies: activists, 168–169; educators, 88–91, 102, 137–138, 197–198, 200–201; training, 121, 139–140, 207. *See also* AVID; GEAR UP
Alva-Brito, Griselda, 11, 127, 210, 220
American Civil Liberties Union (ACLU), 37, 42, 49, 128, 204
American, feeling, 123–124, 194. *See also* Identity
American dream, 12, 67, 102, 123, 193, 194
Amnesty, 21, 40
Anti-immigrant community, 128–129
Arizona, 29–30, 31, 37, 149; Arizona State University, 139; Phoenix, 178; Sheriff Joe Arpaio, 178; University of Arizona, 220
Asian American, 97, 128, 228
Asian Students Promoting Immigrant Rights Through Education, 177
Aspirations, research on, 228
At-promise, 69
At-risk. *See* At-promise
Avery-Merker, Rhonda, 11, 43, 212, 216

Baile folkórico, 72, 81, 100
Bias, high school, 96–99, 83
Bilingual: assessment, 182; bias, 83; hiring, 80; services, 75–76, 117, 179, 220; teachers, 186–188; tutors, 75. *See also* Welcome Center
Border crossing, 17, 19, 21, 47, 148, 199, 202, 203; game of, 1–2
Border Patrol, 1, 3, 6, 10, 47, 52, 85, 99, 100–101, 114. *See also* Immigration and Customs Enforcement (ICE); *Migra*
Border Protection, Antiterrorism, and Illegal Immigration Control Act of 2005, 165
Bracero (farmworker) Program, 17–19, 38, 42
Broward Detention Center (Florida), 174. *See also* Detention Facilities
Brown, Edmund Gerald "Jerry," 37, 159

Cal Grant Program, 24; AB 540, 176
California: budget cuts, 74; college prerequisites, 97, 229; community college transfer rate, 228; community college tuition, 110; DACA applicants, 37; Department of Education, 65; Department of Motor Vehicles, 37; driver's license, 233; eligibility to attend institutions of public higher education by undocumented students, 93; in-state tuition for undocumented students, 28; middle school dropout rate, 64; nonresident tuition exemption, 176; number of community college students, 107; Proposition 187, 22; "push-out" rate, 7; research participants, 143, 157; undocumented populations, 21; US Supreme Court cases, 24
California Assembly Bill 60 (AB 60), Safe and Responsible Driver Act, 37, 114
California Assembly Bill 130 (AB 130), California Dream Act of 2011, 29, 176, 222
California Assembly Bill 131 (AB 131), Student Financial Aid, 29, 176
California Assembly Bill 540 (AB 540), Nonresident Tuition Exemption, 26, 28, 93–94, 102, 109–110, 113, 126, 131, 176, 222; college club, 136; costs of college without, 109–111; Task Force, 138; workshops, 78
California community colleges, 29, 93; cost, 230; IIRIRA impact, 41; number of students, 107; recommendations to assist undocumented students, 126; research participants from, 108, 112, 235; roles of, 107, 125. *See also* California Assembly Bill 60; California Assembly Bill 130; California Assembly Bill 131; California Assembly Bill 540
California Development, Relief, and Education for Alien Minors (CA DREAM) Act, 29, 50, 120, 152–153, 176
California DREAM Team Alliance, 174
California Immigrant Youth Justice Alliance (CIYJA), 174
California State University system (CSU), 8; AB 130 and AB 131 and student financial aid, 29, 176; in-state tuition eligibility, 24, 28; Office of Diversity, Equity and Educational Inclusion, 140; privately funded scholarship eligibility, 29; undocumented students' needs, 139. *See also* California Assembly Bill 540
California State University, Fullerton: Titans Dreamers Resource Center, 139
California State University, Dominguez Hills, 173
California State University, Long Beach, 139, 220
California State University, San Marcos (CSUSM), 7, 69, 92, 220; AB 540 Task Force, 22–221; Clark-Ibáñez, 223; Department of Sociology, xii; MEChA, 122; Montiel, 122; Standing Together As oNe Dream (STAND), 69, 122, 173, 177
CalWORKS, 122
Campus police, 141
Canseco, Omar, 1–2, 5, 12, 54, 143, 207, 212–213
Career Exploration Conference, 121
Carlsbad, 7; graduation rate, 8, 86; high school graduates' college readiness, 96
Catholic Church, 100
Center for Labor Research and Education (UCLA), 232
Chaparrito Crew, 72–73
Checkpoints, 39, 71–72, 79, 128, 129, 171, 199
Childhood, undocumented, 197
Children's Health Insurance Plan (CHIP), 36
Citizens Brigade, 128
Civic engagement, research on, 232
Clark-Ibáñez, Marisol, 43, 63, 83, 107, 127, 143
Cleaning houses, undocumented student working, 92, 135, 144, 149. *See also* Work

Climate: campus, 116, 120, 220; classroom, 134; gender, 134; high school, 97–99; fear, 202; safe, 103, 130; services, 118, 141
Clinton, William Jefferson "Bill," 22, 205
Coachella: city, 120; valley, 108, 120
College Assistance Migrant Program (CAMP), 116, 138
College Board, 4, 105
College of the Desert, 110, 117, 119, 121–122, 124–125
Color blind, 49, 60
Coming out, 131
Coming Out of the Shadows, 170, 172, 177
Commencement speech, 145
Community-Based Block (CBB), 192
Community engagement, 220–223
Commuting to school, 129–130
Comprehensive immigration reform (CIR), 10, 33, 34–35, 36, 39–40, 142, 150, 152, 153–155, 161, 166–168, 203–206
Comprehensive Immigration Reform Act (2006 and 2007), 36; DREAM Act, 26
Concerted cultivation, 56–57
Construction, undocumented student working, 55, 144, 147, 185. *See also* Work
Convention on the Rights of the Child (CRC), United Nations, 195, 206
Cooling out, educational aspirations, 64, 228
Costa Rica, 143, 146, 236
Counselor, school, 15, 67, 69, 70–71, 77–78, 83, 88–91, 97, 102, 103–105, 113, 117, 201; general counselors, 120–121; research on, 228; transfer counselor, 126; university, 137. *See also* Alas Con Futuro; Allies; Community-Based Block; Puente Club
Covered California, 126
Cultural capital, 123, 228
Cultural citizenship, 130
Cultural competency, 60; counseling 140–141; financial aid, 105; teachers, 191–192; family style pedagogy, 120
Cultural funds of knowledge, 199–200
Cultural wealth, 102, 199–200

Davis, Joseph Graham "Gray," Jr.: AB 540, 26
Defense Authorization Bill (2008), DREAM Act, 26
Deferred Action for Childhood Arrivals (DACA), 35–38, 94, 111, 122, 150–151, 158; activism, 163, 166–169, 174, 178; caution, 153–155; Deferred Action for Parents of Americans and Lawful Permanent Residents (DAPA), 40; impact, 109, 143, 152–154, 161, 195–196, 208, 218, 232
Deferred Action for Parents of Americans and Lawful Permanent Residents (DAPA), 40
Defining the situation, symbolic interaction, 91–92
Deportation, 22–23, 38–40, 49, 198–199; activism against, 169–170, 174–176; brother, 2, 115; children, 197; community college, 113–116; elementary school, 4; high school, 79, 95, 99–101; laws, 31–32; parents, 49, 54, 129; postgraduates, 15, 145; unaccompanied minors, 202–203; university, 129, 132–133. *See also* Deferred Action for Childhood Arrivals (DACA); Detention facility; Fear
Depression. *See* Sadness.
Desert Hot Springs, 109, 120
Detention facility, 39, 49, 174–175, 198–199, 202, 204
Development, Relief, and Education for Alien Minors (DREAM) Act [federal]: activism, 12, 159, 163, 165–166, 168–170, 173–174, 176–177, 210; Border Security, Economic Opportunity, and Immigration Modernization Act of 2013, 35; California DREAM Act, 29, 50; congressional testimony by Tam Tran, 169; creation, 12, 25–26, 165; Deferred Action for Childhood Arrivals (DACA), 35; hope for, 136; importance, 152–154; knowledge of, 94; Maryland

DREAM Act, 29; proposed, 27; public support, 40; similar legislation, 276
Discouraged, feeling, 92, 96, 157
Domestic labor rights, activism, 158–159
DreamACTivist.org, 164, 168–169, 172, 174
DREAM Act Portal (DAP), 166–167
DREAMer: activism: 163–178; activists, 159–160; deportations, 175; Garía-Alverdín, 15, 41; high school students, 83–84; Valdivia-Odorica, 12, 213; name, 165
DREAMER Assistance Network, 122
Dream in Mexico, 159
DREAM keeper, undocumented students, 12, 179, 192, 201
Driver's license: apprehension, 38, 39; driving without one, 113, 114, 133, 141, 150, 153, 154, 233; law, 22, 35, 49, 126. *See also* California Assembly Bill 60
Drop out, 64, 85. *See* Push-out rates

Educational citizenship, 130
Educational Opportunity Program (EOP), 116, 122, 138–139, 198
Educational pipeline: all students, 5–6; undocumented students, 6–7
Educational Talent Search (ETS), 69, 82
Education Without Borders, 140. *See also* Allies, training
Educators 4 Fair Consideration, 105
Elementary school: Hillside Elementary School, 43–50, 51, 103; Individual Educational Plan (IEP), 47; legislation, 23–25; photo-elicitation study, 52–60, 225
Emotions, researcher, 210
Encinitas, 2, 7
Encuentros: classes and curriculum, 65; Leadership Club, 121–122
English as a Second Language program (ESL), 72, 201. *See also* Spanish-speakers
English-language Development (ELD) program, 70–71, 75, 83, 89–90, 96, 109
English-learner Advisory Committee (ELAC), 189
English-only policies, 180
Equity, 52
Escondido, 3, 7–8, 33, 67–69, 86; graduation rate, 8; high school graduates' college readiness, 9
Extended Opportunity Programs and Services (EOPS), 116, 122

Fallbrook, 7; graduation rate, 8; high school graduates' college readiness, 9
Familismo, 59–60
Family reunification, 204. *See also* Deportation
Fast food, undocumented student working, 144, 146, 161. *See also* Work
Fear, deportation, 53, 79, 231–232
Financial aid: advocate for awareness of, 94, 174; applying for, 120; culturally competent, 105; designated staff for undocumented students, 141; need, 230; policies, 28–29, 109–111, 176; task force membership, 138; unaware of, 93–94, 229; workshops, 95, 126, 222. *See also* Financial challenges
Financial challenges, 11–13, 155–156, 230
First-generation college student, 43, 116–117, 136, 145, 146, 218
Foster care, 31, 202
Free Application for Federal Student Aid (FAFSA), 68, 105, 117
Freedom University (Georgia), 177
Friends: activists, 165; children, 55–56; hide status from, 24, 133, 148–149; support from, 28, 90, 91, 94–95, 99–100, 116, 158. *See also* Allies
Fresno, student activism, 165
Friends of the Border Patrol, 128
Fútbol, 72–73, 79

García-Alverdín, Fredi, 5, 11, 15, 105, 127, 209–212, 219
Gatekeepers, 107, 229
Ganas, *échale* (have determination), 85, 86, 90, 91, 96, 108, 112, 221
Gay Straight Alliance (GSA), 121

GEAR UP (Gaining Early Awareness and Readiness for Undergraduate Programs), 63, 79; best practices, 74–79, 221–222; importance, 198, 200; recommendations, 80–82
Georgia, 177
Ghana, 143, 237
Goffman, Erving, 91, 214
Graduate school, 136, 155–156
Graduation, 144–148
Grandparents, 197; death of, 47, 87, 147–148, 160; living with, 88; role of, 55, 88, 96, 103; separated from, 50, 55, 197, 204; visiting 17, 19
Green card, 133
Grossmont Community College, 191
Guatemala, 37, 143, 148, 153, 160, 236–237
Guggenheim, David, 178

Hopelessness, 115, 135, 136, 147, 145–148, 151. *See also* Sadness
Hughes, Langston, 224
Human capital, 144
Humanizing research, 11, 215

ICE. *See* Immigration and Customs Enforcement (US Department of Homeland Security)
Identity, 10, 123–124; managing, 131
Illegal Immigration Reform and Immigrant Responsibility Act of 1996 (IIRIRA): impact on students, 41; passage, 22–23, Section 505, 25
Illegality, 61, 164, 197, 233
Immigrant Youth Justice League (IYJL), 170
Immigration Act of 1990, 22
Immigration and Customs Enforcement (ICE), US Department of Homeland Security: apprehensions, 99; detention center length of stay, 204; enforcement policies, 34, 38–39, 128, 174, 198; fear of, 49, 79, 85, 114, 129; impact on undocumented youth and families, 100, 134, 144, 169, 175–176, 196, 202, 205, 231; personal experiences with, 1–3, 10, 15, 20, 47, 52, 90, 103, 207
Immigration and Nationality Act of 1952, 20
Immigration and Nationality Act of 1965, 17, 19, 20
Immigration law, overview, 16–17; restrictive, 18–19; anti-immigrant, 29–30
Immigration Reform and Control Act (IRCA) of 1986, 20–21, 210
Indio, 120
INS. *See* US Citizenship and Immigration Service
In-state tuition. *See* California Assembly Bill 540; Tuition
Invisibility, 110, 118, 132–134, 141. *See also* Passing
Isolation, social, 145–146, 148–149
Institutional Review Board (IRB), 13, 210, 212, 214–217
Interview, methodology, 214–217

Jewish Family Services, 105

Kindergarten, 179, 181–182. *See also* Elementary School

Lal, Prerna, 172
La Quinta, 120
Lara, Luke, xii. *See also* Puente Club
Latino/a educational rates, 7–9
Legal Aid, 105; San Diego, 222
Legal liminality, 131, 232
Leticia A. v. University of California Board of Regents and California State University Board of Trustees, 23, 41
Levins Morales, Ricardo, xi
Libraries, 89, 96,198, 230; cards, 117; classroom library, 184
Life course theory, 232
Local anti-immigration laws, 30–33
Los Angeles, 108, 160; California DREAM applicants from, 29; immigrant youth activism, 165, 205; South Central, 224; study of undocumented students, 229; US Supreme Court case, 24
Low-income families, 45. *See also* Families
Loyola University, Chicago, 139

Mann, Horace, 194

May Day Immigrant Rights marches, 165
Mecca, 120
MEChA. *See* Movimiento Estudiantil Chicano/a de Aztlán
Mechanic, undocumented student working as, 145. *See also* Work
Media, undocumented immigrant portrayal, 84, 170, 203, 206–207
Medicaid, 36
Mental health, 10, 55, 90, 96, 142, 161, 206; counseling services, 141; Institutional Review Board, 210
Mentor, 137; AVID, 82, 88–89, 102; GEAR UP, 75; Latino/as, 81; Latino male, 73; Puente, 121. *See also* Allies
Mexican American Legal Defense and Educational Fund (MALDEF), 37
Mexico, 2, 15, 17, 47, 50, 71, 86, 94, 95, 100–101, 121, 124, 158–159, 183, 185; border issues, 40, 52; economy, 23; Guanajuato, 86; Guerrero, 55; guest worker program, 19; Jalisco, 87–88; Mexico City, 20, 86, 224; Oaxaca, 17, 19, 148, 207, 212–213; research participants from, 143–149, 151–152, 155, 157, 160, 167, 191, 236–237; return to, 151–152; Tijuana, 2, 5,12, 15, 191
Middle school, 64; college readiness programs, 73–79; push-out rates, 6–7, 64–65; undocumented students, 66–73. *See also* GEAR UP
Migra, 2, 47, 49, 54, 61, 100. *See also* Immigration and Customs Enforcement (ICE, US Department of Homeland Security)
Migrant Education Program, 15, 80, 90, 94, 97, 101–103, 198, 221
Migrant labor, child and youth, *v*, 2–3, 206
Minutemen, 128, 130
MiraCosta College (MCC), 7, 106, 111, 117–118, 125, 221, 222; DACA workshop, 122, 223; Encuentros Leadership Club, 121–122
Misinformation, higher education opportunities: 92, 93–94
Mixed status families, 37, 135, 202
Model minority, undocumented, 83–84, 228
Montiel, Yeraldín, 11, 83, 208, 212, 219–220
Movimiento Estudiantil Chicano/a de Aztlán (MEChA), 108, 122, 159, 191, 196, 221

Nahualt, 183
National Council of La Raza, 35, 39, 85
National Defense Authorization (2011): DREAM Act, 26
National Immigration Law Center, 37
National Immigration Youth Alliance (NIYA), 174–175
National Latino Research Center, San Marcos, 7
Napolitano, Janet, 36, 139
Native American/Alaskan Native, 97, 120, 128
New Mexico, 28, 176, 178
New York, 28, 28; research participants from, 143, 146, 148, 154, 160
Ninth Circuit Court, US Court of Appeals, 24, 37
North American Free Trade Agreement (NAFTA), 23
North County, San Diego: xi, xii, 7, 8, 63, 73, 83, 86, 108, 122, 196, 210; educational context, 7–9; GEAR UP, 73

Obama, Barack Hussein, 11, 34, 36, 42, 175, 203; Affordable Care Act, 205; Deferred Action for Childhood Arrivals (DACA), 35, 143, 153, 163, 174; Deferred Action for Parents of Americans and Lawful Permanent Residents (DAPA), 40; Deporter-in-Chief, 35; Secure Communities Program, 39, 198
Occupy movement, 159
Oceanside, 7–8, 8, 9, 86, 96; Human Rights Committee, 122
Oregon, 20; activism, 168, 176–177; in-state tuition, 28

Pacific Islander, 44, 97
Palm Desert, 3, 108, 120
Palm Springs: city, 120; High School, 120–121

Palomar College, 7, 92, 113, 118, 122, 207, 221–222
Parent Institute for Quality Education (PIQE), 74, 77–78
Parents: incarcerated, 68–69; left out of legislation, 155; participation 80–81, 95; supportive, 86–87; training, 74, 189; undocumented, 45, 54–55, 146,180, 182–186, 188–189, 229–230; unsupportive, 88
Participatory research, 218–220
Passing, symbolic interaction, 132–135. *See also* Invisible
Pedagogy, 65, 140
Personal Responsibility and Work Opportunity Act of 1996 (PWORA), 22
Peru, 27, 143, 152, 236; Ayacucho, 224; Lima, 223
Philippines, 37, 143, 237
Photo-elicitation interviews, 52–43, 224. *See also* Research Methods
Play, 1–2, 54, 56–57, 58–59, 79
Plyler v. Doe, 2, 4, 23, 25, 41–46, 194, 205; violations of, 4. *See also* US Supreme Court
Poverty: Latino children, 182
Priority Enforcement Program, 39. *See also* Secure Communities Program
Professional workforce, joining, 149–150
Provisional Unlawful Presence Waiver, 38–41
Public Sociology, 4–5, 94, 222–223
Puente Club, 121. *See also* Student clubs
Puente Project, 121
Push-out rates, 6, 13

Ramona, Unified School District, 7–9
Regents of the University of California v. Bakke, 24
Regents of the University of California v. Superior Court (Bradford), 24
Research assistants, 211–213
Research ethics: 214–215; undocumented children, 216; using photographs, 224
Research methods, 10–11, 143, 129; research collaborator training, 213–219; self-selection bias, 159
Resiliency, 59, 148, 153, 157–159, 177
Resistance capital, 103, 200
Resource Center, 139
Riverside, 3–4, 108, 196, 221
Rocha, Cecilia, 11–12, 63, 217, 221
Role conflict, 135, 199, 232
Ruiz-Pohlert, Alma, 12, 60, 179, 198

Sadness, 94–95, 112, 114, 144–145, 148, 157–159, 164, 197. *See also* Hopelessness
Safe-Space Training for the Undocumented Student Population, 104, 139. *See also* Allies, training
San Diego, 3, 49, 179, 221, 223; County of, 29, 47, 64, 82, 151; Grossmont Community College, 191; ICE detention center, 39; Legal Aid, 222; traveling through, 167; undocumented youth activism, 170, 173–174, 176
San Diego DREAM Team (SDDT), 170, 173–175, 208
San Diego Legal Aid, 222
San Diego Padres, 67
San Diego State University (SDSU), 16, 192, 213, 236; Community-Based Block, 192
San Marcos: city of, 7; elementary school teacher, 4; study participants from, 86; Unified School District, 8–9
Scholarship audit, 106
School leavers, 201. *See also* Push-out rates
School to prison pipeline, 6, 13, 68, 85
Secure Communities Program, 15, 34, 38–39, 61, 198, 204. *See also* Priority Enforcement Program
Self motivation, 91–93, 125–125, 136
Serna, Bettina, 11, 107, 212
Sikh, farmworker children, 200. *See also* Migrant labor
Soccer. *See* Fútbol
Social capital, 102, 129–130, 132, 157, 231
Social location, 10
Social media activism, 165–169, 171–172, 175–178
Social network sites, 143, 148
Social Security number: benefits and IIRIRA, 23; DACA, 153; Illinois

SB 957, 37; need, 16, 48, 69, 90, 93, 95, 104–105, 117–118, 132, 135, 146, 150, 164
Sociological imagination, 9–10, 198
Spanish-speakers, 44, 117; interviews, 62
Standing Together as oNe Dream (STAND), 82; activism, 173, 175, 196; Alva-Brito, 210, 220; CSUSM, 122, 221; middle school, 69, 77; Montiel, 208, 220; Valdivia-Odorica, 220. *See also* Alas Con Futuro; United for Education
State University of New York (SUNY), 25
Status, symbolic interaction, 130, 232–233. *See also* Role conflict
Stereotype, 57, 91, 103, 125, 200, 232
Stereotype threat, 99
Stress, 33, 49, 53, 59, 90, 112, 115, 134–135, 140, 147, 157, 164, 204, 231–232. *See also* Deportation; Financial challenges
Student clubs, undocumented focus. *See* Alas Con Futuro; Standing Together as oNe Dream; United for Education
Student clubs, undocumented support. See Alas Con Futuros; Standing Together as oNe Dream
Suicide, 144–145
Summer slide, 189–191

Task force, 138
Teachers: anti-immigrant, 50–51; bias, 97–98, 186; bilingual, 186–188; misinformed, 48; of undocumented students, 46–47, 57–58. *See also* Allies, educator
Teen pregnancy, 74, 84
Texas, 143, 145, 147, 202, 224; access to education, 24, 26, 28; community colleges, 230; DACA applicants, 37; financial aid to undocumented students, 176; Immigration Reform and Control Act (IRCA) impact, 21; local anti-immigration ordinance, 33; Secure Communities Program participation, 39
Thermal, 120
Tijuana, 14, 17, 24, 27, 302, 223
Training, ally, 121, 139–140, 207; need for, 60, 74, 126, 139–140, 201. *See also* Allies
Tran, Tam: congressional testimony on DREAM Act, 169
Transfer, community college, 90, 97, 107, 125–126; rates 109, 111, 121; research on, 228
Trilingual, 183
Trinidad, 143, 146, 237
Tuition: in-state, 28, 25, 26–29; misinformation about, 93, 94, 102, 109–111, 123, 135, 140, 145, 152, 160, 166; none available, 177–178; requirements for 104, 176. *See also* California Assembly Bill 540 (AB 540)
Tutoring, 67, 75, 101, 232. *See also* GEAR UP

Unaccompanied minors, 2, 99, 202–203
UndocuBus tour, 178
Undocumented and Awkward, video series, 177
UndocuPickUpLines, 176–177
United for Education, 130, 137–138. *See also* Alas Con Futuro; Standing Together as oNe Dream
United Nations: Convention on the Rights of the Child, 195, 206; General Declaration of Human Rights, 195; Global Action Week on Education, 201; High Commissioner for Refugees, 2, 203
United We Dream (UWD), 164, 168–169, 174
University of Arizona, 220
University of California (UC), 8; AB 130, 176; AB 131, 176; AB 540, 176; in-state tuition, 24; undocumented students, 139
University of California, Berkeley, 139, 220, 223
University of California, Davis, xii, 139, 224
University of California, Los Angeles, 48, 69, 70, 127
University of California, San Diego, 24, 76, 224

US Citizenship and Immigration Service (USCIS), US Department of Homeland Security, 22, 37
US Department of Education, 73
US Department of Health and Human Services, 36
US Department of Homeland Security, 15, 38, 139
US House of Representatives Immigration Bills, 27, 35, 36, 165–166
US Immigration and Naturalization Service (INS). *See* US Citizenship and Immigration Service (USCIS, US Department of Homeland Security)
US Senate Immigration Bills, 25–26, 27, 35, 165
US Supreme Court, 2, 4, 23, 25, 37, 43, 194, 205; Latino education, 24

Valdivia Ordorica, Carolina, 12, 163, 213, 220
Valley Center, 8–9
Vista, 7–9, 33, 71, 86
Voluntary departure, 27, 54, 211, 223
Vote, Latino/a, 34–35, 160, 232

Welcome Center, school, 191
White: access to college support services, 228; community college students, 118, 125; GEAR UP program assistant, 73; Hillside Elementary School, 44–45, 50–51; median household income, 230; middle school staff and faculty, 81; National Assessment of Educational Progress, 227; preschool, 182; privilege in high school, 96–98; researcher, 43
Work, by undocumented students: cleaning houses, 92, 135, 144, 149; construction, 55, 144, 147, 185; fast food, 144, 146, 161; mechanic, 145. *See also* Professional workforce
World War II, 17, 19

Xenophobic, 128

Youth-led undocumented activism: California Immigrant Youth Justice Alliance, 174; DREAMActivist, 168, 174; DREAM Act Portal, 166–168; Immigrant Youth Justice League, 170; National Immigrant Youth Alliance, 174–175; San Diego Dream Team, 170, 173; Standing Together As oNe Dream, 173; UndocuBus, 178; UndocuPickUp Lines, 176–177; Undocumented and Awkward, 177; United We Dream, 168, 174

Zone of proximal development, 181

About the Book

Though often overlooked in heated debates, nearly 1.8 million undocumented immigrants are under the age of eighteen. How do immigration policies shape the lives of these young people? How do local and state laws seemingly unrelated to undocumented communities negatively affect them? Marisol Clark-Ibáñez delivers an intimate look at growing up as an undocumented Latino/a immigrant, analyzing the social and legal dynamics that shape everyday life in and out of school.

Marisol Clark-Ibáñez is associate professor of sociology at California State University, San Marcos.